TWO GENTLEMEN TO SEE YOU, SIR

The Autobiography of a Villain

by

VICTOR CARASOV

With a Foreword by
Michael Young

LONDON
VICTOR GOLLANCZ LIMITED
1971

ISBN 0 575 00597 1

MADE AND PRINTED IN GREAT BRITAIN BY
THE GARDEN CITY PRESS LIMITED
LETCHWORTH, HERTFORDSHIRE

TWO GENTLEMEN TO SEE YOU, SIR

AUTHOR'S NOTE

This is an *explanation* of *words* and *phrases* used in my *story* . . .

Wherever and whenever I use the words: homeless, friendless and penniless, I am not seeking *pity* or *sympathy* . . I'm merely stating a *fact* . . *ironically*, as in a Gilbert and Sullivan Opera . . being fully aware that the state of *deprivation* has been brought upon myself . . *by* myself.

Wherever and whenever I use the words—*Two gentlemen to see you, Sir*—I am doing so in the manner of that ancient *Greek chorus*. After all, *my life has been punctuated* down through the years by these very, very *fatal* words.

If *any pity* is aroused by this story of mine, let it go out to those men, women and children who assuredly . . *barring accidents* . . will be right where *I am now*: *Prison*.

1969 VICTOR CARASOV

SLANG WORDS AND ABBREVIATIONS

Slang Words and Expressions

To case	to look a house over before burgling it
Chokey	solitary confinement
Gear	stolen goods
Pad	a padded cell
Peter	a cell
Put the pot on	pretend to be mad
On the game	to be a prostitute
Screw	a prison warder
Stripped cell	a cell with the minimum of furniture
Ticket	sentence
Tom-foolery	jewellery
Villainy	crime
Sticks	suburbs

Abbreviations

H.L.	hard labour
P.D.	preventive detention
P.O.	principal officer
P.S.	penal servitude

FOREWORD

50 Years in Prison

by Michael Young

'Despotism and lies so disfigured our childhood that it makes me sick and horrified to think of it. . . . I remember father began to teach me, or to put it more plainly, whip me, when I was only five years old. He whipped me, boxed my ears, hit me over the head, and the first question I asked myself on awakening every morning was, "Will I be whipped again today".' Anton Chekhov wrote this about his childhood. He is one of a multitude of writers and others who have overcome the disadvantages of a miserable childhood. How have they succeeded when so many others with all the initial advantages of a stable family have failed? It is one of the great mysteries.

The story of Victor Carasov—Russian name, Russian father—also illustrates the puzzle. As he says, his 'cards were well and truly marked'. After a childhood like Chekhov's, almost all the rest of his life has been as terrible. Such a childhood *should* have led to such a life, and has. Such a life *should* have petered out in continued misery, and has not. He has in the end broken away from the 'recidivist compulsion' which has controlled his life—the repetition of crime–prison–misery—crime–prison–misery.

The manner of his accomplishment was immediately clear the first time I saw him in the Governor's office at Blundeston Prison. The Governor was a very large man with the advantage of a large desk to sit behind. Mr. Carasov was a small man in prison clothes. But he, not the Governor, filled the room by his presence and dominated the conversation from the start. He did it by marrying great aggressive energy to great intelligence. He was no more tamed by authority, after he had spent 50 out of his 65 years in a long chain of prisons, than he had been when he was consigned as a small boy to the training ship which was the first of them. By countering external authority with inner authority, he has kept his integrity; he has even kept his youth. Most men of his age, retiring after 50 years in *their* occupations (as he said he was now hoping to retire from his) have little trace of youth left. If the prison service were advertising itself, it might publish Mr. Carasov's photograph as one of its successful products—'50 years inside our prisons and still a young man'. But the achievement is his, not theirs. They tried to break him, and failed. Every time they put the 'mad bastard' down below in the punishment cells, he emerged the victor.

It was only when the authorities stopped trying to break his spirit and reversed direction that they had their first success. The move for reform is one of the refrains of the book. He has had an inside view for longer than almost anyone—certainly longer than any warder—and he recognises the changes over his lifetime. When he returns to one prison after another he notices that the regime has become a little more liberal than it was when he was there before. Some of the old brutality has gone. And eventually he finds himself in one of the new kinds of prison which the reformers have been struggling to create. Almost the only luck Mr. Carasov has had in his life was being sent to Blundeston. It gave him hope. It broke the chain of repetition.

M.Y.

I

IT ALL STARTED on that *train* . . June 8, 1904. Mother was on her way to present *me* to her ever-loving family, but I . . I could *not* wait, so *out* I came, bawling and shouting, no doubt, as I've done so many times since.

Mother was Welsh . . Father, a Russian Jew . . and from *that* mixture comes *me*.

Sitting here, trying to recall what I can of days gone by, I find it hard to see things clear and distinct. I've none of that vivid past-recall so common to writers of *autobiography*.

Looking back, I can't remember much home-life, but there is a clear recollection of the city of Glasgow where my father, then, had a photographic studio, and Mother, some kind of theatrical work. As time marched on, I began to realise that Mother and Father were not happy together. I recall the night when I was awakened by screaming and shouting. Outside my small bedroom, on the landing, there was this noise . . terrifying . . it scared me. I got out of bed, opened the door and *there, there* was Mother in a long night-dress . . lovely, golden hair, loose, all over her shoulders . . in her bare feet. She . . she was struggling to escape from my father who held her by one hand and *beat her* with the other. Nearby stood the little maid-of-all-work who stayed with us in the house . . she looked scared out of her wits.

I rushed over to my father, grabbed him by the legs, and begged him to leave my mother alone. Father stopped beating Mother, got hold of me and picked me up . . then threw me away . . just like that . . threw me away.

It was years before I fully understood just exactly *why* Father was beating Mother. This man, my father, was, it seems, a kind of *sex-maniac* . . he hadn't married Mother because he *loved* her . . *all he* wanted was to get her in bed. As this fellow, my father, couldn't stay with Mother in bed *all night* and *day*, he turned to the maid for *extra sex* . . On *this* occasion my mother must have disturbed him in the bathroom . . he immediately turned on her and accused her of *spying on him.* Then he brutally set about her. In this way I . . I learnt quite early in my young life what a dreadful force of *evil sex* and *violence can be.*

During the many separations between Father and Mother, when both were living apart, I usually stayed with Mother, and she would go back to show-business. And so I began to learn something of the tragedy and gaiety of show-business people. Mother would go on tour, and take me with her. We usually travelled on a Sunday . . one *big family,* mostly *girls,* and all of them lovely to look at. On these tours we put up at theatrical digs which for *me* meant fish-and-chips, fleas, bugs, and drunken landladies. Mother was not a *star* . . not a *star* . . just a common little chorus girl . . but *full* of *gaiety* and *personality.*

I remember the night when Mother took me behind the scenes of the theatre for the *first* time. The *lights* . . the *mirrors* . . the crowded dressing-tables . . the *powder* and *paint* . . the lovely girls . . the *laughter* . . the *chatter* . . the *all-pervading smell* of *bodies* which, in some fashion, thrilled me and excited me too. An old gramophone would be started up, and I . . I would be picked up by one of the girls, placed on a dressing-table and told: "*Dance . . dance, Victor . . like your Mummy does.*"

Came the day when Father said: "Victor, I'm taking you away from here. You will have a *new mother,* a kind of foster mother. You will stay in one place. You will go to a regular school, and you will be a *good boy.*"

In due course, I was introduced to my *new mother* and the *new house* and to school, too. *But* a *new mother* is *not* like the *old mother* . . a *house,* even a *new one,* is *not* a *home* . . and as for that school, *I hated it.*

This foster mother was *tall* . . *scraggy* . . and *vicious.* She seemed to *hate my guts* and made up her mind to *starve me* . . *make* me attend *Church-services, morning, noon, and night* . . join the *Boys' Brigade* . . the *Boy Scouts. . . In* fact, this woman was determined to drive that *devil right out* of *my immoral soul* which *she* considered *damned . . damned . .* You see, all this happened in Scotland many years ago, when religious people had the notion that *divorce was a sinful thing* and *children* of *divorced parents* were *sinful,* too. I don't say *all* religious people in Scotland were like this, but my *foster mother was.*

The time came when I'd had enough of all this enforced *religion*, this *spartan* regime. I missed my mother . . I'd begun to hate my father, and the very name of *God* I'd associated with this horrible *christian* woman, my foster mother . . . So, I run away . . I run away . . I run away. Outside the house I saw a bicycle leaning against a railing . . I took it, mounted it, and pedalled away for life, liberty and *happiness*.

And so we arrive at my eleventh year . . 1915 . . and my first offence against the *law* . . though at that time, I'd *no* idea I had broken the *law*.

There I was, in a large room, a large *bare* room, furnished with the minimum of furniture . . a table, a bench, a bucket to piss in. With me, in this room, are about a dozen boys, *all* of whom had offended the *law*, just like me.

"Wot you in for, mate?" . . . "Nick somethin'?" . . . "Hit a copper?" . . . "Got a *fag*?".

This room *stank* . . *stank* . . and was stone-cold. These kids were a *wild* lot, but likeable.

"Victor Carasov, you are charged with stealing a bicycle, running away from school, and being in need of care. Neither your father nor mother wants anything to do with you. You appear to be quite uncontrollable, so the sentence of this court is: *You will go to reform school* . . to *reform school* . . for five years."

At this distance of time, I just can't recall *exactly* what I felt about all this, but I *do* recall, at the back of that court, behind this old man, my *judge*, there was on the wall a kind of heraldic device on which I could clearly see the words: "*Justice* . . *justice* . . *tempered* with *mercy* . . . Afterwards, down below in that cell, I just *laughed* . . I just *laughed*.

I soon discovered that reform school was an old wooden-side, sails-before-the-mast kind of ship, dating from the Napoleonic Wars, and anchored on the River Clyde near Row, Dunbartonshire, Scotland.

The night was dark, the water rough, and that small boat *rocked*. I sat in the stern, cold, miserable and a bit scared. We were on the way to that reform school, riding high, out there on the River Clyde, lights glimmering in the distance. The boat got alongside, was tied up to the gangway, and we jumped out, climbed those stairs, and there we were, on board the reform school, *Empress*. *Empress Training Ship* she was called, and *this* was to be my home for the next five years.

The old *Empress* was a vivid reminder of all the tales I'd read about the sea, and the sea-faring life of Nelson's day. Wooden decks, soaring masts, brass guns, and fo'c'sle-heads which *stank to heaven*.

I was soon initiated into the *Empress* life—medical inspection . . issue-of-kit . . assignment to a mess below deck—and learnt to knot-and-splice, scrub the decks with holystone, get around winter and summer bare-footed and cropped-headed.

As this story is to concern a period of many years, I must necessarily be selective in what I relate. So I'll cut short this part of the story and summarise: The life on the *Empress* was hard, crude and deprived . . deprived of everything that growing boys should have.

No love, affection, guidance or friendly counsel for them. In short: "You've got five years *to do*. *This* is the way *we do it*, and *this* is the *way you'll do it*." I got on that old ship a *wild one,* and as time went on, I got *wilder*. For shore-going we were given shoes to wear . . on board we went bare-foot. One day, looking for my shoes, ready for kit-inspection, I found they were missing. I . . I concluded someone had nicked them. I looked around to see if there was a pair that I could nick. I nick somebody's shoes . . after all, somebody had taken *mine* . . and I am caught, charged with stealing shoes, and am ordered to be flogged in the presence of the whole ship's company.

Down there, on the middle-deck, was a battery of small brass guns, and on one of these they tied me. I was tied up at both ends, stripped to the knees, then flogged. As I was being flogged, I thought: Next time I nick a pair of shoes, I'll take care the bastards *don't catch me*.

The day came when I was fed up with knots-and-splices, scrubbing decks, and going to school. Having found out that a boy could join the band and get excused *all* ship-board chores, *and* school, too, after the age of fourteen, I ask to join the band. After certain tests, I was accepted. I started on clarinet . . rather liked it . . soon reached *solo* clarinet . . became a band sergeant . . stood in for the bandmaster when he was off duty . . took rehearsals, and when the band went ashore to take engagements playing for private dances and public performances in the parks, as often as not, I'd stand in there, too.

We were ashore on a public performance, down there on the Pier Head at Helensburgh. During the interval, when we boys were allowed to take time off for a stroll in the town, I noticed a pretty girl standing at a window, looking out. I found a bit of paper and a pencil, and wrote a brief note: "I saw you at the window. I like the look of you. Will you, please, come out and meet *me*?" I marched up to the door of this house and rang that bell. The door opened and *there* was a fearsome-looking woman glaring at me.

"Well, *what do you want*?" she says.

"Will you, please, give this note to the pretty girl I saw at the window?"

"How dare you bring this filthy note to me. Go away at once, before I call the police." This woman's hostility I *did not understand* . . but, realising that *once* again I was up against *authority*, I just turned away, more in sorrow than anger, thinking: In future, I'll do a *Romeo and Juliet* act. No more letter-writing for *me*.

The wind was blowing up a gale . . I could hear it whistling in the rigging . . for all that the order was: "All blankets up for airing", which meant: "Get up there on deck, put your blankets on the rigging", the weekly procedure on the *Empress* for airing blankets . . *That* being cheaper than laundering.

I get up on deck, start fixing those blankets, when I hear the words: "*Man overboard . . man overboard.*" I run to the starboard chains, and from there I can see them, fishing somebody out of the water. They get him aboard, water running out of him at *both* ends . . head and face a mass of bleeding flesh and bone. In spite of this boy's condition, I recognised my ship-mate as a boy I had fought with in the ring . . a boy I had eaten with in the mess . . in fact this mate of mine could have been *me* . . and *now*, he was dead.

Next morning we are told: "Friends and mates of the dead boy to parade outside the sick-bay cabin if they would like to see him." We walked in, one at a time, and *there he was* . . all wrapped up in white sheets . . head and face in bandages, only the eyes to be seen, or rather, the place where his eyes should have been. Covering his eyes were *two bright new pennies*. I was a bit scared . . this was the *first* time I'd ever seen *death*.

On board the *Empress*, we had a daily and a weekly routine. It was war-time . . the Great War, 1914-1918 . . the *war* to *end all wars*. We were on a starvation ration, and to get some excitement *and* some food, we often raided the food-stores. If caught, it was a *sure flogging*.

There was school for some of the boys, until the age of fourteen. The rest of the boys spread around the ship on various seamanship courses, scrubbing decks, polishing mess-cans and, for me and others, band practice which I liked very much.

Looking back now, with adult understanding, I'm surprised to recall so little of the *sex* lark. Apart from a kind of mutual masturbation and occasional curiosity as to the *size* of each other's pricks, I recall nothing whatever to compare with the obsession with sex, so common today. By now I'm getting on for sixteen . . it's 1920 . . . and the question being asked is: "What are you going to *do* when you leave here, as you must do, when your time is up?"

During *all* these years on the *Empress*, I'd never seen or heard of my father, and only heard from Mother once or twice. Strangely enough, though I was playing clarinet and conducting the band when standing in for the bandmaster, *and* getting Press notices, too, I don't recall *any fancy notions* of becoming a *top bandsman*. The truth is, I think, I'd none of that inner urge to *be something* that *all* promising young musicians are supposed to have.

Release Day came, and I . . I was told: "As your parents don't want you, we've decided to put you in an army band." And so, willy-nilly, I'm in the Army as a bandsman, a boy bandsman. It didn't take *me* long to discover that the Army . . for *me* . . was *hell*. What with my 'dear' violent father and that 'ever-loving' foster mother . . the bloody judge who gave *me* five years' reform school, where I got that public flogging . . *no* parents to forget and forgive my peccadilloes, *not even after I'd done my punishment* . . all this, topped off with a big dollop of Army life, made *me* feel I was a *dead duck*.

II

"DO THIS, YOU bastard. You are *not* on the *Empress now.*"

"Do that, you bastard, you are *not a band-sergeant here.*"

"How about a bit of *prick*? Here, take this . . nice and juicy, *all* ready for sailor boys . . *you are in the Army, my son . . .*"

Yes . . yes . . I *was* in that *army* all right, but I had *no* intention of staying there . . .

I had just returned from a short leave and, getting into the barracks, I found my locker had been broken into. *This . . this* was all I needed . . all I needed to set that *fire alight.* I smashed up that bloody barracks . . dashed out across the yard into that officers' mess where a ceremonial dinner was taking place. The *piper* was walking around playing some *lament*, for God knows what. I spotted the *adjutant* in all his *sartorial glory* and, grabbing him by the collar, I demanded to know why he couldn't stop *lockers* in the barracks being *burgled.*

Pandemonium . . pandemonium . . .

The *piper* stops playing . .

Crockery is smashed . . Glasses are broken.

All is confusion and noise . . and *me . . me*, I'm grabbed by the mess-servants, hustled away, pushed and kicked . . and thrown into the detention cell.

In due course, I took my trial, and was told: "*Get out of this Army . . you are discharged with ignominy.*"

So here I am, out of that bloody Army, homeless, friendless, and penniless. Where to go? What to do? That's the question. Strangely enough, *now* free of the *Army*, I'm thinking of music. In my pocket-book I have a collection of Press-cuttings, dating from the *Empress* days, in which I am described as an "up and comin' " clarinettist . . and a band-conductor too . . and recalling that my mother had once told me that Father was in London, now, where he had a photographic studio, I decided to go there, find my father, show him the Press-cuttings, and ask him to help me get into a *good school* of *music* to finish off my musical education.

I had a few shillings in my pocket, was a bit bewildered at all the things happening to me, didn't really know much about this town called *London* . . but I set out just the same. I walked till I was tired . . I begged lifts . . I slept rough . . finally, I'm in *London* . . but *no bells are ringing for Victor.*

How to find my father? I look around . . . there is a shop over there and I go in. "I'm looking for my father," I said. "Can you help me?" I am invited into a little room, behind the shop, and told to be seated, given tea and sandwiches. . and then told: "We'll soon find your father . . don't worry." The person doing all this talking was a little man who might have stepped straight out of a tale by Hans Andersen. Dried-up-apple for a face . . . *all* crinkles and crunkles . . with shining *bright* laughing eyes. I watched this man as he riffled through a large book which, he said, was a trade directory. "I've got it," he said: "Mr. Samuel Carasov . . Photographer . . Notting Hill Gate."

I thanked the kindly old man for his help, took the piece of paper with my father's address on it, stepped out into the street, got on a bus . . and there I was, outside my father's shop. I go straight in, see a girl at the counter, ask: "Is Mr. *Carasov* in?" The girl points to the back of the shop . . I go in . . and *there* . . *there* . . he is . . this father of mine whom I've *not* seen since he planted me on that damned foster mother when I was very young. He is sitting in front of a fire, this father of mine. Behind him is a tall wardrobe, the door of which is partly open, and sticking out of this door, I can see the sharply pointed *shoes* of a woman. I think: This bastard is *still at it*. He throws my lovely mother away and *goes for this shit, behind* the *wardrobe door*.

"What do you want?" this fellow, my father, says.

"I've been thrown out of the Army, Father, and I've come to you with these Press-cuttings, hoping you'll get me to a good school of music so that I can get on with my musical education." I stood there, looking at this man, my father, watching him riffle through my Press-cuttings, and thinking: What a *bastard*. Father looked up at me, and said: "Get out of here. Go to your mother if you wish." At the same time as he spoke to me, he threw the Press-cuttings into the fire. For a moment, the briefest of moments, I felt like hitting this man, my father, but I turned away and walked out of that shop, thinking:

What a pity . . what a pity. . . Whom I was pitying, my father or myself, I don't know. To the best of my knowledge *that* was the *last* time I ever saw my father.

We have now arrived at a most crucial point in my somewhat erratic life. I'm seventeen years of age . . been to reform school . . *in* and *out* of the Army . . *in* quick . . *out* quick . . turned to my father for help which I did not get . . and I'm getting a bit angry with myself *and* the world, too. I don't recall thinking very deeply about *all* this in those days. I just felt sort of puzzled . . and very angry.

I find my way to the docks . . get me a ship in a coastal line going to Liverpool and Dublin . . *me* I am a cabin boy. The smell of the ship, the smell of the sea, the smell of my small cabin, down below, thrilled me, *it was good*. The cook was a great big coloured man, with a great big smile, a great big mouthful of teeth, and a great big bellowing voice.

Getting into Liverpool, I was making some coffee . . the cook comes into the galley, takes a cup of coffee, has a sip and spits it out. He slings that cup overboard and says to me: "For *two pins, I'd throw you overboard, too. That coffee* is the *worst I've ever drank*." From this moment on I'd made up my mind: *No coloured cooks for me.*

Ship-board life on a coaster with a coloured cook was *not* for me . . not at all *because* of his *colour* . . but . . *because of his taste in coffee*! So, when we docked in Liverpool, I took my wages, went ashore and stayed there. I didn't have *much* money, but enough to get me a modest lodging and a meal or two.

I'm taking a look round the waterfront, and I notice a steamer about to leave for the Isle of Man. I go aboard, seek out the steward, and ask him: "Can I work my passage to the Isle of Man?" After a bit of arguing and barguing, he says: "O.K., help me in the saloon." The trip's a short one, but I make myself useful, serve a little food and some drink. I arrive at Douglas, Isle of Man . . it's a sunny day . . the pier is crowded with holiday-seeking people loaded with luggage, children, and hopes for a *good* holiday. I step ashore, get off that pier, on to the promenade, look around me, and wonder what next? Over there I see the words: *Empress Hotel* . . Proprietors: Mr. and Mrs. *Boyd*. What a strange thing . . *Empress Hotel* . . and *me* . . just recently left the *Empress* Training Ship, that old River Clyde Reform School. I ask myself, *is this a good omen*?

I go up those steps, over to the desk there, and ask: "Can I see Mr. or Mrs. Boyd?" I'm told to take a seat. I wait a few minutes . . and *there* is Mrs. Boyd, a nice little woman with a smiling face, quick bird-like movements and a pleasant manner.

"What can I *do* for you?"

"I'm looking for a job," I say.

"Please come into the office, will you?" and "*Do* sit down. Tell me something about yourself." I tell Mrs. Boyd something about my recent past, and I notice, when I'm talking to her, she is looking at me, as if . . as if she, were seeking an answer to an inner question.

"Will you please wait a moment, whilst I go and get my husband?" Mrs. Boyd comes back with a little man, no bigger than herself . . getting a bit fat, perhaps . . but cheerful and friendly in manner. "My husband," she says. "John, John, *isn't he like our boy*?"

It was explained to me that the Boyds had lost a son, in the recent war, and, by some freakish chance . . I . . I was very like him, or so they believed. I was engaged on the spot, told: "You'll start in the pantry, take a turn in the kitchen, do a bit of office-work, and learn the business, as our boy would have done."

I'm thinking: *What a break . . what a break.*

I'm given a small room, at the top of the hotel, shown the bathroom, on the same floor . . given a white jacket . . told to settle down, take it easy, look around, and get to know my way about the hotel. "Tomorrow," Mrs. Boyd said. "You can start in the pantry."

So, here we are . . a new start in life . . a new job . . . *most* promising. According to that fairy-tale, I . . I should *never* have looked back. I should have become a *top hotel man*, son and heir of the Boyds. I regret, dear reader, it did not go like that.

One morning, in the pantry, about 7 a.m. I'm getting ready the early morning teas . . boiling the water, putting out the cups and saucers, getting some biscuits, when the rush starts: "Two teas, please" . . . "One tea and a biscuit, please". . . "One tea, but *no milk*, please". . . "Oh, *bother*, didn't I tell you, *no sugar, Victor*." By now I'm getting just a bit worked-up. Never *too* good at the patience lark, never *too* good at the noble self-control lark, I suddenly *explode like a bomb* . . smash the cups and saucers, throw the biscuits on the floor . . bawl, shout and rave at the defenceless girls waiting for those teas . . and, throwing my white jacket on the floor, I dash away upstairs . . put on my own jacket, leap down the stairs, through the corridor, down the steps, past the bewildered porter out into that street . . . And I'm back where I started . . homeless, friendless and penniless . . and . . *myself to blame.*

Quick to anger . . quick to cool off . . but a somewhat vain and proud young man, though I knew I was in the wrong. I just couldn't go back, and so my one and *only* chance to learn the hotel-business, and *repay* the Boyds for their kindness, was *lost for ever.*

I look *back* on all this, my life so far, and what do I see? I see a human being, a young man, heading for *disaster* and *he did not know it.* Worse still for him, there was no one around caring enough to put him right. In the *books*, all those *text-books*, it says: "*When all the world around you is* tottering and bonkering, *keep thy head up, man* and *be a man.*" For what it's worth, I . . I was *not a man*, just a bloody fool.

Having a few shillings in my pocket, I get down to the pier, and learn that a boat will be leaving for Liverpool in an hour or so. Whilst awaiting the boat, my feelings are mixed. I'm sorry for myself . . a bit angry with I know not what, and bewildered too, as I am not so sure *why* all this is happening to me. I get on that boat . . we steam across the sea . . I smell that old, familiar sea-smell . . the boat-smell . . and I experience a kind of nostalgia for boyhood days and boyhood memories, way back on that River Clyde. Unknown to me, I must have got more involved with the sea, and all its mysteries, on that old boat, the *Empress*, than I was aware of at the time.

Liverpool . . there it was . . the *old* Liverpool of days so long ago: the waterfront, Pitt Street, China-town . . a busy thriving port. You'd meet them *all* there: Americans, Swedes, Africans, Indians . . yes, whores, thieves, pimps and vagabonds too . . and to this rip-roaring town I come. Unknown to me, *somebody up there* (or is it *down there?*) was busily plotting my very next step towards *that* life which has been mine ever since . . a thief, a fool and a *nutter.*

In passing Lime Street Station, I hear a voice: "What cheer, *chum*? Stranger?" I stopped in my tracks. After all *this* was a friendly voice.

"Yes, quite a stranger to this town," I say. I'm invited to come and have a coffee in a nearby 'caff'. This fellow tells me there is plenty of money in Liverpool. "*But*," he says, "you have to nick it."

My new found friend had just come out of Liverpool Jail, so he said, doing bird for some kind of hotel theft. Up till now, I'd done *no* villainy since that bicycle theft as a boy of eleven for which I got a reform school sentence of five years. At this particular time in my life—I was barely eighteen years of age, had no friends, no home—I was in a somewhat confused state of mind and, in a sort of way, I suppose I was an angry man. But *don't ask me why* . . *why* I was an angry man . . that I did not discover for many years.

I agreed to go in with this fellow as a sort of partner. I booked in at the Great Western Hotel. My job was to get *any* gear such as jewellery . . 'tom-foolery' he called it . . bring it out and he would sell it.

I go to this hotel, take keys from the porter's desk when he is absent for a moment . . go upstairs . . open a door . . enter . . look around in *this* drawer, in *that* drawer . . and I find some gear. I go downstairs . . don't pay that bill: this *last* act, the *hallmark* of the amateur thief. *Hotels should always be paid.*

I'm out in the street . . look around . . there he is . . same place I saw him last, outside the station. "Got the foolery?" he says. Me, I suddenly decide to leave this man . . have nothing to do with him . . so I say: "I've got nothing, and I'm getting out of here. Goodbye." I find a buyer for the gear in one of Liverpool's backstreets . . and I . . I become a *professional thief*.

Liverpool City . . money in my pocket . . and the town is mine. I walk along Dale Street looking in the shop-windows, not a care on my mind. It is a strange thing, but I must confess to having no misgivings and *no* premonitions as to the course I was taking. The money in my pocket *might* have got there from honest labour, for all I knew. That I was a *thief*, setting out on a dangerous course which *could* be disaster for *me* and *hurt* and *loss* for others, I did not know *or* think about.

I go over the water to New Brighton, get me a modest bedsitter; buy a few clothes, stow all my things away, nice and tidy; have a bath, change my clothes, and go for a night out. Looking around me I notice a poster . . "Tower and Gardens for Fun and Games". I soon find this "Fun and Games" place, buy a ticket and walk in. Music . . music . . whirring-machines . . swings and roundabouts . . pretty girls . . *all* the fun of the fair. A kind of *zoo . . lions, tigers, snakes* and *toads* . . queer smells, too.

"Enjoying yourself?" I turn round . . and there was such a pretty girl, actually talking to *me.*

"Yes . . yes . . I am enjoying myself. Are *you*?" Thus I met Jean, rather small, rather nice, rather young. We got talking. Jean had a half-day off, worked in a tobacco shop, was only seventeen, was living at home with her parents.

At this time in my life, I was not at all experienced in a boy and girl situation, and can only say this: Jean and I went around those gardens, and on the merry-go-rounds. We looked at those poor caged animals, ate ice-creams, drank lemonade and came to the end of that day as innocent . . as natural . . as completely inoffensive, as a couple of kids.

I left Jean outside the Tower Gates later in the day . . feeling somewhat odd and disturbed, not quite sure if I had failed in some way or another. Truth is, I suppose, *unknown* to *me,* I was a sort of *lost* one, seeking I know not what. Time marched on . . I'd go in a café, order something to eat or drink . . sit adreaming . . get up, go out . . wander around. I'd go down to the docks . . look at those ships . . stare down there into the river . . *no plans* . . *no schemes* . . just drifting . . .

I got to my last ten shillings as usual, *dreaming,* when I hear: "Like to come home with me, ducks?" The voice was a woman's . . soft and alluring. I look up . . there she was: a nice one, indeed . . fair . . no hat on . . hair down to her shoulders . . a neat, trim little body . . buttoned up in a very smart suit. "Sure I'll come with you. Sure."

This woman takes me by the arm and leads the way. Here it is. Up a few steps, she opens a door . . invites me in . . we climb a stairway . . rather a ricketty-racketty, paint-peeling-off sort of house, this. Another door is opened . . and we are in. What a contrast to *all* that shabbiness out there . . soft lights . . soft carpets . . soft chairs . . and a soft bed. I'm looking around, somewhat unsure of myself . . and *she* starts taking all her clothes off . . right down to stockings and panties. *Me* I'm sitting on the edge of the bed . . pleased to be up here, *never* having had an invitation like *this* before. The woman sits down beside me . . puts an arm round my shoulder and says: "What are you going to give me, ducks?" I . . I just sat there, not quite knowing *what* she meant.

"Come on, ducks . . *money* . . *money* . . *money*." I look at this woman . . I don't quite get it . . Money? Money? I put my hand in my pocket, bring out that ten shilling note . . offer it to the woman . . and *she* . . *she* . . recoils in a kind of horror and rage . . bawls and screams: "How dare you, you young bastard . . offering *me* ten shillings? *Do* you think I'd let you fuck *me* for ten shillings? Get out of this house . . get out of here."

I . . I got out of *there* . . as she told me. So begins my *education* . . . as *playboy* . . *thief* . . and *mug*. This woman was a whore and I did not know it. Don't ever tell me whores are fine, warm-hearted, gentle creatures, taking young innocents into their large comforting bosoms. *This* one was hard, mean and ruthless. I don't have to say that never happened again. I learnt quite a lesson . . . you pay for what you get in this world.

At this moment in time, in Liverpool Town . . still unknown to me, undreamt of by me . . the *fates* were busily planning my next step, down . . down . . down. Not that I'm suggesting I'm a defenceless victim of *invisible powers* . . only this: as my life unfolds, there does appear to be more in the notion than just the foolish choice of a foolish man. I'm penniless, homeless and friendless . . and that old anger . . that old anger against everything and everybody . . takes over. I cross the river by ferry . . land at New Brighton . . find a small hotel . . book in . . look around for an unlocked room . . and start the old thieving lark again . . knocking off anything I can sell. Not very selective as yet . . just a beginner . . a petty thief.

I go from hotel to hotel . . booking in, stealing what I can get . . leaving the hotel without paying the bill . . selling the 'gear' for what it will fetch. After all there is *plenty where that came from* . . or so the bloody thief thinks. I live in this absurd world of fantasy and folly, getting money where I can steal it or gear which one sells to the ever-ready buyer or *fence*, as he is called. Then one goes on a spree, spending the money on wine, women and song . . *kidding oneself* . . one is a very *fine fellow* . . *a villain*.

All this time, on the way down that road . . I make no friends . . go out and steal . . sell the gear . . spend the money . . find comfort *of a kind* in some whore's bed . . drink that wine, never caring for beer. I soon got a taste for *good wine*, in fact the day came when, much later in my life, I became an authority on wine.

III

I WAS IN this hotel, sitting in the lounge, when the receptionist comes over to me and says: "There are *two gentlemen* to *see you, Sir*. They are in the hallway." When a thief hears these words—"*Two gentlemen to see you, Sir*"—*something happens to his heart* .. it seems to *drop down* .. *drop down* .. right *down* through that floor .. and .. you just ain't got no heart.

I don't suppose I'm any more of a coward than most fellows in the thieving lark, but I must confess, that old heart of mine had gone for a *Burton*. There they were ...

"We are police officers, making enquiries into certain offences concerned with thefts from hotels .. and *you* are like the man we are looking for. Will you come quietly or must we hand-cuff you?" For a moment or two I was desperate. I looked over there at the *open* door, thinking of a wild dash for *freedom*, but those fellows closed in on me .. and I was *done*. This was my *first* contact with the *law* since the day, long ago, when I was arrested for taking a *bicycle*, for which offence I got five years' reform school.

As I've reached a significant point in my life .. a sort of *wild* and *dangerous no-man's land* .. let me try to convey the inner turmoil that I *now* experienced.

I was barely eighteen years of age .. I'd had a somewhat deprived boyhood .. met up with a few bits-and-pieces of unsolicited punishment .. been to reform school .. *in* and *out* of the Army .. drifted *or* dropped *right* into that *villainy lark* .. and yet .. and yet I was *not* .. was *not* .. was not a *cold, calculating scoundrel* .. and *this* is said with no *intent* to *dodge* the *consequences* of my behaviour. Almost everything I did in those days .. in fact, *in all* my days as a *villain* .. sprang from *anger* .. from *rage* .. from *frustration* and from *impulse. This is no excuse*, but it *is* the *fact* ...

So here I am feeling rather as if this thing was *not happening to me*, the *real me*. I was puzzled .. bewildered .. also .. I was angry .. angry with *what* exactly, *I know not*. In this alien state of mind, this disturbed state of mind, I'm confronted with the police. It's *assumed by the police* I'm quite *guilty*, even without the *formality* of a *trial*. I harden in my attitude to the police . . . I get hard and tough, and say, in effect: *Fuck you, do your worst*. I'm taken to the Dale Street Police Centre . . am charged with various petty thefts . . . and down that corridor . . in that cell . . empty of *all* furniture . . except a bench fixed to the wall . . a stinking *open* W.C. in the corner . . they *bang* that door on *me*. As a story has to be told concerning a thief, a fool and a nutter, I won't write *any* tear-jerking stuff regarding that stinking Dale Street lock-up. Suffice it to say: *Whatever criminal tendency I may* have had, it was *confirmed* by *my experience there*. In due course, I took my *trial* . . I was sentenced to twelve months' Hard Labour, and was transported to *Walton Prison* . . a grim, cold fortress, my *home* for the next year.

My *first* jail experience ever: a mixture of *bad* smells . . *bad* food . . *bad* bastards . . and yet . . and yet I must confess it was I who took those steps which led to Walton Jail.

"Stand there, shut your mouth up, empty your pockets . . strip off . . any ailments? Turn round . . bend down . ." he looks *up* your arsehole . . "cough . ." he looks at your prick . . "All right, you can go."

"Put this on . ." vest and pants . . a dirty grey sort of stuff, heavy, and stinking to heaven. A shirt more like a sack . . jacket, breeches, long stockings . . heavy boots, the boots *smelling* of the *feet* of every man or boy who had done time in that prison for the *last* twenty years.

Walton Prison, as *all* prisons in those days, was a grim and primitive place. As *this* is not an *old lag's tale* nor a prison documentary, I'll just say this: the food, the work, the general conditions, the overall climate of jail-life, was designed to *kill* or *cure*. In my case it did neither: what it did do to me was strengthen my every hatred, every resentment . . every and *any anti-social thought* in my mind.

I was in the Boys' Wing, working in a labour-gang on a building-site outside the prison-wall, with an electrified railway on the other side of a separating fence. I go up to some of the fellows working farther down the site, look right and left . . see where those 'screws' are . . and whisper: "Have a 'barney' . . a punch-up . . get that screw's *attention* . . I am going to scarper."

Those boys set up an *unholy din* . . belted each other . . for all the world as if they really *meant it*. *Me* . . *me* . . I note the screws running towards this punch-up . . I dash to the fence . . scramble over it . . down that embankment . . *leap . . leap* . . over the railway line . . up the opposite embankment . . over another fence, and . . and I am *free*. Behind me I can hear whistles, shouts, threats . . threats to *murder* me when I am caught.

There is a lorry coming along . . I put my thumb up, for a lift, and much to my *joy* that lorry slows up. I get on the back of the lorry . . feel *safe* . . *secure* . . and *happy*. We are approaching a built-up area and the lorry slows down . . I drop off, wave a thank-you to the driver . . and start walking . . walking into that town . . feeling like a *king* who had *lost* his *throne* and *found it again*. There is an alley-way . . down there, down the side of a row of shops. I go to this alley . . try *that* door . . try *this* door . . try *this* window . . that window . . finally, a small window . . at the back . . I take my shoe off . . smash the window . . start climbing in . . and I hear a voice: *"What are you up to, me lad?"*

My feet and legs were held in a vice-like grip, and I knew *this* was it . . . I . . I . . was *done*. I had an impulse to *kick out*, but: "*Come quietly. It's a fair cop*," said a voice, and I came quietly. That's *him* . . the *law* in *all his majesty* . . I'm thinking. A fat copper, big-fisted . . big-bellied . . big-voiced. I was held firmly by this fellow and asked to come with him to the police station.

I'm soon identified as *wanted* for *escaping legal custody* . . . They forwent charging me with shop-breaking, took me back to Walton Prison, and left me to the tender mercies of my jailers.

So here we are . . you just *can't beat them*, can you? I take my trial before the visiting magistrates, am sentenced to *one* month's *loss* of Remission, 15 days No. 1 diet, 28 days No. 2 diet and "take away his mattress for a month" . . and *unofficially*: "give the young bastard a tanning."

I won't tear-jerk you . . that punishment was hard . . practically . . starvation. The cell was *cold* . . empty of *all* furniture . . bed and pot for night use . . pot *only* for day use. I'd walk up and down . . up and up . . down and down . . till my feet were sore . . then sit on the floor *or* the hard piece of wood stuck into the wall, there . . till my *arse was sore* . . then I'd *repeat* this rigmarole *all* day . . .

You get bread and water three times a day, but when on No. 2 diet, some 'skilly' and potatoes with the mid-day bread. You get *cold* down there . . you toss yourself 'off' *to get warm*, to get a little excitement in that boring *hole*. You *plot* . . you *plan* . . how to make up for *all* this? You *don't get repentant,* nor do you *get sorry for yourself.* You *get angry . . angry . .* and the end of it all? You make your mind up to get your own back.

The day when I finished that punishment, I was taken upstairs, and told: "You are not going back to the Boys' Wing . . you'll be put in the Men's Wing. You'll work in the weaving-shed . . and *give us any more trouble, you are for it.*"

I find myself in the weaving-shed, making rough-sheeting, and bed-coverlets for prison use. I liked this work. Strangely enough, the rhythm of the machine . . the weft and the wooft of it, and the resultant product, sheets and coverlets for *tired prisoners . .* all this pleased me . . quite a change from those stinking mail-bags and that humiliating oakum-picking. In the weaving-shed, at this time . . 1922-1923 . . were many Irishmen doing time for 'trouble' in Ireland and elsewhere. The *silent system* of those days *forbade all talking . .* but communication was possible . . and sometimes I had a word or two with these Irish fellows . . friendly, cheerful, and intensely loyal, one to another. I cared nought for the politics of the Irish at that time, but I respected them, as men dedicated to their cause.

The day came, when my time was up, and I was *asked*: "Where do you want to go to, when you leave here?" For no special reason, I said: "*Glasgow.*" I get a ticket to Glasgow and half-a-crown in cash, leaving that prison determined to *make someone pay, for this . . 'this'* being a sort of *fantasy thing* born of *all that fall-out* from *mine own actions . . .* not knowing, at that time, *it was I* who was my *own executioner . . mine own worst enemy.*

So here we go again: a young man getting on for nineteen years of age . . reform school . . jail . . the Army as an unwilling recruit . . . no friends . . no home . . no *objective* worth *fivepence,* and *itching . . itching* to square that account.

Strangely, *it never occurred to me* in *those days* that it was I . . I with *whom* an *account had to be settled.* There I am in *Glasgow.* That two shillings and sixpence wouldn't go very far. I'd *nothing* but what I stood up in. So straight into the *first hotel I saw . . I went.* Thus, I renew my thieving activities . . entering and leaving hotels, knocking off *anything* of *value* I could find. Quickly I begin to accumulate gear . . quickly I sell it, to the ever-ready *fence . .* quickly I get the notion I'm a *clever guy . .* a *'lucky guy' . . sure to beat that rap. . .* Invariably, when a thief gets this notion . . that he's *clever*, he's *lucky* . . he's *in danger*, but *does not know it* . . and he gets careless. *Me* . . *me* . . get careless . . *drunk with an illusion* of *freedom* and *opulence.* I go back to that *hotel once too often* . . and I'm *done* . . *done* . . *done.*

"Two gentlemen to see you, Sir."

I'm taken to the lock-up . . am charged with stealing jewellery . . and *also* getting food and lodgings by false pretences. I'm ignorant of many things . . . I'm stupid . . defenceless . . soft clay in that policeman's hands . . *no* difficulty in *convicting me* . . I'm a *bastard* from the start.

I'm tried in due course . . I have *no* counsel . . am sentenced to three years' *Borstal* . . and *so* . . I take another step *down* . . . another step *down* . . almost like Pilgrim's Progress in *reverse*, eh?

Here it is . . the *Borstal Institute* . . somewhere in Scotland. Another home-from-home . . the bloody place, I soon discover, is a *den* of *thieves. I ought to have fitted* in, but I did not care for this place masquerading as a *public school* for *working-class delinquents*: *spit* and *polish* . . *fake culture* . . *studies* . . *classes* . . *housemasters* . . and *buggery galore.* I'm *soon* in trouble. Some bastard takes *me* for a *queer* . . I threaten to *kill* him. I'm involved in a battle . . am grabbed . . taken down below . . get a going-over . . and find myself on the way to the tough and dreaded *Barlinnie Prison*, where they tame *lions*, so they say. Except for a few weeks . . I spent *three years* in *Barlinnie* . . and *this* for the record: *they did not tame me* . . . but then, I am *not a lion.*

Always, when writing of prison, I hesitate somewhat. After all, I put myself in it. I was *not* an *innocent man*, nor was I a *victim* of the *establishment* . . also, *society must be protected* from the *marauder* and from the likes of *me.* Having said all this . . let's face it . . *prison is not an intelligent remedy* for *crime* and *criminality. My life proves that.* If any man in all this world has had the prison-treatment, I am *that man* . . and yet at sixty-four years of age I was *still in prison* . . though I started *out* on this *life* of *crime* and *criminality* so many years before.

Barlinnie Prison, when I arrived at that grim institution way back in 1923, was *cold* . . *hard* and *tough.* And though it *never* made me *cold*, it *did* make *me* both *hard* and *tough. Tough* and *hard* in the *wrong kind* of *way. This place* was designed, *first* and *last*, as a place of *security* for *holding* and *keeping* any unfortunate man getting in there for a jail-sentence. Also, I would say an element of sheer *sadism* went into the *making* of this jail . . as in all such places the world over. *I must put it on record* that today in England, Scotland, the U.S.A., Scandinavia, and elsewhere in the civilised world, *jails are being built* for *human beings* rather than for *animals* . . . Not that I would put either *man* or *animal* in *jail*, be it *modern* or *otherwise*.

I arrive at Barlinnie very much a *marked man* . . in other words, a trouble-maker, so-called and so-named.

They put me in the stone-yard, and I'm told: "14 cwt. of road-metal a day we want from *you* . . and be sure you break it up so the pieces go through a sieve, two by two inches." It's *mid-winter* . . and I am out there in the stone-yard . . a huge pile of *stone*, in massive lumps . . *all* to be broken up into pieces no bigger than two by two *inches*. I have *never done this before* . . don't like it at all . . *it smacks* of *slavery* . . . *slavery*.

A two-pound hammer in my hand, I grab a big lump of stone . . place it down there, right on that solid earth, and give it *one bang* . . another . . another *bang*, and it slips from under that *hammer* . . just *rolls away* . . almost in *contempt*. I try again . . finally, I succeed in getting *one little chip* off that mountain of rock. By now I'm getting blisters on my hands and a kind of blister on my patience. I begin to curse *me*, the jail, the whole bloody world.

"Get on with your work, there, and shut your mouth" . . this remark from a screw on a bridge-like platform. It seems, even talking to yourself is an offence. I throw the hammer down, go over to the screw and say: "Fuck you, if you want this work done . . *do it yourself*." Talk about *pandemonium* . . the screw blows his 'flute' . . bawls and shouts: "Get this man down below." I'm jumped on by several screws . . pushed, hustled and bustled . . kneed and elbowed down to the 'separates' . . stripped of jacket, shoes, belt . . thrown into an empty cell . . and that door *bangs shut*.

I look around this cell . . brick-and-cement . . a piece of wood fixed to the wall to sit on . . a piece of wood let into the floor to lie down on. A pot without a lid to piss in . . and *up there*, a very small barred window covered with so much dirt a mere glimmer of light came through. Half the walls of this brick-and-cement box, this cell, were painted a dirty kind of yellow. On them I noticed a fine collection of *graffiti*: *"Fuck you, John", "This nick is a bad one", "I can do it, on my head", "Four more days to go"*.

It is getting dark .. it is very quiet. I .. I am thinking what next? when the door opens, a screw says, "Take your bed in." Outside was a lumpy, smelly mattress, two blankets and a pillow. I take these things in the 'peter' .. this empty, cold box .. sling them down on the floor .. and that door *bangs* shut.

It's getting cold, down there .. I walk up and down .. I sit down .. I get up .. spread those blankets on the mattress. A light goes on .. a *gas light*, out there .. separated from this cell by a thick pane of glass let into the wall. The gas flickered .. *up* .. *down* .. *up* .. *down*. You could smell that gas .. *almost like a gas chamber*, in which *you* were going to die. In the door, a Judas hole through which that screw .. can *watch* your every move. *Me* .. I think: He must have seen some *strange larks* in *this peter*. Funnily enough, I wasn't thinking too much of what would happen to *me* the following day. *All I* thought of was: *Wait till I get out of this.*

It's morning .. "put your bed *out* .. slop *out* .. here is a basin of water, soap-and-towel .. get washed."

A mug of tea, cob of bread smeared with margarine .. and that door *bangs*. I may note, as a matter of interest to the reader, bread and margarine was a *luxury*. For years and years porridge and sour milk had been the standard breakfast at Barlinnie .. but, the wind of change was coming .. so, bread and margarine was allowed.

"Give your name and number to the Governor. You are charged with refusing to labour, using bad language and threatening an officer." The evidence is given by the screw .. and I'm asked: "What have you to say, in your defence?" Having heard that screw, I knew that anything I said would be *useless*, so I answered: "Nothing to say."

"Three days No. 1 diet, and seven days No. 2 diet .. and take *away* his mattress for seven days .. *about turn* .. *quick march*."

Back in that peter .. there you stay till end of punishment except for a brief period, perhaps twenty minutes, morning and afternoon, out there in that yard ... for what they call *exercise*. No. 1 diet is bread and water—16 ounces of bread a day .. as *much water as you want* ... *if* it's *cold, you don't want water* that is cold too. No. 2 diet is bread and water plus, for mid-day meal, some gruel and potatoes. If you wish, whilst on punishment, you could *pick oakum* or make a sort of coir-rope . . . *Me* . . *me* . . I wanted *none* of their work . . . *all* I wanted was to be left *alone*. I did my punishment, quite content to stay down there for the rest of my time if necessary, *dreaming* of *freedom* and a settlement of accounts. You just walk up and down . . up and down . . dreaming of successful villainy . . then, come night-time, you lie on that stinking, lumpy mattress, and you *dream again*.

In due course, I finished that piece of punishment, went upstairs, and back to that stone-yard . . . where I got to like that stone-breaking, funnily enough, turning out 16 cwt a day instead of 14cwt, thus getting 2 ounces of bread *extra*.

In the meantime, whilst working in the stone-yard, I have periodic explosions . . go down below . . serve *that* punishment . . *as if I liked it*. They even try the *dark cells* . . in an effort to break and tame my recalcitrant spirit . . but I just go on *dreaming* of *glory* . . I see myself as a *top villain* in *Dartmoor Prison one day* . . and *that* is the effect of punishment on *me*.

Between punishments and work in the stone-yard, I was reading quite a lot from *Dickens* . . *all* the way *up* and *down* . . . Shakespeare . . Burns . . Shaw . . *yes* . . *Josephus's history of the Jews* . . . too and, do you know something? I remember in Josephus a passage concerning the *man Christ* . . and, as I had previously thought that *man* was a mere *invention* of the *church*, finding that Josephus seriously wrote of *Him* as a *real man*, I was very very excited. And yet I was hardly a religious young man.

To the list of *my favourite authors* of those days, I must add Mr. *Phillips Oppenheim* . . that writer of the *Opulent Life* . . fine hotels, fine women, fine wine . . . In short . . I'm living in a world of fantasy and folly in an effort to escape from the intolerable life of a prisoner, from the essential sordidness of my *actual* life. I suppose, in a kind of way, *I knew* . . *I knew* that my life was a *dead loss* . . so I reached out into fantasy and folly in a *blind* effort at compensation.

One day, towards the end of my time, I was told that the Governor had ordered my transfer from the stone-yard to the library . . but I refused to go, and was told: "If *no* library, you must go down below." I stayed below for weeks and weeks until they let me go back to that stone-yard. Funnily enough, *what* I once hated, that breaking up of stones . . *slavery*, I called it, I would not now give up.

Looking back at *all* this seeming folly and wilfulness . . refusing to take the library-job, refusing to leave the stone-yard . . I *now* realise that my choice of villainy as a career, and the consequent punishment when caught, was beginning to take effect. In my case this life of mine and its outcome *confirmed* every single defect in my make-up. Not being an expert in human behaviour, I don't know why *crime* and *punishment, together,* confirmed me in this course . . instead of *deflecting me away* from it.

Finally I take the library-job . . and from *one book a week,* and *no noting-system,* I start a brand-new system, permitting every man a choice of his own books . . . *three books* a *week* and a *noting-system* too. This book-changing and noting system, the *new system,* was a revolutionary change for Barlinnie . . and I *must* put *this* on record: had it not been for the collaboration of the screw nominally in charge of the library, this change *could not have taken place* . . a mere prisoner could not have done it on his own.

I like this library-work. I met a lot of the fellows I would not otherwise have met; also, for the *first* time in my life as a villain and jail-bird, I met an intelligent and humane screw.

There was a concert in the chapel, one of the few that ever took place in Barlinnie, whilst I was there: Herman Darewski and his band, a top band of that era. At the end of the show, the governor asked me to give a vote of thanks. Having said my piece, a wonderful show, etcetera, I was introduced to Herman Darewski as a one-time clarinettist and boy-conductor, the governor having found *this* out from my record, I suppose. Darewski told me he was going, with his band, on a coast-to-coast tour of the U.S.A., and said: "If the Governor will allow you, I'll take you with me as 'featured boy-clarinettist'. I might even let you have a go on the *rostrum.*" I was near the end of my time. The Governor promised to communicate with the Prison Commissioners for Scotland. So I *await* the Commissioners' reply, which, in due course, arrived: *"We will not permit a boy in our care to join a band of strolling players." This* was said of the famous Herman Darewski band.

I take my discharge from Barlinnie Prison. I'm offered a place in a Church Army Hostel which I refuse, and a ticket to anywhere I like, in England or Scotland. I elect to go to *England*, and that was a *fatal choice* though *I did not know it* then.

IV

BACK IN ENGLAND, where I got my *first* Prison sentence—no friends, no home, about five shillings in my pocket, *still* failing to see the way I was *heading*, still itching to put that account right, still seeing myself as a potential *big shot* in the villainy-world—I plunge back into the old activities, get me some gear . . and I'm on the way *back . . back . . back*.

Harrogate, City-of-*opulence* . . after the city of *Leeds*, a kind of *sacred city* for the *high priests of finance, retired*. I register in this hotel, I look around, find a retired banker staying there . . I rob him of stocks, shares, money and jewellery . . I leave the hotel, go to *Leeds*, sell some gear, stay around for a while . . have some wine, women and song just like the *old tale* . . you know, that *Oppenheim novel* which I read down there in old Barlinnie-town. I say this in *all* seriousness: *Don't put a budding thief in jail . . with leisure to read books concerning the life of the rich* and *opulent* . . you make him very *discontented with his lot* . . .

I go to Carlisle . . find a stockbroker with whom I make an appointment for the next day. I had bought a rather dangerous-looking Webley Scott Air Pistol which, for some absurd reason, I fancied. I carried this gun in a small bag, along with the share certificates.

My plan for handling the stocks and shares was very amateurish. I really knew *nothing about* stocks and shares but, impressed by all the fancy-stampings, the signatures, the *figures*, running into *thousands*, I imagined, in my *ignorance*, I could *borrow money* under pretence of *owning* the shares, wishing to *sell* them ultimately.

Staying the night in a small hotel, I go to the stockbrokers next morning . . am received by a polite clerk who tells me. "My principal is out for the morning, but if you will call this afternoon he will be in." At this time in my life, I had not learnt the lesson of *never . . never* going *back, later*. *That* way, you walk *right into the trap*.

Come the afternoon, I get the small bag, the *gun*, the paper-stuff, and off I go . . . *walking on air*, in the illusion . . I . . I . .

* *

was a clever and successful thief. Up those stairs . . in that office . . a big desk . . behind it . . a *big man . . too bloody big* for *my taste* . . . "Please take a seat," says the man. "You want to borrow some money, eh? and later, sell the shares?" I'm looking at this man . . and, if that fellow is a stockbroker, I'm a *bishop*, I'm thinking. As if the fellow had read my thoughts, he says: "I won't waste any more time, Sir. I'll tell you right *now* . . *I am a police officer* and I have reason to believe these shares are *not yours* . . and you are *not* Mr. Harrison, whose name is on the shares." For a moment or two that old heart of mine goes *down there* . . down there . . I have that *old* familiar feeling of being *done . . done . . done.*

I remember that gun . . . only a toy, but dangerous-looking. "Oh, Mr. Harrison, as you call yourself, what have you got in that little bag?" *This* . . *this* was it . . . I open the bag . . . I pull out the gun and say: "Stick your hands up, you bastard." . . *Yes*, that's *what I said*, just like those damned movies . . . I rise from the table . . back towards the door . . the man, this police officer, dives under the table, *screaming* . . . *screaming* . . "Get *this* fellow, *before he kills me*." . . . *Unknown* to me, two men had been posted behind a nearby door, and I was grabbed from behind, the gun being knocked out of my hand. And so . . and so . . I'm *done again.*

In writing this story, I'm governed by two considerations. *One*: to tell the truth. *Two*: *not* to give the impression that I deserve a *medal* . . that I'm a kind of *underworld hero* . . that I'm a *victim* of a *remorseless society*. Having made *all* this clear, I'll resume the story.

I'm taken to Police Headquarters, Carlisle . . am formally charged . . locked up. I'm in that old familiar *peter* in the jail lock-up. The *same old smells* . . the same old glimmer of light through that small window . . W.C. in the corner . . *stink* . . *stink*. Plank-bed fixed to the wall . . and the *graffiti* . . . so common . . so common to the *excommunicated*: *"I love Jean", "Fuck you, I can do my bird."*

I hear keys rattling . . footsteps, down the corridor. I stand back against that wall, expecting trouble. After all . . I tried to *gun* that copper. The door is unlocked . . and *there* is what appears to be the whole police force of Carlisle. The policeman who arrested me in that stockbroker's office came towards me, hand outstretched to shake mine, saying: "We are sorry, Mr.

Thomas X., you are in this trouble. We thought you had finished with all this kind of thing when you left Borstal, five years ago."

Me . . me . . I'm puzzled. Is this a new kind of police-trap? Are they kidding me for some secret reason? This police-fellow and the others soon make it clear to me . . I'm mistaken for another man, who, it appears, had been to Borstal, come *out*, and become a successful writer, specialising in crime and criminality. All this struck me as rather absurd, and yet it *could* serve my purpose. In due course, I'm taken back to Harrogate . . there to be formally charged . . and committed for trial.

All this time I'm letting them think I'm really this Mr. X., . . after all, if they think I am Thomas X., *only* one lapse since that Borstal sentence, I could get off quite lightly. I'm sent to Leeds Prison, there to await my next appearance in Court; but, coming down in the meantime with a shattering dose of the pox, I was put in the jail-hospital, which meant somewhat less harshness. The day came when I was summoned to the Magistrates' Court, Harrogate . . and there I am, in that *box*, facing the court, once more having to answer for my behaviour.

"Mr. Thomas X., you are charged with stealing jewellery, cash, and stock shares, to the value of £30,000. You are also charged with using a dangerous weapon in an effort to escape arrest. What is your answer to these charges?"

In that *box*, looking around me at all these people . . the court, the police, the onlookers . . I'm thinking: *Why continue this farce?* I'm *not* Mr. Thomas X. . . I'll take the rap . . I'll pay the price *alone* and unprotected by someone else's name.

My answer to the charges? "I am *not* Mr. Thomas X. . . the police have made a blunder . . and I plead guilty to the charges, *except* the 'dangerous-weapon' one, to which I plead *not* guilty, as this weapon was a *toy gun*, an *air pistol*, not dangerous as far as I know."

At once there is *laughter . . talking . . loud comment.* The police looked rather *sheepish.* After all, it isn't often one gets a chance to catch the police out.

"*Order . . order . .* in this court. Quiet, please . . *this* is *not* a *music hall.*" When order is restored, I'm told: "*You* will be *remanded* for a *week* . . perhaps, by then, the police will *know* who you are."

I return to Leeds Prison for one week's remand and, as I'm

down with that *pox* thing, I go straight into hospital to continue treatment. This *pox* . . is not, in itself, of great importance to this anecdote . . but . . as you will read, later, it does have some relevance to the story. Many men get this pox thing . . ignorance, stupidity, thoughtlessness, folly or just inexperience . . you get it. And for *me*, at this time of my life, I must confess, I was *both ashamed and afraid.*

Next morning, in hospital, I'm visited by the governor and the chaplain, and I'm told: "There is a Special Delivery letter here for you . . it's from a Mr. Thomas X. It appears that he saw something in the Press regarding your words in court yesterday, and he is impressed by your refusal to hide behind his name." I read this letter: . . "Thanks for disassociating yourself from my name . . . Thank you for a kind of honesty very unusual in cases like yours . . . Is there any kind of help I can give you?" I answered: "Thank you, there is nothing you can do for me", and, from that day to this, I've never heard of or from that Mr. X.

The week's remand soon passed, and I again appeared before the Harrogate Court, where I was formally charged in my adopted name of *Rogers*, and committed for trial to the notorious *West Riding Quarter Sessions*, where, it is said, the magistrates will hang you for stealing a *rabbit*. I return to the prison hospital . . and resume treatment. I'm told to go downstairs for *irrigation* of which I . . I knew absolutely *nothing*.

It's a long corridor, on one side of which is a row of open cubicles, with a kind of inverted glass-jar, hanging up there, and a long, rubber tube, dangling from there. In this jar, a purple-coloured fluid which was released from the tube through a nozzle at *this* end . . . to be inserted in that offending organ. Well . . well . . I *look* at this contraption . . I *look* right and left . . notice . . about a dozen other men . . and *each* of these fellows, using the tube, as to the *manner born*.

I think: *Jesus* . . *Jesus* . . have I got to do this in *public*? A male nurse comes along, opens up my trousers, takes out that bloody thing . . inserts that nozzle, turns on the fluid and says: "*Now you know* . . *get on with it*" . . and I get on with it.

In these days I'm writing about . . strictly speaking . . *talking* was *not allowed* in prison . . but down there, in the hospital department, things were *not too strict, so* . . you could talk a little.

"I say . . I say . . are you that fellow they mistook for Tom X.?

Are you the fellow that stuck those coppers up with the *toy pistol*?" In the next cubicle to me . . there is a young fellow buttoning up his trousers, and it seems I am the guy he's talking to. "Sure," I say. "I'm that fellow . . *why*?"

"*Gee* . . *gee* . . . I think you are great . . fancy tackling those coppers with a *toy pistol* . . . and *all* that stuff, from the Harrogate hotel." It was clear to me . . this youngster had a bad dose of *hero-worship*. He had it *all* wrong, of course . . I was *no hero*, and *villainy is not heroic*. Funnily enough, though I was engaged *in villainy*, and with some kind of addiction, I none the less *knew*, none the less *felt*, this thing was not for me *nor* for that youngster either.

I have some time to wait, before I go for trial, and during this time I got to know this young man. I learnt the lad was a Jew, son and heir of a local tailor. He was about my own age, twenty-two, had a nice home, was learning his father's trade . . unmarried, but involved with a girl, to whom he'd given a child . . . And it was on this account he was in jail, serving a short period of time for failing to maintain his child.

As time marched on, and my trial-day approached, my young friend and admirer was nearing the end of *his* time . . and he said to me, one day: "I'm coming to the gate the morning you finish, whatever time you get, and taking you home to meet Mum and Dad . . have breakfast, and then I'm coming away with you." In jail, one often hears people say: "I'll meet you at the gate" . . . but it isn't very often they *do so*. I tell this lad: "Forget *me* . . my kind of life is *not for you*."

This is trial day . . and there they are . . *West Riding Quarter Sessions* . . hard-looking . . tough-looking.

"*Rogers* . . you stand trial before this court for very serious offences . . you steal jewellery . . you steal cash, stocks and shares, and you try to escape lawful arrest by threatening a police officer with what appeared to be a dangerous weapon. What is your answer to these charges?"

I look at this man, my judge . . other men, on each side of him . . and I see . . I see that old familiar Heraldic Device . . on which are the words: *Justice is* . . but nothing is there about *mercy*. I recalled what I'd been told about this court: utterly merciless, even to a *rabbit thief*. I deliberately turn my back on that court, thinking: *Fuck them . . I won't ask for mercy . . I would not get it, anyhow.*

I hear a soft, ageing voice: "*Rogers* . . you don't have to turn your back on *this* court . . you will get justice, never fear." I turn round and face the court, fully expecting to get what *they* called *justice,* but I, by another kind of name.

"The court has considered your case carefully. We make allowance for your age, and other factors. You will go to prison for two years' Hard Labour . . . thus, I hope, learning that your kind of behaviour will not be tolerated in this country."

Well . . well . . well. I thought I would have got at *least ten years* . . .

"You were lucky, *Rogers* . . though I must say I've never known *any man* turn his back on that court before. It took great courage, and folly, too." *This* remark came from one of the escorting prison officers, taking me back to Leeds Prison. I go back to the prison hospital and stay there for most of the two years. As a matter of interest to the reader, who, I hope, has never seen the inside of a prison, I'll say that that prison hospital, in spite of the universal harshness of prisons in general at that time, provided good treatment, good food, good will. And the doctor there, a Dr. Worsley, a fine, well-mannered, kindly man, could not have treated me better, had I been a distinguished free-world *citizen*. As time went on, in this hospital, I got much worse, and the comparatively mild *pox* turned into a sort of rheumatic condition which practically *paralysed* me. However, I've *always* had this *survival-thing*, and towards end of sentence I was fully recovered.

Near the end of my time at Leeds Prison, I met the police surgeon of the Leeds City Police, who used to stand in when the regular prison M.O. went on leave. This police surgeon, for some reason, took an interest in me, and when on his rounds, he would always stop and talk to me.

"Rogers, if you could take up short-hand before you leave this prison, and show some promise, I may get you a job on a local newspaper." *I did* take up short-hand . . made good progress, but never saw the surgeon again.

My release day arrived, and I stepped *out* of that prison, fit and well, to start again, out there . . a bit unsure of myself, but *happy* to be free. There is a car outside the gate, and standing alongside it the young fellow who once told me he'd be there, waiting for me, one day.

"Hullo . . hullo . . I'm here as I promised you, I knew what your sentence was, and figured out when you would be released. You are coming home with me to meet Mum and Dad, have breakfast, then I'm coming with you."

I looked at this young man, so keen to follow in my steps, and not knowing, in his ignorance, what this villainy-thing really is. I felt sorry for this lad, and I said: "I am not coming home with you, and I advise you to forget the likes of me. *Go home . . learn your father's trade . . stay home,* and *keep out of jail.*"

I walk away . . look back . . wave . . wave a *goodbye* . . to this hero-worshipper of mine . . and *that* was the *last* I ever *saw of* him.

V

IT'S 1928, AND I'm back in the free world. The clothes I stood up in . . a bag with a change of under-clothing . . various items of personal use . . about five pounds in cash . . that was my lot. I did *not* want to go back to the villainy lark, but at the same time . . I had *no driving conviction* . . that villainy was *totally wrong for me.* I get me a small bedsitter . . and I look around. I think back . . to Leeds Prison and I recall that police surgeon, who had volunteered to help me if I learnt short-hand. So, I write to this man, care of the Leeds Police Headquarters, reminding him of his offer, and saying: "I'd rather take a newspaper job than go back to thieving."

I waited exactly *one* week, for a reply to my letter to the police surgeon, and getting *no* answer . . I . . I . . in one surging, urging *drive* of contempt for the surgeon, and contempt for *me* . . for having believed in this man and *his* promise . . I *went back to villainy.*

I'm twenty-four years of age, have done three years' *Borstal* . . though *that* was served in a *prison* . . twelve months' H.L. and then two years' H.L. . . on top of *all* that, five years' reform school . . . a villain in the *making* . . . and yet . . and yet . . I have a queer sort of reluctance to return to thieving.

I'm fronted, as I *see* it, with rejection from a Pillar-of-Society, one of a city's *top men* . . a *police surgeon* . . an honourable man who had flagrantly broken his promise to help a man. . . . I *exploded* into the self-destructive, murderous villainy-thing.

I make *no* excuses for this immature reaction to the *seeming rejection* by the police surgeon. *All* I know now is what I *did. Why* I did it, I don't know. It is strange . . I did see the wrongness of villainy for my young hero-worshipper outside that prison gate . . but I don't see the *wrongness* of the villainy-thing for *me.*

I'm now in *London* . . the London of 1928: *Ma Meyrick* and the "43" . . the *Shim Sham* . . the *Gargoyle* . . *Romano's* . . *Café Royal. Dot Dickson* . . *Bea Lillie* . . *Flo Desmond* . . the *Houston*

Sisters .. "*Tea* for *Two*" ... And the seamy side of life, too; *Bow Street* .. *Marlborough Street* .. the *Old Bailey* .. where I was to be a featured *artist* .. right there, in *that dock* ... *Soho*, too and its murky byways, its dirty little joints and *whores to suit all tastes*.

I've just come up to Town from the coast, done a bit of villainy down there, done another bit of villainy here in London Town .. Grosvenor Street .. and I'm on the way to sell the gear to my buyer, better known as *snidy-bastard*.

I see this buyer and his car outside Hammersmith Palais, this being the usual rendezvous. It was his idea for beating the cops: "Get out there in Hammersmith, *away* from the West End, and you're *safe*," he'd say. I get in that car and we drive off. A little way out of London, the car slows up .. stops.

"Let's have a *look* at that gear, Nick. *Jesus* .. *Jesus* .. Where did you get *this* from?" I look at this buyer .. his *eyes popping out of his head* with *greed, anticipation* of *profit*, and *fear* .. *fear* .. *fear* that *he* .. *he* might get mixed up in police procedures. Always this man would take my gear, but never without a show of terror at the mere possibility of *his involvement*.

This buyer takes a ring from the jewel-case, looks at it and turns to me, saying: "Can't give you much for this as I've got to break it up, and reset it, too." Other rings, bracelets, a diamond plaque, get the same *treatment*. I'm beginning to think: This bastard thinks he is doing me *a favour by just taking the gear*. By now, I'm getting fed-up with this fellow's method of doing business .. very common to such as *he* and his kind .. the method of *reduction*. These bastards invariably reduce *all* gear submitted to them, as if it were *valueless*, or so difficult to reset or handle they do you a *favour* by *taking it*.

"Look, Max .. cut the rigmarole .. you know it's *good stuff*. Give me a fair price and let me get out of this car."

The fat bastard puts his hand on his heart, saying: "Nick, for God's sake, *don't start anything* .. my heart's *bad*. *See* .. *see* .." he pulls out of his pocket a bottle containing what appears to be *pink medicine*. And I, not very patient at the best of times, *nor* a *good bargainer*, I say: "O.K., give us the money and let me get away."

The gear I had given this fellow had a newspaper publicity value of FIVE THOUSAND POUNDS .. this bastard offers me ONE HUNDRED POUNDS. For a moment or two I felt like belting this man . . then I think: Oh hell, there is plenty more where that came from; and I took his paltry hundred pounds.

I get back to my flat in Bloomsbury. I find Molly is in. She's a blonde, Irish, very *good* to *look at* . . . even *better in bed*.

"Hello, Nick, I'm just getting ready to go to work. I'm waiting for Jane to come for me. What've you been up to?"

"Just done a deal, Molly . . got a hundred pounds or so to spend. Why go to work? Let's go *out* and *play*."

"What's the *old sod* give you this time, Nick? I'll *bet* he's *robbed you again*." I tell Molly just *what I did get* for the gear . . and *she . . she goes off like a bomb*. "Nick . . Nick . . go back to that robbing bastard, make him give you *more money*. And *why . . why*, don't you *stop* throwing your money away? Buy a fish-and-chip shop. I've told you, again and again, fish-and-chips, where I come from, over in Ireland, they sell like *hot cakes*."

I tell Molly: "O.K. I'll go after the fellow tomorrow. For the present, you and I are going *out* . . going *out* for some fun."

I must explain, Molly was a restaurant-hostess and normally she would go to work afternoon and evening. If I wished to take her out before she finished her turn of duty, I'd *buy her out* by taking *all* her dance-tickets for that day.

So tonight, Molly and her friend Jane are escorted by me to the restaurant, and after a meal, served to me and Molly, I buy her out for the night.

I clearly remember *that* night. It was the day after I had done the job in Grosvenor Street and it was *all* out in the Press. Even the posters were carrying a more or less accurate description of me: "*The dapper little man in brown . . where is he tonight*?" Well . . well . . *here I was tonight*, with Molly, my girl, stepping through the theatre foyer, to see the latest Edgar Wallace play. Both Molly and I are tickled to death at the *absurdity* of *life*. *We* are looking at a *play* all about *fictitious villains* . . and *shady clubs* . . when I myself was the *real thing*. Molly and I enjoyed that *play* all the more for knowing the *play* itself was *not* the *real* thing, but *we were*.

Looking back, after *all* these years, I *now* know how *false*, how stupid, how *childish*, were all my values. I . . I . . was living in a world just as fantastic, as *unrealistic*, as *any* Edgar Wallace *play* . . .

On another occasion I had just returned from a visit to the country, where I had done some villainy, and without waiting to go home, I took a taxi from the station, and gave the driver the address of Molly's place of work.

The taxi stops. I get out, settle with the driver, go up those steps, straight through the foyer, don't even stop off at the cloak-room to leave my hat, coat and gloves. I go right in there, and look around me . . all these people, eating and drinking. Laughter . . soft-music . . lights shining bright . . tinkling glasses . . and *there* . . and *there* . . my *Molly* . . . seated at a table, with a man whose hand she's holding . . a large ice-bucket with a bottle of champagne between them. I cross that dance-floor, not caring whom I bump into. I go over to this table, grab the bottle of champagne, and say: *"Let go that bastard's hand, or I'll crack you with this bottle."* The place *exploded* into noise and din . . screams and shouts . . chairs are knocked over and, before I can carry out my threat, I'm grabbed by the waiters, who *all* know me, of course . . taken outside . . politely helped into a taxi and told: "Go home, and cool off." As the taxi starts off, there is Molly . . she stops that taxi, gets in beside me and we move off. We arrive home, having said *nothing* whatever all this time in the taxi. I unlock the door of the flat . . walk right through into the living-room . . straight on into the bedroom . . where I begin to take my hat, coat and gloves off. Meantime, I'm looking around . . . I see gramophone records *all* over the divan. Presumably Molly, before going out to work, had been playing the gramophone. By now Molly has followed me in, and she too begins to take her things off . . a beautiful evening-wrap . . a silk scarf.

Me . . me . . I'm simmering with rage. I suddenly turn on Molly, and grab her by the throat, and I press . . I press . . I press . . on Molly's throat as if it were the man whose hand she'd held . . and as if it were *she too*. We fall, down there on the divan, with me on top . . still pressing that throat, Molly clawing at my face, struggling to break my hold. Whilst *all* this is going on . . I could hear those gramophone records *breaking* . . *breaking* . . *breaking*.

"What the hell are you doing, Nick?" Through my anger, my rage, my fury, I heard this voice, the voice of Jane . . work-mate and friend of Molly, who, unknown to me, had followed us from the restaurant, knowing what a jealous bastard I was. In our mutual anger, when arriving home from the restaurant, neither Molly nor I had noticed we'd left the front door open, and thus it was Jane was able to come straight in and demand to know: *"What the hell are you doing, Nick?"* I let Molly go, and the next thing I know . . I'm lying on that floor and Molly is holding my head in her hands . . kissing me . . kissing me . . and saying: *"Nick . . Nick . . I'll never, ever hold another man's hand . ."*

I soon learn that on letting Molly go when on that divan choking her, I had konked right *out* into a dead faint, only to come to, hearing Molly say: *"Nick . . Nick . . I'll never, ever hold another man's hand."* For the record: *Molly never did hold another man's hand,* so far as I know.

London was getting very *hot* for me. The Bogeys were right on my tail. As often as not, when I went *in* at *one* door of my favourite eating-place, the old Queen's or the Café Royal, the Bogeys would be going *out* the *other* door, having just been *looking* for *me*.

One Saturday morning I'm going into the Queen's Hotel to settle-up for the previous week's food and wine, it being then my custom just to sign a bill and settle later. I'm walking through the corridor, on the way to the manager's office, and I notice *two men*, standing together. As I pass these men, I hear: *"Good morning, Sir."* Me I answer: *"Good morning to you."* In the manager's office, I'm asked: *"Did you see those two men in the corridor? They . . are police officers, enquiring after you."*

"What did you tell them?" I ask.

"Well," said the manager . . "What *could* I tell them? I'm a hotel manager, *not* a police officer . . *all I know* is you eat here sometimes . . you are a *good* customer . . and *that's all I know*."

I settle my account . . leave the office . . go my way . . *hoping, hoping,* those police officers *don't* have a very accurate description of *me*, which, as it happens, is so. Years later I met one of these police officers, and he then told me: "At the time we were looking for you, our knowledge of *you* was vague, though we *did* know *something* of your *eating habits* . . said to be rather fancy."

Getting out of that hotel, I decided, there and then, the *old town* was getting too *hot for me* and, without telling Molly *or* anyone else, I packed my bags and left for Edinburgh, en route for Holland . . Belgium . . and France, where I proposed to join the Foreign Legion and thus make a fresh start in life.

I get into Edinburgh, find a small hotel, go to the *North of Scotland Bank* . . ask if I could have my money, then in a

London bank, transferred to them. Having arranged this money-business . . *incidentally*, the *one* and *only* time I ever had money in a *bank* . . I go to Leith to get a boat for *Holland*.

I don't find it so easy to persuade that Dutch skipper to let me sail with him to Holland . . he's a suspicious sort of fellow . . so I return to my small hotel, to think things over.

I'm walking along Princes Street . . and there in a jeweller's shop . . I see in the window . . a fine diamond ring . . resting on a black velvet pad. On impulse, I go into the shop . . ask to see that ring in the window . . as I'm thinking of buying something, for my fiancée, so I say.

"I'm sorry, *Sir* . . that ring is not for sale . . but we can show you other rings just as fine."

I'm brought a tray of rings and invited to examine them. These rings were magnificent . . the stones were fine, good colour, free of all flaws and brilliant-cut. Whilst looking at these rings, I note the shop-assistant walking away to attend another customer. I pocket one of these rings . . then openly select another . . give it to the shop-assistant when he returns to me . . and say: "Please, keep this ring for me . . I'll bring my fiancée in tomorrow to try it on."

I leave the shop . . *walking on air* . . . after all, I've got a marvellous diamond ring . . *and* for *nothing*.

All this, I must point out, totally *unnecessary* . . I've got money . . I'm leaving the country about to start a *new life*. In other words . . I love things of beauty . . I'm an addicted *thief* but *don't know it* . . I see this lovely ring and, without rhyme or reason, pocket it like any petty shop-lifter.

I return to my hotel . . exhilarated by the notion of getting a beautiful ring so easily and for *nothing*. All my plans for going abroad, joining the Foreign Legion, finishing with the villainy lark. . . *all* these things, I jeopardise for *one bloody ring* . . and, I must confess, I was not even *aware of this absurdity*.

I'm in the bathroom, washing my hands, when the maid comes upstairs, saying: *"Two gentlemen to see you, Sir . . . two gentlemen to see you, Sir."*

For one moment my heart *stops* . . I recover quickly . . dry my hands . . take the ring out of my pocket . . break the tablet of soap in two . . put the ring in there . . put the two pieces together . . place the soap back on the wash bowl . . and, picking the towel up, I leave that bathroom . . as it were drying my hands . . and I'm confronted with the "*two gentlemen*".

I walk into my room . . invite the men to come in.

"What can I do for you, gentlemen?"

"We are police officers making certain enquiries, Sir. I believe you visited a jeweller's shop in Princes Street . . asked to see some rings, promising to return tomorrow, with your fiancée?"

In situations like this the thief usually tries to bluff it out . . he pretends *anger* or *surprise* or *indignation* . . *me* . . *me* . . I want to know "what's wrong with a piece of ordinary shopping for a *ring*?"

The police don't say *anything* about a missing ring. *All* they say is: *"Who are you? What is your business in this city?"* and *"where is this fiancée of yours?"*

I'm doing some quick thinking . . *it occurs to me that no one* in the shop *actually saw me take that ring*. But, after I left the shop, the ring was missed and the shop-assistant must then have immediately phoned the police who, right on the ball, got into the shop almost as soon as I left it. When they came out they must have seen *me* down there in Princes Street and followed me to the hotel.

Finally . . after some more talk . . *still no reference to that ring* . . the police say: "Before we go, Sir . . as a matter of form . . just to satisfy us that you are quite a bona fide visitor to this city . . may we just look around a bit?" *Me* . . *me*, I have never been what you would call a wide-boy, so . . feeling quite safe . . after all, I'd hid the ring . . I say: "O.K., look around. I don't mind."

Those police officers *did* look around. I stood watching them, feeling a bit amused. They look under the bed . . pull that case out . . open it . . and . . and . . *there* . . *there* . . forgotten by *me* . . a single-shot, long-barrelled *pistol* . . which I had bought in a Windsor pub . . for a pound or so.

"Have you got a licence, for this, Sir?" I tell them: "*No.*" "I'm afraid, Sir, you'll have to accompany us to the police station . . *this is Edinburgh* . . we don't allow people to go around *here* with *firearms*."

Once again I experience that old, old feeling . . my heart goes for a Burton . . I recover . . think of a wild dash . . for freedom . . then I think: *To hell* . . I'll face it out . . .

I'm in the police station . . standing in front of the station-sergeant's desk . . being formally charged with being in possession of a firearm without a licence. As I'm waiting there a tall man in a well-cut suit, nicely-fitting shoes, and, under his arm, a document file, comes over to the desk. This man looks at me, opens that file . . looks at me again, turns to the arresting police officers . . and says: "*Drop that charge . . London . . London . . wants this man very badly . . lock him up.*"

And so . . and so . . *here I am again* . . . *All* for a bloody ring that I take a fancy to . . .

Same old lock-up . . same old smell . . same old *graffiti. "Fuck you, I can do my bird", "I love Nelly", "I'll get three months."*

I'm walking up and down . . that door opens . . in comes the man with the file . . "Very *unlucky, Victor*, the *Yard* wants you. Did you know that your father resides in this city? We'll phone him, if you like, tell him you are here."

I say: "*Fuck my Father.*"

The door opens again. "*Victor*, we phoned your father . . and *he says: 'Give him anything he wants to eat, but otherwise I don't want anything to do with him'.*"

Me . . me, I answer: "To hell with my father and his bloody food."

That was the *last message I ever got from my dear father* . . .

Later that evening I was informed: "The Yard will be sending two officers for you tomorrow. You'll probably travel back by the night train."

The next morning I'm awakened early, am given the usual lock-up breakfast . . bread, margarine and tea . . wash in the place provided . . a sort of back-yard enclosed by high walls . . and I return to that cell, remaining there until the evening.

The door opens again. "*Victor*, we phoned your father . . and Victor, out you come. They are taking you to London, by the night train." I step out of the peter into the cold corridor, go up those stairs into that office . . and *there* are the "*Two gentlemen to see you, Sir*".

"Hello, Victor, we nearly lost you. *Bad luck* for *you.*"

After some more of this playful talk, I'm hand-cuffed . . led into a waiting car and driven to the station, where we are guided by a porter to the train, a special compartment having been reserved for us. On the way to this train . . we have to pass through the people standing around, awaiting their trains . . and *that*, funnily enough, I *enjoyed*. You see, in *my* situation . . likely to be put away for many years . . one tends to see everything around one that belongs to the free world as *if it will never be seen again.*

We are in that compartment . . it's First Class . . and the door is *locked.* Clearly . . the police are "doing themselves *proud*". All modern conveniences. *But . . lock that door.* The train starts moving, I look out that window, I note the passing scene . . the tea-wagon . . the pretty girl pushing it along . . the newspaper-kiosk . . *all* those lovely glossy magazines . . that couple over there, *very* much in love . . *honeymoon?* We get out of the station into the *open.*

As the train picks up speed and we get into the country, the police officers *relax,* and the senior of the two offers me a cigarette, saying: "Victor, we have a long trip, and if you promise to behave yourself, I'm prepared to take the cuffs off, and we can all travel in comfort. *Me . . me,* I like to travel in comfort so I agree to this friendly proposition.

I won't bore the reader with all the details of this trip to London. Suffice it to say: the police treated me as if I were an honoured guest . . they dined and wined me in that diner . . they provided the cigarettes of my choice . . they rambled on about this and that . . my presumed travels . . my bits and pieces of villainy . . . *and* conveyed to me clearly it was not *me* they *really* wanted, but that buyer, that fence whom they *knew* to be crooked but so far had not been able to catch.

We arrive in London . . it's raining . . the traffic . . old London's traffic . . buses . . taxis . . lorries . . above *all* those *people . . all free* . . so busy about their daily chores. Whilst waiting for the police-car, I'm *breathing* . . I'm *breathing that London air* . . which I've always found so *stimulating.* The car stops. *This . . this* . . is Marlborough Street Police Centre as it was *then* (it's now Savile Row), planted right there in London's sweetly-smelling *Mayfair.* I go up those steps *almost gaily.* After all, I'm an honoured guest . . the police are *actually cultivating me . . me . . me.*

I'm booked in, but not charged . . placed in a detention-room, not a *cell,* and told: "Settle down, Victor . . somebody will be coming to see you shortly."

So . . here we are again. Locked up . . not *quite a cell* . . a kind of cubicle . . *no furniture* . . just a W.C. in the corner . . a wooden bench fastened to the wall . . and up there . . an unusually *large* window. It's barred and opaque, but I note a vague outline of a stairway, a sort of fire-escape. I'm looking around . . a bit nervous . . a bit worried. There on the door I see: *"I'll get away with it", "This place stinks"* . . and with that remark, I *agreed*.

I hear footsteps . . *heavy* footsteps the other side of that window. I see *shadow feet* . . *legs* . . *leggings* . . and *all* going *up* that fire-escape. . . . I listen . . and it seems to me . . those feet . . those legs . . going *up there* . . a never-ending *regiment* of *feet* . . *big feet* . . *armoured feet* . . belong to invisible *men coming for me*. I learnt later . . these *feet* . . these *legs* . . belonged to the police attached to this police centre. Up and down that shadow-staircase . . the police had to go . . to reach their canteen or assembly station.

The door opens . . a very well-dressed man . . tall and quite distinguished . . comes in, and offers to shake my hand, saying: "Victor, I'm from the 'Yard'. I've got a piece of paper here on which is written a *name*. We believe this is the name of the man who has been buying all the gear you've been stealing. And *if you will sign this paper* testifying that it is the name of your buyer, we'll *let you go*."

With these words the Yard man left me to think it over. This buyer . . this man the police wanted *more* than they wanted *me* . . was a bastard. He'd treated *me* as if I were a mug . . he'd robbed me right and left . . even Molly had said: "*That* man, Nick . . your buyer . . is a *bastard*." I'm thinking . . thinking that *freedom* . . *freedom* could be mine if I signed that paper.

Then the door opens . . and there are Molly and Jane. "Nick . . Nick . . the police have let us in to plead with you to sign that paper," said Molly. Jane just stood there looking at me.

I stood there looking at Molly . . then at the piece of paper . . my ticket-of-leave . . but I *could not bring myself* to sign that paper. I tear it up, saying: "I can't do it, Molly." She looks at *me*, gives me one slap right across my chops, and flounces out of the room, Jane following her, but giving *me* such a very *regretful look*. I never saw Molly again . . .

As soon as Molly and Jane had left me, in comes the Yard man, and *he* says: "All right, Victor, if you are *not* with us, you are *against us* and will have to *take the consequences*." With those words the man went out, and *banged that door*.

In due course, I'm taken from the detention-room, formally

charged with various jewel thefts, put back into a cell. I stay there for the night . . am brought up the next morning to Marlborough Street Police Court . . am again charged . . and, after hearing some evidence, the court remands me to Brixton Prison for one week.

So . . here I am twenty-four years of age . . quite a bit of 'form' behind me . . getting a name for slick, successful jewel stealing . . have offended the police by not collaborating . . in putting that buyer in jail . . and I'm faced with my *first* London court appearance, which *could be* an *Old Bailey trial* . . . and *that* could be serious for me.

VI

Brixton Prison in the days I'm now writing about was not much different from the other jails I'd been in, except for the fact that it was reserved for remand and *trial* prisoners . . with a small number of debtors, too. Some prisoners wore their own clothes, others did not. Cells were exactly the same as in all other jails . . food, the same . . and the time locked-up was very considerable. There has been so much written around and about the *prison scene,* so much that is quite untrue and completely misleading. I'm reluctant to *add* to all this controversial stuff . . in fact, if this story wasn't *inescapably* a part of the prison scene, *I would not so much as refer to it.*

Anyhow . . here I am . . in prison . . same old conditions . . same old *waste of human life* . . but I, too, am the *same old fool* . . same old *mug* . . .

You see, dear reader, though I was aware of the vileness of the life of a prisoner . . its sordidness . . its utter waste of human power . . its destruction of every decent thought . . feeling . . idea and notion, I did not think deeply about all this. I was caught-up in a kind of *fantasy thing*, born of the life I was living. In other words, *crime* and *punishment* in *my life* was *reproducing itself*. Out of my villainies was coming a sort of *desire* to *perpetuate this very same thing* . . all mixed up in a desire for getting-one's-own-back . . *hit out* . . *hit out* . . not realising then what I was doing to *me* . . *me* . . and to the people and the world around me.

I'm summoned back to the police court and committed for trial at the *Old Bailey* . . for the first time in my life; I have Arthur Comyns-Carr as my Counsel . . I'm elated . . elated. At last *I'm in the big time* . . *starring* at the *Old Bailey* . . *hobnobbing* with the *big shots* . . . In short, I'm *lost* . . *lost* . . in *fantasy* . . in *vanity* and *conceit* . . . I'm *nuts*.

"Victor Carasov, you are charged with stealing jewellery to the value of five thousand pounds. There are other similar charges. You've given the police quite a run . . well . . that run has ended. I've listened to your Counsel . . very interesting indeed . . but I am not impressed. I intend to teach you a lesson. You appear to think you have a licence to rob as long as the people whom you rob are what *you* call *rich people*. This kind of thinking is *ridiculous*. You will go to prison for four years' *penal servitude*."

In these days, way back in 1928, *penal servitude* was considered to be *almost a death sentence*. It was synonymous with the old sentence of *transportation*. For a man to get four *years'* P.S., it was thought he had a very, very *bad deal*. *Today* . . the bastards *laugh*, if somebody gets *thirty years*.

I must confess, even *my absurd ego* went down there. *All my conceits* were momentarily busted . . *but* . . *but* . . only *momentarily*. I recovered a bit—after all, I was *now* . . indisputably . . *a real villain*.

I go to *Parkhurst Prison* . . 'the *Island*', almost as notorious as *Devil's Island*, the infamous French Penal Colony. This is the traditional *old lag's resting place*, this is where he *recovers* all his strength and goes *back* to the *fray* . . or *he dies* . . and *never goes back*.

At the time I get to the Island, things have been going very *badly* there . . the men are getting restless . . beginning to protest . . there are smash-ups . . attacks on screws . . . the whole place is in an uproar. It is *rare* for the *English criminal to hit out* in the English jail . . he tends to be *discreet* . . *prudent* . . *philosophical*. He tends to *avoid fighting it out with authority* . . but *sometimes*, the pressure of jail-life . . the arrival of a *new governor* with ideas for *repression* . . a *new chief officer* with notions of *tightening up* . . *this* will start a riot . . . and *that* was just what was going on at the Island when I got there.

I was young . . only twenty-four . . and, though I had a little courage and *spirit* too, I *was* rather nervous in this *new climate* of a *lag's own colony* . . something *sinister* about it . . something *frightening*.

I'm put through the reception, given the kit specially devised for the long-term prisoner as if he was on a *long, long journey* and had to be equipped for *all* emergencies. The clothes were rough, *broad-arrowed,* mittens for *cold weather*, very heavy boots for *wet weather*. The cells were sparsely-furnished . . the windows, very small and barred . . the same old Judas hole in the door . . and . . *silence* . . *silence* . . *talking is forbidden.*

I walk up and down that peter. I hear all the shouting, the cursing, the screaming . . the doors are being kicked and battered . . screws are bawling and shouting . . men are being dragged down below . . the jail is in a state of near-mutiny . . most of the men are refusing to go to labour. After a while things seem to get quieter. I'm taken to the tailor shop, and given a place on a long bench with other men seated on either side of me. I soon discover that this shop is a sort of *quiet shop,* in which the noisier kind of prisoner is not allowed. Also, it is run by a screw of the old kind: *he* doesn't want *any* trouble . . so tends to be very mild and temperate . . what the old lag calls a *good screw.*

The work given to me in that old tailor's shop was, much to my surprise, *knitting socks.*

"Here you are, two needles and a ball of wool. That man there, sitting next to you, will show you what to do." With these words, the screw hands me the needles and wool, and walks away.

" 'Ere, let me show you, it's *easy.*" I look up, and there is an old man . . thin and grey . . steel-rimmed spectacles . . and crinkly dried-up old hands. I'm shown how to knit . . soon pick it up. I rather like it, *much* better than mailbags or oakum-picking.

" 'Ow long you doing? You look very young. Get out of this place, mate, if you can. I'll tell you 'ow to do it."

I'm listening to the old lag, looking at his wrinkled face, those old hands, his pale bespectacled eyes . . and *I* think: Jesus . . *I must never get like that.*

"Look, mate, this place 'as got a *new governor.* He's a real bastard . . the men will give him a lot of trouble . . but *they will lose in the end* . . and *he,* the bastard, will then get his own way. Ever heard of *Broadmoor*? The *loony house*? See here, mate, you'll be better off in Broadmoor, in the loony-bin, than *here* . . I'm telling you. Put 'the pot on' . . make out you're *mental* . . act *daft* . . they'll soon get shut of you."

I finish the day's work, return to my peter, and I think over the old lag's advice . . . I do *not* like the set-up *here.* This is not what I used to dream about in those punishment cells. This is *not* a place for *heroic* villains.

All my life I have quickly made my mind up on deciding a course to follow. Until *now* . . 1968 . . I've *never thought too much on any contemplated course of action.* I've had the idea one minute and have acted the next. So, having heard the old lag's advice, finding it to my liking, I proceeded to act.

I refuse to work . . I threaten to act violently . . I throw fits . . I get a petition . . I say *I'll kill that judge who sentenced me to four years.* Funnily enough, looking *back* on all this, I wonder at my *nerve* . . my *courage* . . my *desperation* . . because . . *I could have been given a real bashing.* The jail was in an uproar . . near mutiny. *I could* have qualified for a flogging. Also, what a risk I was taking . . actually in danger of a flogging on the one hand . . or *certification* as *insane* on the other. Whatever the odds, I persisted in my chosen course.

They put me in hospital . . matted cell . . *no* furniture . . papier-mâché *pot* . . papier-mâché *mug* . . *gated cell* . . *observation* night and day . . *also* . . *sedatives* . . . *paraldehyde* . . Jesus, shall *I ever forget the smell of that?*

I'm sent for, down to the M.O.'s office, escorted by two screws.

A very *nice* office . . rug on that floor . . big shiny desk . . two comfortable chairs, one on this side of the desk, one on the other, and, in the other chair, a very distinguished man . . hair, carefully brushed . . suit, very neat . . hands, very clean, clasped and resting on that desk.

"Take a seat, Carasov. Have a cigarette? Now tell me, Carasov, *why* do you want to kill the man who sentenced you to *four years?* And tell me, have you had these fits before? Ever been under treatment for mental trouble? Any *insanity* in your family? Why did you *steal?* Did you think *rich people fair game?* Um . . um . . . um . . .

"Strip off . . breathe in . . out . . in . . out. Um . . um . . drop your trousers . . cough . . um . . um. Ever had *any venereal disease?* All right, Carasov, put your things on. You can go now."

I'm escorted back to my peter. I ask one of the screws: "Who is that fellow, back there?"

"He is the prison medical commissioner."

I stay around in that hospital cell for a further period of weeks, am examined several times by the resident M.O. and some of his assistants. All this time I'm getting *almost to believe in the masquerade I'm putting on* . . my *fits* are almost *real* . . my *anger is real* . . I'm getting to hate the whole rigmarole . . *me* . . the *heads* . . the *world* . . .

The day came when I was told: "*You are going away,* tomorrow."

Tomorrow never comes, they say . . well, tomorrow *did* come, and I . . I . . had mixed feelings. I'd beat the bastard who had sentenced me to *penal servitude* . . I'd beat the bastard who was running this jail . . and . . I was off to the '*loony-bin*' . . *Broadmoor Criminal Lunatic Asylum* . . though I was *not insane*.

VII

We take the ferry from the Isle of Wight . . the Island . . then car from Portsmouth to Crowthorne, the village in which *Broadmoor* is situated.

I travelled with two prison officers. The whole trip had an unreal quality . . was a kind of *burial party* for the living. None of us talked. I suppose the screws *knew* the kind of place I was going to . . and just didn't want to talk about it. As for *me*, I was elated . . . after all, I'd beaten the rap, I'd escaped from that inferno of a jail. But, for all that, I was somewhat perturbed . . I was *sane*, yet on the way to the notorious loony-bin . . *Broadmoor*. . . .

The car came to a stop . . the screw says: "Here we are, out you get." I get out, and there . . there was *Broadmoor* . . high walls, double gates, crenellated lodge, uniformed screws, big and *silent* . . .

My first impression of this place was of its *silence* . . the gates swung open and shut *silently* . . the screws' keys appeared to be *padded* . . no one spoke, except in very *low voices*, almost as if they didn't want to disturb the *dead*.

I'm handed over. One of these fellows says: "This way", and *points* to where, I note, is another of these uniformed people. I start walking . . one man in front, another behind . . across a yard, through a double gate, down a corridor, through another gate. The gate is locked behind. In front of me is a passageway . . a door . . and there, beckoning me in, is a screw. I am in a barely furnished sort of cell . . table, chair, a barred window, a weighing-machine . . and, seated there at the table, is a small, pock-faced man, quite undistinguished looking, lumpy hands resting on that table.

I'm told: "Stand in front of the table. Your name? Your age? Do you *know why you were brought here?* Any complaints? Get on that weighing-machine . . um . . all right, take him away."

I'm taken away down another corridor . . through another gate . . out in a yard . . tall, tall walls . . clean, cold cement pathway . . . *Silence* . . . A door is unlocked. I'm told: "Get in there." Another passage . . tiled . . a door-less opening . . a small cubicle . . a *bath* . . and, seated at the top-end of that bath, hand on the tap, another of these big big *silent men* . . .

"Strip off, *quick*, we haven't got *all* day." I look at this man, one of my escort, big ugly brutal-looking. I look around . . there are *now four* of these fellows, *all* looking at me as if I had just *murdered* their *mothers* and *might murder them.* I stripped off . . a bit nervous . . yet *angry too* . . I didn't like this place . . .

"Get in the bath," I'm told. In the meantime I notice the fellow at the top of the bath has turned the water on. I get in the bath, am handed a piece of kitchen-soap, a scrubber not unlike a *floor-scrubber.* Whilst I'm lathering up *all five* of these screws are standing around *glaring at me . . me.* I am thinking: Fuck them. If they start anything, I'll get *one* of them.

I finish bathing, stand up, am given a towel which feels like *canvas.* I'm now handed a sack-like shirt, noticing down there on the front of the shirt a large spreading *stain.* It makes me feel sick . . .

"Come on, wrap this round you" —a dirty, evil-smelling blanket, also stained . . .

They point the way . . I go on, bare-footed, down a long red-cement-floored corridor. There is a screw outside an open door . . *that is my stopping place* . . a bare cell, shuttered window . . mattress on floor . . what appear to be *canvas sheets* . . no pillow. In the corner, a papier-maché *pot* with *no cover* . . and, I discover later, *no toilet paper.* I step into this cell . . and the door *bangs on me.* I stand there . . looking around . . *listening to that silence.*

"If I was you, I'd get into that bed. The *doctor* doesn't like it, if you don't go to bed." *This* . . *this* . . sinister warning came through a long *observation slit* alongside that door. I get into bed, soon discover those sheets *are canvas* and you can't wrap them round you, and it gets *cold down there,* even in late summer . . .

The door opens, a screw comes in, tells me: "*Get up*". I'm given a tin plate, with a thin slice of bread and margarine on it, also a papier-mâché beaker with a luke-warm, weak, sort of tea in it. The screw gives me a dirty look and leaves the cell, banging that door.

I'm not hungry. I am a bit angry . . after all, *this place is supposed to be for mentally sick men*, to put their worries and anxieties to rest. *If I had really been ill*, what would *this treatment have done to cure me?*

I get up . . walk up and down . . up and down. *I know I've asked for this* . . I know I risked this by putting *that pot* on . . but, for all that, I was simmering with rage.

The window is shuttered, but through the cracks I see *bars*. Also, I note it's getting dark . . and *no sign of any light in this cell*. I hear a dull thud, as if someone was banging his *pot* against the door . . I hear voices . . wild voices . . *all* confused and near-hysterical . . then . . someone *screams* . . after that *all hell is let loose* . . *me* . . *me*, I am scared . . scared . . .

The noise gets worse . . I feel as if there are wild animals out there, and they *might break my door down* . . . Wild animals or *wild men* . . the voices are not really *human*. The din is terrific . . I walk up and down . . put my fingers in my ears to escape hearing that noise. Little by little, the noise subsides . . as does *thunder* after a violent storm. It is now very dark. I'm thinking: "These bastard screws don't care what happens to us here . . *no light* . . no attempt to find out *what all that din was about* . . . *Bastards*, I'm thinking. At such moments a man just *can't see reason even if he, himself, is his own executioner* . . he just can't *see* it till long afterwards . . . I get back on that bed . . sleep fitfully . . then the door opens . . and in comes the screw, in his hand a tea-cup, the cup *full to overflowing* of *white mixture*, the mixture so thick you could stand a spoon in it. I'm told: *"Drink this."* For the briefest of moments I felt like hitting out at these inhuman bastards . . but . . tired . . worn out after the night's noise . . *I drink that mixture* . . *I eat* . . *eat* that mixture . . and from *that* day, for nearly a week, I . . I never stopped shitting. I *stank* like a *pole-cat* for a week . . hadn't even any *paper* to *wipe my ass-hole*.

I stayed down in that cell for a week or so. Every night . . the same din . . the same uproar . . the same screaming and shouting. I now know the cause of all the din: where I am confined is the ground floor of Block 6, reserved for Broadmoor's most dangerous inmates. As most of these fellows are stark raving mad, they tend to be quiet by day . . apathetic and silent . . and towards night they seem to get restless. Like wolves out there, they howl by night.

Every morning I'd be told: "Get up, bring your bedding, get in there." 'In there' would be the cell next door . . floor newly-mopped . . empty pot in the corner . . window shuttered . . they'd *bang that door* . . and there I'd stay till the next day . . then back to the original cell. Nothing to read . . no visitors . . stay in that bed . . *think* . . *think* . . . Every now and again, that observation slit would reveal an *eye*. *No one ever talked* except to say: "Get up. Go next door". Breakfast . . mid-day meal . . tea-time . . that's how I marked the passing hour. Night would come and the howling commenced. I was no longer scared but I was disturbed and unaccountably apprehensive, *afraid* of I know not what . . .

The morning came when I was told: "Get up, put these clothes on." The clothes consisted of heavy, thick-clothed jacket and trousers, dirty grey in colour . . long grey stockings . . ill-fitting under-vest and pants . . and a stained shirt. I was a bit reluctant to put the shirt on, but was told: *"Get it on, quick!"* In addition to these clothes, I was given a pair of very old, rather *smelly* slippers.

Having dressed myself, I'm taken down the corridor . . up some stone stairs . . another corridor . . and in there . . a large room, barred windows open about two inches from the top, bare tables all round the room, benches behind each table. *At these tables*, two to each table, sat the strangest collection of men I'd ever seen.

Over there, one man *tossing himself off*, quite unconcerned with all around him . . opposite him, a man fretting and fuming, swearing he'd *murder somebody* . . farther down, a man shaking as if he were having a *fit* . . another man acting as if he were *mounted on a female* . . . But, standing up and above and beyond *all* this, beyond the dreadful *smell* of thousands of *unwashed feet*, unwashed bodies, was, just inside the doorway the *biggest*, the most *brutal looking* screw I'd ever seen in my life.

I stood there, scared out of my life. I just couldn't move. "There is a vacant seat over there. Take it." I go over, look at the man sitting there, and *he* . . just looks through me, saying *nothing* and seemingly *seeing nothing* except *his inner world . . .*

This was my first day in what I learnt was the *refractory ward . . all inmates there supposed to be dangerously insane.*

As time went on, little by little I began to realise this was a loony-bin all right, but with a *difference.* All men here (many of them to be "detained during His Majesty's Pleasure", perhaps for all their lives . . others, like *myself*, having put the pot on to escape the rigour of prison-life) *all* these men were treated *like dangerous animals* . . laughed at . . mocked . . manhandled at the slightest sign of resistance . . put down there in *that ground-floor corridor . . canvas shirt locked behind their necks . . canvas sheets* . . on a dirty, lumpy mattress . . on that cold cold floor . . . All this I learnt in the passage of time, and I was *shocked.* I always thought of *mental cases* as very defenceless and needing *care* . . but *not here in Broadmoor's back-block* 6.

At this point in my story, let me say this: I do not wish to *indict* the penal system of England, a part of which *Broadmoor was* in the days I'm writing about . . nor do I suggest that *all* the things going on *behind the scenes* in prison and Broadmoor were *known to the top men* in the *prison service.* But I did *experience* certain things, and *witness* certain things . . and believe *these things should be known* . . even though some of them have since been *stopped* and *a wind of change* has blown away many of these worst *abuses.*

Above all, I must put it on record, *most of my experience was brought upon myself, by myself.*

I *now* believe that the shock administered to me in *Broadmoor* . . my experience in the Refractory Blocks 6 and 7, where I spent nearly two years of the four-year term, disturbed my mind and my nervous system for years and years. Also, the *anger* . . the *rage* . . the *resentment* engendered *there* was the *motivating force of many of my subsequent crimes.* In other words, I later *hurt people* in the free world as a kind of *transference* of *all that violence I felt* towards the Broadmoor personnel . . at least, that part of it with which I was all too familiar.

In those days, way back in 1929, there was no *radio, no*

television, no relaxation for the back-block inmates. Once a fortnight a broken-down old gramophone was taken round the wards.

On one occasion we are in there, seated all round the ward, the usual high-jinks going on . . men performing like animals . . though some of us, from prison, tried to exercise some self-control. The gramophone is brought in. The screw on duty tonight is a big, brutal, farm-hand, safer with *pigs* than with *men*. He has a perverted sense of humour so, instead of some *gay light music* to cheer and comfort these fellows here, he puts on *"Onward Christian Soldiers"*. And he *keeps it on*. Amongst the men in that ward are some *who hate the very name of Christianity* . . chiefly, I think, because they haven't experienced much practical Christianity. Whatever the reason, these men *hate religion* so, hearing this *hymn* going on and on, they begin to froth at the mouth . . to curse . . to threaten. *Me . . me*, I'm disgusted with this big bully and his cowardly mockery of these poor fellows, so I go right up to him and say: "*Stop that record. Can't you see these fellows don't like it? Why torture them?* You are here as a nurse. Care for these men . . don't torture them."

"Are you talking to me?" this fellow says. *"Get back to your seat."*

I warn this fellow, if he persists in mocking these men, I'll crown him with the gramophone. He gets up . . blows his flute, hollers . . shouts . . other screws come in . . I'm grabbed . . hustled down below and thrown into that cell. Shortly after the door opens. In comes a man I had not seen before . . tall . . very distinguished-looking.

"Well, what are you up to? Why do you threaten my staff!"

I say: "Is it the duty of your staff to torture these helpless men? Is *that* what they are paid for?" This man *looks at me as if he didn't believe his ears.*

"What is your age, young man? . . . Well, this place has been going now for more years than you have lived, and *don't think you are going to change it*. Any more trouble from you and I'll put you in canvas for the rest of the time you are here." With these words he walks out.

I'm allowed upstairs again, *warned by the screws*: *"Watch your step, Carasov."* There are *no more religious gramophone records played in that ward*, and, strange to say, the big farm-hand type was *never seen again in that ward . . .*

One time I was out in the airing-court, the fancy name for the exercise yard in Block 6 . . a barren cement-paved yard with high walls all round . . a stinking W.C. in the corner.

"Hey you," says this fellow to me, "are you feeling run-down?"

I look at him, this fellow . . stringy, bean-stalk body . . unshaven . . unwashed . . a wild gleam in his eyes . . "No, I'm not run-down," I say. *"Why?"*

"Oh, I thought if you were run-down, *I could do some artificial respiration on you . . .*"

Before going out to the airing-court, we inmates had to change from slippers to boots which were kept in small cubby holes in a room just inside the gate opening on to the yard.

I'm in this room putting my boots on, my back turned to the other fellows, and I get one big bash right across the back of my neck. I turn round and there . . there . . is a wild-eyed inmate about to give me another *bash.* I immediately lock this man's arms to his body with his own jacket . . an old trick, learnt long ago. I turn to the screw and say: "Take this fellow away. I don't want to hurt him." They take him away. After I come in from exercise I'm sent for . . the M.O. "wishes to see you".

I go in this room. A little man sits there in a chair, a desk between him and me. I look at this man . . very pale skin . . heavy-set eyes . . dark pouches beneath a serious, studious expression . . I like the look of this man.

"Carasov, I've heard about your behaviour in the locker-room. You didn't strike that man, *that's self-control*, and *I respect self-control.* I'm transferring you to Block 7, semi-refractory ward. If your behaviour is good, I'll transfer you to a front-block later."

In this way I met, briefly, *Dr. Hopwood* . . the *most humane of all the medical men* in *Broadmoor,* a kind well-meaning man, later to become *Broadmoor's finest* and *best superintendent* . . making revolutionary changes in the care and treatment of inmates, though this was long after I had left Broadmoor.

I'm in Block 7 . . semi-refractory . . not so wild as Block 6. The fellows are reasonably sane and self-controlled.

Amongst the inmates in Block 7 were some men from prison, not *all* of whom had "put the pot on" . . some were really disturbed, though not by any means insane. One of the ex-prisoners who had got his time for violence of some kind, was sent to the 'Island' and, when there, had done himself harm. This man ended up at Broadmoor, where I met him. I was barely twenty-five at this time, and *youth* sometimes attracts the older man. Unknown to me this man got to fancying *me*, and was foolish enough to *show* this in his words to me. One day this man said: *"I'd like to fuck you."* To me, in those days, that was an insult . . and I decided to kill this man . . or try to do so . . .

The next morning, in the day-room, I go straight up to this man who fancied me. I grab him . . pull him away from the table . . knock him down . . and . . start to kick his face in with my slippered feet. The man was bigger than I . . harder, tougher . . but the speed of my attack bowled him over. I had him there on the floor . . *kicking* . . *kicking* . . and saying: *"You'll never fuck me . . . never."*

I'm grabbed by staff . . . taken down below . . put in a canvas shirt . . it's *locked* behind my neck. I'm put in canvas sheets . . and *there* . . *there* . . I stay for five days and nights. It's cold . . you *can't wrap those canvas sheets* around you . . you are on that floor . . draughts blow all around . . through the shuttered window . . through the observation-slit . . .

My diet whilst down there in 'solitary' was very light. It was winter-time, and having to stay right there on the floor, I found the cold was inflaming all my face, that being the most exposed part of my body when lying down. I can't recall much of the thoughts I had in those long days and nights. I think the *main thought* in my head was: If I ever meet that bastard again, I'll finish the job. *He* won't ever want to fuck *me* again.

The door opens. In comes the distinguished-looking man . . tall . . well-dressed. He says: "*Carasov*, if you ever attack anybody again in this place, I'll put you in *canvas* for the rest of your time". With those words he walks out.

I'm taken back to Block 7. I never see *that man* again, but *me* . . *me*, I'm getting very nervous . . I'm beginning to think: *much more of this* and *I'll really be nuts.* I ask to see

Dr. Hopwood, am sent for. I tell Dr. Hopwood: "*Much more of this back-block* stuff and I'll go right off my rocker." Dr. Hopwood transfers me to a *front-block*, Block 4, and I remain there for two years, the rest of my time. Thanks to Dr. Hopwood I am saved a complete breakdown.

Front-block 4 had a lovely terrace overlooking the countryside. That was our airing-court. Most of the daylight hours were spent out there on that terrace. At other times we were in the day-room . . rather nice fellows . . *not* a sign of *insanity* . . we could *talk freely* . . wear our own clothes . . buy our own food if we wished.

Whilst in the front-block I met many interesting men. None of these men bore *any outward sign* of *insanity*, though most of them would stay there until they *died.*

There was a doctor . . author of several books . . ex-medical officer . . a slight little man . . very active . . clever and witty . . he liked to talk about Indian food which he claimed he could cook very well.

There was a solicitor . . big . . fat . . unwieldy . . a gluttonous *elephant.*

Another man . . cynical, hard-boiled . . mother's darling . . had the run of the place . . lived like a *gentleman* in the *gentleman's block* . . No. 1.

A little stiff-backed, independent Yorkshireman . . saved up every little penny he could earn so that he could send his beloved sister a birthday present every year.

The ex-butler . . smooth, suave . . *greedy.* He'd buy several ounces of tobacco . . then sit at his table in the day-room, openly flaunting his affluence by emptying *all* the tobacco on the table and teasing it out.

The bathing system was peculiar in Broadmoor, at least in Blocks 4, 6 and 7 . . . a small cubicle . . a bath with a screw sitting at the top end. He would put the water in the bath . . remain there whilst the inmate stripped off and got into the bath . . meanwhile the next inmate in line would be starting to strip off ready to get in next. One day . . *me* . . I go in . . there is a man in the bath . . I note it's the greasy, suave butler . . and he, true to form, is giving a public display . . *how to wash that prick. Me* . . I don't like this, I'm *not interested in his bloody prick,* so I step over to the bath and say: "*Stop that* . . *stop that* . . or I'll *drown you.*" The screw blows his flute . . other screws come in and I am grabbed . . removed quickly to a 'stripped' cell. The tall distinguished man, whom I *now knew* to be the *superintendent*, comes in and says to me: "What is the trouble *now*, Carasov! Why did you threaten to *drown that man*?"

I say: "*Would you* like to be fronted with a *public display* of somebody's *prick*?"

"Carasov, don't you know that this . . this . . is a *mental hospital*? If you *ever* threaten to drown somebody . . again . . *I'll put you in canvas* for the rest of the time you are here."

I'm allowed back to the ward . . I never see that 'butler' again.

"Tomorrow," I'm told, "*You are going away, Carasov. Your time is finished.*"

I get all my clothes, my few bits and pieces of property, and I am on the way *out*. But, it seems, I'm *not* to go *free* . . I have an *escort* . . they are sending me to a free-world mental hospital, in spite of my having confessed, long since, to *having put that pot on* to get *away from jail.* On the way out of Broadmoor . . down those stairs . . along that corridor . . I meet some of the old Brigade, screws from the back-blocks 6 and 7, and one of these fellows says to me: "Carasov, *If you ever come back here, we will kill you.*" I say: "I've been here for nearly four years, and you *failed to kill me. I don't think you will ever kill me.*"

So this is the end of my Broadmoor chapter. I never *did* go back there, but I very nearly got sent there *without my asking* several years later . . and, strangely enough, it was a *prison M.O.* who saved me from *that dreadful fate . . .*

VIII

THERE IS A car waiting for us . . two screws and I, we get in . . and the journey begins. I'm now, it seems, a *real loony*, on the way to a *real loony-bin* . . this is how I was thinking.

I tried to find out where we were going, but those screws were *not talking* . . the trip was completed in *silence* . . . *Me* . . I just sit in the car . . thinking back on all the things that have happened to me, almost as if these things concern somebody else. The countryside was pleasant and restful, though being in a moving car made any considered view impossible. We arrived at Esher, a lovely Surrey town. At that time no modern building was to be seen, and, apart from the town-centre, Esher was really a country village.

Down a side-road . . trees on either side . . a gate . . a lodge. *This is it* . . a free-world mental hospital . . a loony-bin. The car drives through the open lodge-gate. We are directed to take a turn to the right . . then straight down the drive . . a lovely flower-bordered pathway . . trees all around . . a country-house sort of place. Here we are . . *no screws* . . *no locked gates* . . a large house, with steps leading to an open porch . . smartly-uniformed, cheerful-looking nurses . . white-coated men with stethoscopes hanging out of their pockets . . all the appearance of an ordinary hospital with nurses and doctors going about their everyday business. *No sign whatever of the sights and sounds expected* in a loony-bin, a mental hospital. The contrast with the Broadmoor Reception Centre was terrific and very *reassuring*.

We are standing there in the hallway . . my escort clearly puzzled . . no one is attending to us . . *no one*, it seems, even *interested*. Doors all round . . busy people going in and out . . a shining bright tiled floor . . flowers in tall vases, not unlike a hotel reception hall.

"Can I do anything for you?" This enquiry comes from a pretty little nurse. One of my escorts says: "We have to deliver this man here from *Broadmoor*."

"*Broadmoor* . . *Broadmoor* . . *What's Broadmoor?*" The escort explains. "Oh, I see. This gentleman is a *patient from Broadmoor*, to be admitted *here*? Please come this way."

We are shown into a bright, cheerful, pleasantly furnished room. I am told to take a seat, my escort told: "Please give me what papers you have in connection with this patient, and then you can go. We will look after this gentleman". The escort was not at all pleased with this procedure, so vastly different to their experience, but the little nurse firmly *showed them the door* . . .

I sit down, rather surprised at all this informality, this courtesy, wondering what next?

"I see by these papers your name is Mr. Carasov. Well, Mr. Carasov, let me tell you we'll make you quite comfortable here. A nurse will be coming for you in a moment. She will take you to the reception villa."

That nurse arrived, neatly uniformed, fair hair with a starched white cap . . very attractive. I liked the look of this nurse. I'm escorted out of this building into the grounds . . well-kept pathways . . shrubs, flowers, trees . . and *birds galore* . . chirping, yodelling, chattering as *if life was just great* . . .

Up some steps . . through a door . . and I'm in an office. At the desk is another nurse. "This is a new patient, Nurse O'Shay," says my escort. She hands over the papers and leaves me there.

"Sit down, Mr. Carasov. I'm Charge-Nurse O'Shay. I'll be looking after you whilst you are in this villa, this being for Receptions. You'll want a bath, something to eat, and then I'll show you to your room. Tomorrow you'll see the doctor." And that's how I met Charge-Nurse O'Shay, an Irish woman of great charm, great kindness, great humour, and a very competent nurse.

So I get acquainted with Banstead Mental Hospital and its dedicated staff . . men-nurses . . women-nurses . . its doctors . . Dr. Ruthven . . a fine warm-hearted man . . a doctor of distinction . . a bon-viveur . . a lover of all things *Human*; Dr. *Petrie* . . Superintendent . . quiet . . thoughtful . . considerate and kind . . a very learned man, in his own field, the care and treatment of disturbed men and women . . care and treatment of the so-called *mental case*.

I got very fond of Nurse O'Shay. I used to tease her. I'd see her in there in the office . . through the top-glazed part of the door . . she'd be working at the desk . . I'd open the door very quietly . . sneak in . . go up to the desk . . go down on my knee . .

and say: *"Lily O'Shay, say your name. Say your name. I like the sound of your lovely Irish name."*

"How dare you come in here, Mr. Carasov. You'll get me in trouble. If the male nurses see you, they'll be annoyed. I *never* let *them* come in here except on business. Now, *please* . . *please* . . leave this office." I'd look at Lily O'Shay and I'd notice the humour in her Irish eyes. I'd notice she was *really amused*, so I'd say: *"Please say Lily O'Shay,"* and she'd say: "L.I.L.Y. O.S.H.A.Y." Then we'd *both burst out laughing*.

I once said to Lily O'Shay: "When I get away from here, I'm coming back for you. I'll grab you and throw you in the back of my car, and I'll *abduct you*." And she would laugh . . laugh . . laugh.

Then there was Ryan, Charge-Nurse Ryan . . tall, dark, cool, calm, intelligent and charming. She was the very opposite to Nurse O'Shay: you could *love* O'Shay, but Ryan I found you could *like* and *respect*.

My first interview with *Dr. Petrie* took place some time after my arrival. I found this man very impressive. He asked me many questions. He was interested in my early experiences . . curious about my choice of crime as a way of living . . curious about my experience at Broadmoor. He thought my survival of that experience without a complete breakdown was something to *marvel* at. He seemed to have a contempt for the 'Broadmoor Method'. In fact, later he would lecture his student-nurses and doctors about the *destructive* Broadmoor Method of dealing with mental illness, comparing it with the method to be seen there in Banstead. In Dr. Petrie's opinion, I was *lucky to come out of it without permanent injury*.

At the time I met Dr. Petrie I was still a young man and *not* by any means free of *fantasy* notions. I was asked: "What school did you attend, Mr. Carasov?" and I, so vain . . so stupid, not caring to admit I'd *never* been to *any decent school*, I said: "Edinburgh Academy." *Why* I said Edinburgh Academy and not Eton, or something like that, I don't know. What I *do* recall is the response to this bare-faced lie by Dr. Petrie. He just appeared to accept it as *if it was true*, not even trying to prove me a liar. *So shamed* was I by Dr. Petrie's attitude that I have never repeated that lie. Nowadays, if asked: "What school did you go to?" I answer: "No school. I'm an uneducated tramp. *Reform school . . Borstal . . prison . . that's my 'school'.*"

The opinion of the medical staff regarding my mental state soon became clear to me: I was *not insane* but in a *disturbed emotional state*, needing *rest* for a sure recovery or relief. In fact, I was repeatedly told: "You must stay with us for some time, Mr. Carasov. You need rest, especially after the Broadmoor experience." *Me* . . *me*, I was still hankering after that settlement of accounts. I was still hankering after the *flesh-pots*. My long years, my lean years in Broadmoor had made all the more *demanding* the appetite for the things I'd been denied. It takes years to teach certain lessons, and I had *not yet learnt* that things I valued in those days, apart from fundamental things such as *freedom*, had *no real permanent value* . . that *anger* . . *resentment* . . *revenge* . . *all* those things could be destructive. At this time in my life I was still a learner.

One day I'm told: "Your mother is coming to see you." I thought my mother was dead . . .

Mother comes to see me . . we are *strangers* . . she volunteers to take me out for the day . . we go to a neighbouring town to do some shopping . . see a film . . have tea . . then Mother goes back to town . . London or somewhere . . leaving *me* to find my way back to Banstead. I don't go back . . I get a taxi and ask the driver to take me to a hotel that I knew, and where I was once a welcome guest.

All the way back to London, where I had not been for over four years, I was thinking back to All My Yesterdays . . Molly . . Jane . . the headwaiter . . the owner of this hotel. Yes, I was thinking of things I'd better have forgotten. . . The taxi stops . . I get out . . see Bob the doorman . . I say: "Settle with the taxi-man, Bob." He touches his hat, says: "Certainly, Sir", and I go up those steps . . along the old familiar corridor . . don't bother to go in the cloak-room . . go right in there . . the same old restaurant . . same old lights . . tinkling glasses . . happy voices . . soft music. I look around hoping to see Molly or Jane . . *anyone* from the old days. The headwaiter comes over to me, hand outstretched to shake mine.

"So pleased to see you, again, Mr. Carasov. Sit down. Have something to eat . . to drink."

I say: "I've got *no* money. Bob out there has paid the taxi-man for me . . . And where is Molly?"

"My dear Mr. Carasov, you don't have to bother about

money. We'll look after the taxi fare, and you can eat and drink anything you like. Leave the bill to be settled later. As for Molly, she's married very well . . we hardly ever see her nowadays . . Jane . . she's *disappeared.*" I sit there, *lost* in memories. *Everything has changed* except the kindness and goodwill of this old man. I get up, thank him for his hospitality, and Bob, too, and go out into the night . . .

I'm up there, in a top floor bedsitter . . it's cold . . I've done some petty villainy . . I've got a few bob. The prospect before me is not good . . I have qualms about walking out on my Banstead friends . . I wonder just where that mother of mine lives . . but I'm young, proud, vain . . after all I'm *me* . . surely I'll get by?

I remember reading somewhere about a mental hospital story. I thought the publisher was Gollancz so I think: *Why shouldn't I write a story?* I go to Henrietta Street . . in there. "Can I see Mr. Gollancz, please?" In my innocence, my ignorance, I thought you could just walk in there and see anybody you like. "Have you an appointment?" I'm asked. At that moment in comes a greying, ageing man . . dignified . . very much of a person, a man of substance. The girl tells him what I want and he says: "Come in here, young man. I'm Mr. Gollancz." I follow, am invited to sit down and asked my business. Gollancz rings a bell . . the girl comes in. "Please fetch some manuscript paper and some pencils." The girl comes back bringing a pile of paper and some pencils. "Take this paper and these pencils, and go away and *write* . . *write,*" says Mr. Gollancz.

I return to the top-floor room . . *It's cold in there* . . I look at the pile of paper . . and put it in the empty fireplace . . set it alight . . and warm myself by its heat. And that was the *last* time, for years and years, I ever thought of the *writing lark.*

I'm waiting my turn to use the phone . . in my hand is a copy of Evelyn Waugh's *Vile Bodies* . . I hear a soft woman's voice: "I like your taste in books." I turn round and there is a little woman, straight out of a spy novel . . chic . . svelte . . dark and beautiful. We get talking and, as usual with me, I'm frank and unconcealing. I tell her of my writing fiasco . . my near poverty . . no money for food or coal . . rent overdue . . and I tell her about my recent experience at Banstead. She immediately says: "*You must go back there* . . those people are *good* people . . they will help you." I let my new-found friend phone the Banstead authorities, and they say: "Let him come back to us. He can take his own discharge later if he wishes." My beautiful 'spy' friend takes me to the station, puts me on that train and waves *goodbye .. goodbye ...*

I get back to Banstead rather late. The night sister is on duty. She expresses regret that I should have left them in this irregular fashion but says: "We are *all* glad you have come back. You must stay with us for some time. You need rest and care."

Next day I'm interviewed by Dr. Ruthven. He advises *against* immediate discharge, but says: "None of the doctors here will *stop* you going if you wish."

I'm young, foolish, headstrong .. *famished* for *freedom*. I insist on taking my discharge, *all* concerned at *Banstead deeply regretting* this ...

IX

I NOW ENTER a phase of my life, between 1932 and 1935, which I might describe as the *phase of indecision*, the point of departure for renewal. I'd been to jail . . reform school . . Borstal . . and been marked as a nutter, even though I confessed to putting that pot on to get to the *house of nutters,* Broadmoor . . I'd been to a free-world mental hospital and experienced *nothing* but kindness there . . and yet I'm still immersed in a sea of feelings . . ideas . . notions . . peculiar to the world of *jail,* and to those who live in such places.

A part of me was very disturbed, like a man in a storm-tossed boat . . another part of me was seemingly quite *normal.* In this uncertain state of mind I drift . . drift . . start back there . . in the villainy thing . . I work the boat-train . . Victoria . . the famous Golden Arrow. I'm soon caught . . I get done for stealing a fur-coat and a dispatch-case. They give me six months . . and six months . . twelve months in all . . I go to Wandsworth . . *cold . . harsh . . brutal.* I'm in a kind of daze . . I just don't register . . things there have a kind of dream quality. I just go through with it all as if *sleep-walking.* All I remember is one night in my peter when I heard someone singing "Blues in the Night", though talking and singing was *strictly forbidden.*

I finish my time in Wandsworth. I'm free again . . with about two pounds in cash and the clothes I stood up in. I'm walking past the old Lyons' Corner House . . Coventry Street . . in those days, the haunt of all sorts of characters from whores to *High Society.* I go in for a coffee, and there is Dora. I'd known her in my pre-Broadmoor days of affluence. She appeared to be ill.

"Hello, hello," Dora says to me. I join her . . yes, she's ill all right . . lives round the corner in Rupert Street . . has been very ill. I ask her: "Can I get you anything from Boots, over there?" "Yes, Nick, get me some Aspirin." I cross the Circus . . no traffic . . it's long after midnight. I'm thinking: I must help this girl . . get her away from this part of London.

I come back, with the Aspirins, and am invited to come round to Dora's place. I go with her . . and there it is . . *one room* . . a bed . . a chair . . a table . . *no window* . . from this room . . a small, very small, bathroom. We talk . . we make love. The bathroom door opens, and there is a dark, hair-cropped girl wearing a dressing-gown. She looks at me as *if she would like to kill me* . . then goes back into the bathroom.

"Who's *that*, Dora?"

"Oh, just a friend, Nick . . a bit jealous perhaps."

It comes to me . . Dora has sunk very low . . *she must now be a sort of lesbian* . . .

I tell Dora: "I'm taking you away from here. This life is not for you. But I, Dora, must go and get some money. I'll meet you at the Blue Café, Greek Street, tomorrow about three in the afternoon."

I leave Dora . . go to a hotel in Pall Mall . . the old *Garland's* Hotel . . since bombed. I get away with some gear which I put in a railway station left-luggage office, intending to meet Dora the next day . . take her to my small flat . . sell the gear. Then *both* of us will leave London for some place in the country.

Next day I'm there at the Blue Café . . and . . and . . I'm nicked. The Bogeys are waiting for me. They tell me a *phone call* came to them . . a girl's voice saying: "*You will find a crook* at the Blue Café tomorrow. *He may be wanted by you.*"

In short, Dora's friend was jealous, had resented my arrival on the scene and had learnt from Dora where we were to meet. The rest is sheer melodrama. The police find the luggage-ticket, prove I'm the *thief* but *don't want to rub it in* because they admire my effort to get Dora *away* from this sordid set-up.

I'm up before the Marlborough Street magistrate. The police just give the evidence and say: "All this property has been recovered. We don't know anything about this man. For the last four or five years we think he has been out of this country."

Me, I'm thinking: What *luck* . . the police *don't want to know*. The magistrate, not knowing *why* the police are so unenthusiastic about my getting convicted and jailed, is curious to know just where I have been during the *blank years*.

He remands me for a week and *bang* goes *all my luck*. During the remand the Yard comes into the picture, my record is *uncovered* and, on return to the police court, I'm sentenced to eighteen months' H.L. and am transported to Pentonville Prison, a dark, gloomy, filthy prison . . like a Medieval Fortress.

I'm in my peter on the bed . . I'm restless . . sleepless . . my mind *full* of yet another *failure* . . brought upon myself *by* myself . . when I feel an *itch*, a *hot stinging itch* on my neck . . my arms . . my legs. I get out of bed . . the light's out . . but some sort of light comes through the window . . and *there . . there is an army* of *blood-red ant-like creatures*, hurrying and scurrying up and down those sheets. I'd *never ever* seen these creatures before, except years and years ago when as a kid I lived in theatrical digs with my mother. I now recognised . . *bugs* . . *bugs* . . and I went stark raving mad . . got my stool . . and started *killing* those bloody bastards . . *bashing . . bashing . . bashing . . and screaming my head off*. The light went on, a screw looks through the spy-hole. *He bawls*: "Stop that din. Stop that din. Get into bed."

By now I'm frantic . . *mad*. Those bugs have *scared me. I can't go back to bed*. I look at the window, see the bars. I tear a big piece of sheeting, get the stool, put it under the window, stand on it and proceed to tie that sheeting round my neck. I intended to hang myself. That door opens . . screws come in . . I'm knocked off the stool, grabbed, carried down below and slung right in there . . *solitary* . . a bare stripped cell . . *nothing* in there but mattress, blankets and a papier-mâché pot. I'm told: "*Another sound out of you* and we'll kick your teeth out." The door *bangs shut* and there I stay, sleepless, till next morning . . .

"Come on you, put these clothes on. You are going into hospital." And so they put me in hospital . . a stripped cell . . *no* breakable furniture, *no* belt, *no* laces . . *barred gate* instead of a *steel door*.

The gate opens. "The doctor wants you, come on." I get up from the bed, dress myself and follow this screw. An office . . desk littered with papers . . at the desk a little, red-cheeked, balding man wearing old-fashioned steel-rimmed spectacles. *That* was the famous Dr. Sass . . .

"Sit down, please." I sit down rather reluctantly . . I'm now getting a bit wary of *all* prison personnel. I'm beginning to think that I . . I am on *one side* of that wall and the *others,* the prison authorities, are on the *opposite side.*

"Tell me, what disturbed you last night? And why did you tie the sheeting round your neck?" I looked at this little man. He didn't appear to be a killer, not an *executioner.* I talked to this man, I began to like him . . *no* threats from *him* . . *no* brush-off for my vagaries, my stupidities. "You go back to your room. We will look after you. There won't be *any bugs here.*"

I stayed in hospital for some time, had good food and always a cheerful word from Dr. Sass. In fact I got quite fond of this kindly man. I used to do sketches of him sitting at his desk or coming up the drive to the prison in his car. One day I'm sent for. "Carasov, I'm thinking of sending you back to the prison, but we will get you a job over there, something light and not too monotonous."

When back in the prison I was given a clean cell and, thanks to Dr. Sass, an *iron bedstead* so there were no more *bugs.*

I'm over in the jail, Desk Orderly to Mr. Higginbottom, Senior Officer, A Wing. I like this screw . . intelligent, understanding, competent. The bread for breakfast and tea always came to me for arranging in floors, in the separate baskets.

On the landing where I was Desk Orderly was a small cell . . this was our office. The bread for the men would come up in baskets and I would count those loaves. The bread in those days was *not* sliced up . . we got rather nice little loaves, which, when *fresh,* were very *good.* Always, if there was a loaf or two over my Desk Officer and I would share it, just like *good friends . . .*

On A Wing was the Condemned Cell, in those days very often in use. The morning a man had been hanged, it was *my* job, after the Condemned Cell had been 'vacated', to clean it out, remove all debris, rearrange the furniture.

One morning I go in to the C.C. and I'm *uneasy* . . I'm even a bit *afraid* of I know not what. There is this *big double cell* . . a bed . . *all* the bed-clothes on the floor. Clothes, prison clothes, lying all over the place as if they had been *forcibly taken off* and just thrown down there . . bits and pieces of food *partly eaten* . . a papier-mâché *mug* half filled with tea. Over there a fallen table . . playing cards *all over the place*. I feel queasy and *sorry, sorry* for the man who had died that morning. I look in the bathing-alcove, *no* bath-plug . . the W.C., *no chain*. I think: "They will hang him, but *he* must *not hang himself*. I quickly finish my cleaning, *resolved never to clean that room again* . . .

The prison barber used to put his stool right opposite A Wing desk . . so one morning I asked him to give me a hair-cut. He answered: "You wait your turn. I'm busy." I could see the barber was *not* busy at that moment, and I resented his tone. The Chief Officer, Mr. Walker, was at that moment coming down the landing. I say: "Chief, tell this fellow to give me a hair-cut." The old Chief was a decent sort of fellow and guessed the trouble, so he says: "Barber, give Carasov a hair-cut." I sit on the barber's stool, he puts the towel round my neck and says to me: "*Friend* of the *Chief*, eh?" I say nothing. While the barber was cutting my hair I noticed he took his glasses *off* . . he finished the job, put his glasses *on* and I . . I grabbed him by the shirt-front and I *bashed* . . *bashed* his face . . his eyes . . the glasses splintering to bits . . and *he* . . *he* screaming: "You'll *blind me*. You'll *blind me*, you bastard." The man's face was streaming with blood . . I was held firmly by several screws . . pulled . . pushed . . *carried*, straight over to the hospital . . stripped . . and thrown into the 'pad'.

Later that day Dr. Sass comes in the pad. "Why did you attack the barber, Carasov?" I tell Dr. Sass just *why*. I made it clear that the barber took a liberty with me, was treating *me* as if I were a *mug* . . also this barber was well known in the jail for this kind of thing. Dr. Sass ordered my removal to a stripped cell, matted floor, papier-mâché pot and *gate* instead of *door* . . .

I resumed the old hospital life down there in that stripped cell. I'd read, mostly classics . . I'd sketch, the Doctor, the screws. *Me* . . in that cell . . I'd *day-dream* . . hardly ever think of the man I'd injured. If I did I'd say: It was *his fault. He shouldn't take liberties*. It seems my *personal* experiences of *violence* . . in *jail* . . in *Broadmoor* . . were *making me adopt the same methods of violence* . . .

I'm walking up and down that peter *singing* . . I hear a voice: "Shut up, you bastard." I go to the gate, look out and there is a cleaner with a brush in his hand . . I say: "Was that you who told me to shut up?" "Yes, you bastard." Later we are opened up for slopping-out. I notice the cleaner in a kind of store-room piled up with china-pots, buckets, etcetera . . I go in the store, pick a pot up and *crack* . . *crack* that cleaner right across his head. There is a *shout* . . a *scream* . . broken pots *all* over the place . . and I'm rushed by screws . . stripped . . put in the pad . . and they *strait-jacket* me . . .

I'd had experience of canvas shirts *locked* behind your neck, but with those you *could* use your arms, you could use that pot. With a *jacket* your arms are pinioned, you are strapped *round the neck, between the legs* . . you are *trussed up like a chicken* for the *cooker* . . you are thrown down there on the rubber floor with *stiff canvas sheets* your *only* protection from the cold. The screws go out, bang that *safe-like door*. I lie there looking up at the ceiling. From where I lie I can hear *outside traffic noises,* the back of this pad abutting the outer wall of the prison. I hear motorbikes . . cars . . buses . . *roar* . . *bang* . . *crash* . . I hear children's voices . . they are *playing* out there. I'm thinking: *They will end up where I am now* one day or they will be *screws*. The light begins to fail . . there is a very small window up there . . dirty and barred . . the light seeping through. In the ceiling . . way up there . . a dark red light goes on . . I note a glass panel up there, and through that I'm *observed* by a *stealthy eye* . . .

The traffic is lessening out there, no more children's voices . . . But there is a tired *tweet* . . *tweet* . . *t w e e t* . . *birds* on the top of the wall about to retire for the night . . . All is now *silent* . . *silent*.

I'm wondering: What if I want to *piss* . . shit . . ? Must I do it in this *jacket*? I begin to worry. I'm *afraid* I . . I *might make a mess of myself* . . I can't get up to call for help . . I can't signal. I begin to *hate the inhuman bastards who put me in this jacket* . . careless of *what I may have to do* in the damned thing.

A little light comes through the window. *That* light up there begins to fade . . it goes out . . it's *morning* . . *tweet* . . *tweet* . . the *birds are awake* . . I listen *spellbound* forgetting all my troubles. I hear the milk-cart on its *rounds* . . the buses starting the day . . a motorbike *roars* past. The door opens . . screws are there. I say: "Let me out of this, *I want to shit*. They take the jacket off, go away, *I rush for that pot* just in time. Later I see Dr. Sass and tell him: "If they *ever* put me in a jacket again, I'll *kill one of the bastards when I get out.*" I tell him of my *horror* of messing myself in that jacket. I'm moved back into the old peter.

The gate opens . . I'm told: "You are wanted in the doctor's office, Carasov." In there is a strange man . . *very important-looking* . . he *fills* that chair . . he seems to *fill* the whole room. "We are going to send you away, Carasov. You will be well cared for. You don't appear to be very *happy here.*" I never saw that man again nor did I see Dr. Sass again . . .

They come for me next morning, give me my own clothes. We go out there to a waiting taxi, get in. The car moves off. I'm thinking: What *now*? Another loony-bin? The screws don't talk . . they appear to be *lost* in their own *private world*. Me, I look at the *passing scene*. Everything I see from the taxi window . . *is quite as wonderful* as it is *when one sees it every day of one's life . . trees . . fields . . homes in their own grounds . . people*. I look . . look . . *nostalgically . . all . . all . . wonderful* . . but *not* for *me*.

Here we are, another mental hospital. *This* time, *no friendly welcome . . this is not a Banstead . . this is a* kind of *Little Broadmoor*. I'm coldly received, taken to a sort of *gathering place*. Later I learn *this* is the *reception ward*.

I'm put to bed. Over there in bed is an old man . . moaning . . moaning . . in pain. Two male nurses proceed to give the old man an *enema* . . they handle him roughly . . they *shoot* that *enema right into him* . . he moans . . he moans. Next morning the screens are round the old man's bed . . later a trolley comes . . they put that old man in it . . he's *now dead*.

In the place of the old man a younger one . . *asleep* most of the time. Every time he wakes up the nurses start to *pummel* and *beat* him . . *he hits back*. They send for the doctor . . he gives *another injection* . . the man goes to sleep. I note every time this young man *wakes up*, these *nurses* start to *pummel him . . he* hits back . . then they give him *another injection*. There are screens around the young man's bed . . a trolley comes . . they put him in it . . *he is now dead* . . . I am wondering: What sort of place is *this*? I'm getting a bit nervous and *angry*, too. I'm foolish enough to say to one of these nurses: *"If you try anything with me, I will not be so easy to kill."* I was *warned*: "Be careful what you say. You *may get into trouble ...*"

I'm allowed up .. go into a kind of day-room. Many kinds of patients here .. old and young .. but so far I've seen no really violent people. *The nurses seem to me to be the most dangerous men in the place ...*

I'm in the wash-house and there is a very young fellow there, Jewish-looking. He's washing himself .. an *attendant,* a so-called nurse, comes in, grabs this boy, tells him to get a move on and pushes him around. I go up to the nurse and say: "If you want to bully somebody, why not start with *me*?" I'm warned to mind my own business, but they leave the boy alone after that.

I'm in the day-room one afternoon when I'm told: "A lady visitor wants to see you, Carasov." I go in the visiting room and *there* is a very handsome woman with the boy I'd stopped them bullying. This lady introduces herself as the boy's mother. She thanks me for protecting the boy, says she'll take him away from there. We talk .. we share tea and cakes .. I take my leave of her .. I never see her again .. or the boy.

I begin to feel this place is not for *me* .. the staff are hostile, brutal and indifferent to the welfare of the patients in their care. I have been helping in the pantry separating the male side from the female side with a hatch in between (through this hatch, I had the *only* glimpse I ever had of the female nurses). One day I decided to barricade myself in the pantry and *challenge* the bloody bullying male nurses to *come for* me. Amongst the male nurses there is *one* nurse of a very fine type .. intelligent .. self-disciplined .. sympathetic. I liked him .. we often talked together, and it was clear *he* had a very *low opinion of his fellow nurses*. "Nick," he says to me, "don't challenge these people. *You*, Nick are a *certified lunatic* so far as *they* are concerned and *you could get hurt. Don't fight them.*" I took his advice, but those nurses just didn't want *me* around so they report me to the ward-doctor for *threatening behaviour*, and I'm sent for.

"Please sit down, Mr. Carasov." This Doctor is rather young .. good-looking .. very *alert*. "You don't appear to be very *popular* in this ward. The staff are very hostile to you. In your own interest, I propose to transfer you to another ward.

Yes . . yes . . I understand, Carasov, but I *must co-operate with my staff. They do a lot of my work.* I *know some* of the staff here are not good, but it's hard to get the *right men* in this service so we have to put up with quite a lot of unsuitable men. However, where you are going, I think you will be *all right.*"

I'm taken away by two nurses . . through the yards . . the grounds . . down those corridors . . here we are . . a small building on its own . . a gate and a door. My escort ring the bell . . the inner door opens . . then the gate . . and the escort say: "*One* from the reception, Mr. Smith." This man, *big . . tough-looking* . . jacket off, sleeves rolled-up . . cigar in his mouth . . he looks at me, says: "O.K., leave him with me. You can go." The escort goes. "Come in, into the office," says Mr. Smith, locking the door and gate, then leading the way into quite a pleasant office. He sits down, puts his *feet up on the desk,* takes a big puff at the cigar and just quietly looks me over . . .

"I like people of your sort, Carasov. Plenty of spirit. This is the *refractory ward* . . quite a few *tough* characters here, and sometimes I have to take a firm line, but you and I will get on quite well, I'm sure. You can help in the pantry, and as soon as I can, I'll get you a ground parole ticket which means you can go out in the grounds any time you like." As Mr. Smith said this, he *actually* winked. It was clear to me that he did not want me to stay around here too long.

The refractory ward here differed from that of *Broadmoor*: here the staff used the *minimum* of *force* for the occasionally violent . . there was *no* manhandling, *no* canvas shirt, *no* strait-jacket . . just an injection and a clean bed in a reasonably warm and well-ventilated room. Afterwards, on the patient's recovery, there were *no reprisals.* I liked this Smith . . he was dreaming of retirement and a pub where he would be mine host.

I got my parole-ticket . . went out through the gardens . . over the hedge . . and I was *free . . free* . . In my mind was a big "thank you" to Mr. Smith . . .

I have *nothing* but what I stand up in . . a few shillings . . and *all* the time in the world to find my way about. I see a road sign: *Brighton . . Lewes. I* decide to go there if I walk the whole way . . which, in fact, I *do,* arriving at Brighton foot-blistered and weary but *free . . free.*

X

DOWN THERE ON that coast the air . . the sea . . the sense of freedom blew away *all* my accumulated ills, almost as if I'd never ever been in jail . . mental hospital . . Borstal or reform school. In fact, for the moment, I was a king with not a care in the world . . .

There is a notice up there . . "Domestic Service Agency". I decide to seek a job. I go up those stairs into the office and I ask: "Are there any jobs going for house-servants?" This person is rather nice, a motherly sort of woman. She asks me: "What kind of job have you done before? You don't look like a house-servant."

I tell a tale . . trouble at home . . no money . . willing to take anything . . .

I'm told: "I have a vacancy here for a temporary houseman in a house outside Lewes. The owners are away at the Dublin Horse Show, only the son-in-law, the gardener and his wife, and a housemaid are in residence." I'm given the address of this place, a letter of introduction, and the money for the bus fare.

The bus stops . . I get off, walk through the lodge-gate up the beautiful, tree-lined drive, and there it is . . a fine Georgian country mansion . . surrounded by trees, shrubs and flowers . . with hounds, a whole pack of them, sniffling and snuffling around the side-entrance. I felt *as if I had come home* . . .

I meet the son-in-law who accepts my services. He is a bit curious at my having *no* working-clothes and *no* luggage, but says: "I'll take you down to the cook, the gardener's wife. She will find you some working clothes and show you to your room. Also, she will tell you what to do." I meet the cook, the maid, the gardener . . nice people, but very reserved . . and a bit wary of *me* . . so *unlike* the usual man-servant . . and, seemingly, quite ignorant of *my place in the servant's world*. It seems a servant should *never look like a master, talk like one or behave like one*.

I soon discover that this house is a veritable *museum* . . the hallway: antlered heads, armour, rich and opulent rugs, polished wood-work . . upstairs: living-rooms with tall glass-fronted cases filled with objets-d'art, old drinking-horns, antique watches, and *pictures galore* . . in the main bedroom, furnished like a queen's bedroom, on the wide window-seat is an unlocked jewel-case with a few lovely diamond and ruby rings. There are many empty compartments, the jewellery from which has no doubt gone to the Dublin Horse Show. All this I discover on the first day I'm on duty. My job is general house-cleaning, *not* intended to overlap the maid's work. The maid I like, but she is very very *reserved.*

I am settling down to this job more as if it were a kind of hobby for me, the son and heir of the house. I haven't had much dalliance with the fair sex for some time and I try to 'make' this maid, so fair, so attractive. *She* doesn't like my rushing tactics. Apparently, in the servant world, *one goes slow* to start with. *Me,* I'm not a *go-slow performer.* The maid complains to the son-in-law . . he gets *indignant.* That I . . I, a mere servant, should *dare to have any sex life* seemed to outrage this bastard. He *sacks me on the spot.* I think: O.K., *if this is the way of it,* I'll make the bastard pay for it. I go upstairs, empty the jewel-case, select some portable objets-d'art . . watches, a few bits of Georgian silver. I walk out of the house, *sorry* the dream has ended. I am *not* a *servant,* nor am I a *master,* for whom, no doubt, *maid-servants* are tasty perquisites . . .

I go down the drive . . look back at this lovely *domaine* . . and wonder . . and wonder: How does it come about, *all* for *them* and *nothing* for *me*?

I sell the rings here and there in the open market . . *no more crooked dealers* for *me.* I buy some clothes, some shoes, a good bag . . then, *walking on air . . prison forgotten,* I entrain for Llandudno . . a Welsh holiday for me.

I don't know why I chose Wales for my holiday, but that is where I went . . and, booking in at the *best* hotel, I settle down to *lose myself* in sheer self-indulgence. There was good food, good wine, and very pretty women. I don't recall *any* profound *thinking* . . it was just to be a *past-forgetting holiday.*

At the end of a week or two I am thinking of returning to London, which *still* had a very *strong pull on my heart-strings.* Whilst at this hotel, I'd noticed (professionally, as it were) that the rooms on my floor had *balconies* and . . you could step over one on to the other if you didn't mind being *seen* from below. The day before I left the hotel I did in fact explore this balcony thing. Entering a nearby room, I find it quite unoccupied. There is a wardrobe . . I open the door . . a drawer used for studs and cufflinks . . and, believe it or not, a *roll* of *pound-notes.* I pocket the roll thinking: *These will pay my expenses.* I spare no thought for the *dishonesty of the whole business* nor for the owner's *loss.*

I'm on the train *back* to London but stop off at the beautiful old city of Chester. I walk around, enjoying the period stuff of that old city. I buy some more clothes, noting that Chester's shops are as *good* as any in London.

I'm in London again. It's 1935 . . still a swinging town . . clubs: *Murrays*, the "Chez Henri", the Gargoyle . . restaurants: Romano's, the Café Royal, Gennaro's, the Piccadilly Grill . . and the glamorous theatre people: Jessie Matthews, Dorothy Dickson, Sybil Thorndike . . the band world: Joe Loss, Ambrose, Jack Payne . . . a gay swinging *London.*

I'm going down the stairs of the old Brasserie Universal, underneath the Criterion. I fancy a drink before dinner. Seated over there is a very smartly-dressed woman, wearing a most attractive hat. And, to judge by the glass, she is drinking brandy. I am not a brash storm-trooper but, on the other hand, I don't care for *slow tactics.* I look at this woman, catch her eye and *raise my glass* (I'm drinking Dubonnet). This woman responds to my gesture by raising *her* glass. I go straight over and ask to join her. And so I meet *Sarah*, fair, slim, chic, very very smart, but *no chicken* . . mature, married though separated from her husband . . a daughter doing some small-bit stuff for the films. I introduce myself . . "Oh, just a *wanderer* with a *love of beautiful things.*" Sarah and I get on like a house on fire. I soon discover her life has been very unhappy . . the marriage breaking up as soon as the girl was near school-leaving age. Sarah, I gathered, had been some sort of stage personality before her marriage. She *never* told me *who she had been on the stage*, but it was clear to me Sarah had been a *star.*

Sarah tells me she is living alone, her daughter also on her own, and it's soon clear to me that this woman is very lonely . . so am I. I propose that Sarah and I join up, but *she* . . *she* is scared at this sudden departure from a life of convention and "What would my daughter think if she discovered her mother was living with a *stranger*, a man at that?"

Me . . *me*, I have no time for this thing called *convention*, so I practically *abduct* this charming woman. We find a flat in Mayfair. This so-called smart address seemed to reassure Sarah.

After all, she must have thought, *he is not a tramp*. Anyhow, *he has got good taste*.

Sarah and I stayed together for some months. I learnt much of her story, a very unhappy one. We went out wining and dining, we danced . . and wherever Sarah and I went, she was received by the maître d'hôtel, head-waiter or club owner as if she were *royalty. They* always called her *madame* . . welcomed her with bows and smiles. I'm sure *everybody* in this *opulent world* of the *diner-out* would have been uninterested in *me* had I not been escorting this charming woman. At times I got furious with all this attention to Sarah . . it was as *if I had no separate existence* or so it seemed. It was this attention given to Sarah which gave me the idea of her stardom.

This interlude in my life was the *first* ever of its kind. I'd had a wild, furious, crazy love-affair with Molly years before, but Molly, like myself, was not particularly *distinguished* . . we were just ordinary folk . . me, a thief masquerading as a man-about-town . . Molly, a cabaret girl, a hostess. I'm not saying Molly wasn't as *good* as the next one, or I, but what I do say is that for the first time in my life I met one of the 'inner circle', a person with a special kind of *taste* . . *smell* . . *style* . . . This, of course, I now know to be sheer snobbery, but in those days I was younger and, I suppose, very *impressionable*, also very lonely and inexperienced.

Every now and again I'd leave London, go on a foray, return to Sarah, sell the gear on the open market. Then Sarah and I would go on the Town . . eating, drinking, and dancing. Later we would come home and make love *all* night, she acting as if she had *never ever been loved before*. I enjoyed making love to Sarah . . there was *no* mock modesty, *no* prudery . . she was a natural woman, needing natural love.

For some time I did not meet Sarah's daughter. I think Sarah was *scared* of my doing so. *She had this convention thing* . . loved me, but *"let's keep it secret"—that was Sarah's aim*.

Sarah and I were at a dinner-dance, and as we were sitting down between dances, Sarah says to me: "Don't look round, Nick, but my daughter Joan is over there with her fiancé." I don't look round, I'm not really interested, but when we get back home, the phone rings. Sarah takes the call . . I'm looking at her and I notice she's very disturbed in manner and voice. "Who's that on the phone?" I ask. "Oh dear, it's *Joan* and she wants to know *who are you*? She says: 'I've never seen that man before, who the devil is he?' "

Me, I'm annoyed: what's it got to do with *her* whom her mother dances with? "Where does this daughter of yours live?"

"Not far from here . . . Why, why do you want to know this, Nick?"

"Put your things on, Sarah, we are going to visit this daughter of yours. Who does she think she is? *All* this palaver about not *knowing me*!"

Sarah was terrified at the mere *idea* of *me* visiting Joan. I phone for a taxi.

"Stop at the first flower-shop," Sarah orders. "Nick, you must buy some flowers for Joan."

"Flowers? *me* buy *flowers* for *Joan*? Not on your life." Sarah stops the taxi, gets the flowers, *pays for them*, and we continue the journey. Here we are . . a block of fine flats . . in we go . . up on the lift . . out there we ring that bell. A house-keeper who obviously knows Joan's mother lets us in and there is *Joan*.

In spite of the warm weather there is a fire burning away, glowing and cheerful. The room is tastefully furnished. In a chaise-longue kind of love-seat, there is a very handsome young woman . . fair, with hair down to her shoulders . . a smart afternoon-frock a bit *tight* across the up-thrusting breasts . . nice legs. This young woman, looks at her mother, ignoring *me*.

"This . . this . . Joan . . is *Nick* . . Mr. Nick Cranston, my friend. You remember? We were dancing together . . . Oh, Joan, Nick bought these lovely flowers for you . ."

Me . . me, I say: *"I did not buy these flowers for you.* The *only* flowers I would buy for *you, miss*, would be *for your funeral . . ."* Joan looks at me as if she *couldn't believe her ears*, then she *laughs . . laughs* . . and, putting her hand out to shake *mine*, she says: "Mr. Nick Cranston, you are the *first* man *ever to visit me* without bringing flowers or chocolates and I admire you. My mother is lucky to have you as her friend." From that day on till I left London, Joan and I got on very well. In fact, later on she and her mother were given a sort of *family lunch* by me at a restaurant. We sat together as if we were a *closely-knit family* having a gorgeous day out . . .

At this point of the story I would like to explain *why I had to use so many different names*. As a thief, as a hotel jewel-thief, I had to register as a guest and I rarely used my *own* name, so I'd look in the telephone book and select a name or, seeing a reference to a well-known person, writer, artist or journalist, I'd adopt his name and often, for no particular reason, I'd stick to the adopted name for ordinary social purposes . . hence the string of *aliases* in this story. At this time, 1935, I was known as Niki, or Nick, Cranston . . later it was Neal Grayson . . and, later still, my own name, Carasov, Victor Carasov. (Curious, this *last* name . . *Victor* . . from the Latin . . *conqueror* . . and I've *not conquered anything* yet . . .)

Because of my trade I was always moving on from address to address. Sarah found this a bit of a strain as she had the fastidious habit of *always* carrying around with her, wherever we stayed . . flat, bedsitter or hotel . . her own bric-a-brac, candlesticks, vases, etcetera.

One day I went off to Worcestershire to the famous Lygon Arms in Broadway, a place much favoured by the roving, rich American, being a show-place of Elizabethan splendour. In going to the Lygon Arms at this time I failed to note the passing seasons: there are times when *no* tourist traffic is going on and it is out of season. *This* I failed to note . . and, unknown to me, *this* was to lead to my downfall. (I may say, in passing, that *all* my life I seem to have taken certain *fatal steps* which have led . . inevitably . . to *disaster*.)

When I arrive at the Lygon Arms, it's clear the place is all but *empty* . . only a few permanent guests and the resident management. My arrival in the off-season must have puzzled the management. However, I book in, go upstairs. I'm feeling rather *nervous* as *if I knew this was* a *dangerous place for me*. I decide to go to work quickly, get what I can and get the hell out of it back to Town.

I'm up there, foraging around in this room, looking for jewellery, when the door opens and there is the chambermaid come to 'fix' the bed and the curtains for the night. She looks at me, hand to her mouth, *screams* and dashes away. *Me*, I lock that door, leave the key in the lock, collect what gear there is . . not very much . . open the bottom half of the window and climb over the sill. It's now quite dark. I hang there, not knowing what there is below, but I drop down. By some freakish chance, I land on the roof of a glass-house but the glass, being thick and reinforced with embedded wire, doesn't break. I slide right off it, down into what appears to be a sort of vegetable garden in a state of quagmire after rain.

I feel the water soaking into my suede shoes . . my trousers are ruined . . my jacket torn . . and I can hear: "He's round the back. He's jumped out of the window." I see *lights* . . I hear dogs barking . . the *hunt is on* . . and I . . I am the *hunted*. All round me is nothing but vegetable quagmire. I'm soaked and I'm desperate. If I go *this* way I'm lost in wet fields . . if I go *that* way, round to the front of the hotel, I'll be caught in the glare of those car-lights, those torch-lights. Still, if I take the latter course, I *might* find shelter in a neighbouring garden, *maybe* get someone there to get me a taxi. I take the risk, go round to the front hugging the shadows . . .

The road in front of the hotel is packed with cars . . all lights *on* . . people *all* round . . shouting . . talking . . dogs . . dogs . . barking. There is a detached house, a gate, a surrounding hedge. *If* I can get in there, I'm *safe* . . or so I believe. I *do* get in there . . up the path . . ring the bell . . a girl comes to the door: "Will you please phone for a taxi for me? I am a visitor from Stratford and have hurt my foot . . a taxi will get me to the station."

"Certainly, I'll get you a taxi. Won't you come in and rest your foot, whilst waiting for the taxi?"

Me . . me, I feel safer out there *watching* those cars, those *lights*, and the people so eager to catch me. I say: "Thank you, I'll wait here." Then, up the path comes an old man . . he's bent and doubled-up, using a stick . . he reaches me . . and there, on his door-step, he says: "Who be you?" I explain, say I'm waiting for a taxi and he says: "*I don't like strangers*, and *you are not getting a taxi* from *here*." What could I *do*? I dare not start anything. I'm afraid of those people out there. The old man opens the door, gives *me* a *dirty look* and *bangs that door on me*. I go down the path, open the gate intending to dash across the road into the fields . . but, as *if the fates intended my capture*, a car comes *this* way . . a car comes *that* way . . and between the two sets of glaring head-lights . . I'm *done . . done. One big shout of triumph* and they grab me.

I'm taken to the local lock-up . . searched. They find some gear . . a ring or two . . other odds and ends. I'm locked up for the night in the usual kind of cell . . *no* furniture, little or *no* light . . a couple of blankets . . a bed-board, fixed to the wall . . W.C. in the corner, stinking to heaven. I appear at the local Magistrates' Court, am remanded and moved to Gloucester Prison . . a dismal, primitive ancient keep.

A few hours back I was free, a few hours back I was with Sarah. Not being a bemedalled *hero*, not being an ordinary, run-of-the-mill villain, I didn't rejoice at my return to prison. I wasn't coming back to dear old *pals*, dear old *screws*. I was coming back to *purgatory*. Yet, I must confess, *I chose the course which inevitably led back to this purgatory,* so I had to abide by the consequences.

In the jail I get depressed, think of *suicide*. I miss the sight and sound of *Sarah*, to whom I'd got more attached than I was really aware. I walk up and down that cell, looking at a photograph of Sarah which I'd had taken when last in Town and which I always carried around with me . . soft . . sloppy? Yes, perhaps . . . The door opens. "Cranston, don't worry so much. This always happens to people of your trade. You are not dead yet and that woman in the photograph, she won't necessarily leave you. You'll get *out again one day*. Cheer up." This was from the visiting Governor.

Being a remand prisoner, I am wearing my own clothes. They are ruined of course, after that escapade in the vegetable garden behind the Lygon Arms, so I send a visiting order to Sarah, asking her to bring me a change of clothing and enclosing five pounds for incidental expenses on the way down. In due course I'm sent for . . I have a visitor. In the visiting room there is a table with a wall of wire-netting down the middle . . two chairs . . one on either side . . near the door on *my* side is a screw. I sit down and there is Sarah . . smart as usual, half-veil from that dinky little hat . . fur-collared and fur-cuffed jacket, matching skirt . . *all* in great style, which I liked. Now facing the realities of the villainy lark, something we had *never* discussed, Sarah is considerably *shaken*. She even thinks that *she* is in danger. I tell Sarah not to worry, I'd see to it that she was not involved. "Just stay around, look after yourself. Give Joan my best wishes."

Goodbye . . goodbye . . I return to my peter, that cell . . and *sink* . . *sink* into suicidal depression. I'm moved to Birmingham Prison Hospital for *observation* . . . "Watch the bastard, he might commit suicide." In fact, I haven't the courage to commit suicide. I go on *living* . . I'm further remanded . . then committed for trial at the Worcester Quarter Sessions.

Meantime, my mother turns up again. By some queer quirk of fate she is at this time actually living in Birmingham and has seen the Press notices of my case . . .

I hadn't seen Mother since the Banstead days, 1932 that was, three years ago. She then looked very smart, very nice. It's true, I never saw *much* of Mother and she just disappeared, but *now* she was *old* . . *old* . . her hair was *grey* . . her face, that once beautiful face, was wrinkled, lined, weary-looking . . her clothes were shabby, dreadfully ill-fitting. God, I thought, what a change in my lovely young mother! I felt *guilty* . . after all, I should have sought her out, I was her son.

"Victor . . oh, Victor, I'm so sorry. I've been ill, out of work. I didn't know where you were, I thought you had gone back to Banstead . . they were good to you . . and *now* I've seen the doctor here, Victor, and he says: 'We can easily arrange his return to Broadmoor. That might be better than going to prison again.' Victor, go back to Broadmoor."

For a moment or two I nearly struck that woman, my mother. To *think* of letting me go back to Broadmoor was diabolical. Then I recovered my self-control, looked at my poor mother and said: "Mother, I'd rather *die* . . *die* . . than *ever* return to Broadmoor."

She gave me a long, long look, saying: "*Goodbye* . . *goodbye*, Victor," and that was the last time I ever saw my mother.

I take my trial. I have *no* counsel, but a sort of poor prisoners' lawyer who can't care less. "Plead *guilty*," he says. "Don't antagonise the court by any other plea." I stand there, thinking of Mother . . Sarah . . Joan . . wondering whether I will ever see any of these people again?

I hear this voice: "Cranston, Cranston, you appear to be a confirmed *thief*. I'm sending you to prison for ten years . . three years' Penal Servitude, and seven years, Preventive Detention."

I was thus *labelled* forever, at the age of thirty-one, as a *confirmed habitual thief*. And *that label has stuck to me* ever since.

XI

AND SO I'M labelled habitual thief, start a sentence of ten years and go back to the Island to serve it out.

I'm transferred to Wormwood Scrubs for a night . . join other men who are also on the way to the Island . . and the following day we move off . . motor-coach . . ferry . . motor-coach, with a train journey in between . . all of us chained one to the other. The escort of prison officers relaxes a little once we are aboard bus or train, and efforts are made to allow a certain measure of talking and companionship between the travelling cons. With the chain on movement is difficult . . but the ingenuity of the old lag, or the young one, overcomes *all* difficulties.

My nearest neighbour was a tall, good-looking Jew who was technically a first offender, but, having had a motoring offence before this present one, he was classed as a second offender which meant he could be sent to the Island instead of Wakefield Prison.

This Jew and I got friendly. He thought I had had a very bad deal. He'd read all about it in the Press. His own offence concerned selling a hotel which he didn't own.

When cons are travelling together, it's not uncommon for some kind of friendship to develop between them and, under the benign influence of mutual sympathy and mutual interests, promises are sometimes made. Thus my new Jewish friend, having only four years to serve, would be out long before me so he says: "Nick, when I get out I'll send you some books and magazines." *Me*, I'm very *sceptical* so I don't take this promise *too* seriously . . .

The journey is completed. Here we are . . the Island Jail . . where I had my *first* taste of a lag's colony . . and did not like it.

I soon discover, though the jail is still a grim and most undesirable place to live, there have been many changes since I was there last: a new governor, firm but understanding, a man of very real feeling for the prisoner . . a deputy governor of breeding and sympathy, a man of some culture. The whole climate of this Island Jail is now more relaxed, less tense than it was in days gone by.

I always found a kind of excitement in the travelling stage of a prison sentence. This is often the case: a prisoner will almost *forget he is* a *prisoner* and, though he may discuss his villainies and his sentence too, it is as if *this* concerns someone else, *not himself*.

Once in the jail, where sentence is to be served, the prisoner *awakes* . . awakes to *reality*. For me there was a kind of despair, a sort of *death*. I would hate myself, I would despise myself, I would think: To be a villain is in itself a *folly*. To be an unsuccessful villain is a greater folly still. I don't recall thinking of the *moral* aspects of my behaviour, but I *do* recall the reflections on its human and social aspects. *All* of which thoughts and reflections induced in me first a *personal hatred* for *me*, then would come *anger* and *rage*, and I'd get bitter, unreasonable and unreasoning.

I was located on the Observation Landing, the 'Nutters, Wing'. All the most difficult cons were there, the so-called hard cases, the border-line cases. Funnily enough, the so-called nutters had a high percentage of very intelligent men amongst them, also some talented artists (one man, I recall, had a gift for invention . . give 'Smithy' an old shoe, a mousetrap and a tea-spoon, and he'd produce a *motorcar*).

For a time I just got on with my prison chores: I'd do those mail-bags . . I'd clean that landing . . I'd read that book . . . Then, for no immediate reason, I'd smash everything up . . I'd shout . . I'd attack anybody who came my way . . then I'd break down completely . . sob . . sob as if that old heart would break . . and yet I was not the crying type . . .

After one of my periodical breakdowns I began to worry. I was afraid I'd go nuts. I was scared of the complete breakdown, which would mean certifiable insanity. I'd always feared this complete breakdown. I'd seen so many men in this pitiable state where they are at the mercy of utterly merciless men. There was also this notion of *insanity* as a *shameful thing*: you get heart trouble, you get tuberculosis, you get liver trouble and the *world* weeps for you . . but get that *insanity thing*, and the whole world *laughs at you*.

I ask to see the medical officer. I tell him I'm afraid of this breakdown thing. I don't want to be a drooling-at-the-mouth *lunatic* nor a raving madman, hitting out at invisible enemies. I'm advised to come into the hospital for a bit of rest away from the main jail. I'm reluctant, but I take this advice and thus I meet Dr. Walker, a small, dark, energetic man of great kindness, understanding, sympathy and medical competence.

From the moment I entered that hospital I must have been Dr. Walker's greatest *headache*. Looking back now, I wonder at the patience, tolerance and humanity of Dr. Walker. I was violent, I was abusive, I was intolerable. They dosed me with paraldehyde .. chloral .. they tried hot baths .. I was occasionally *padded-cell* confined .. but *never* with vindictiveness or unnecessary harshness.

As an aid to my recovery, I was permitted to join the jail band for a time. I even stood in occasionally for the bandmaster. On one occasion I was sitting in with the band, playing clarinet, and I didn't like the noise coming from the heavy brass .. they were out of tune. *This* maddened me .. I rose from my chair .. struck down the bandmaster with my clarinet for *allowing this infernal noise,* and proceeded to walk out towards the door. I heard a *roar* as of furious animals and saw the whole band coming for me. I didn't run away .. I faced that band, back to the closed door, and fought them off. The bandmaster, meanwhile, got up, blew his flute, pressed the alarm-bell and tried to stop the battle. The door was pushed open from the other side .. I was grabbed and examined for possible injuries, but was *found to have none* much to the amazement of arresting screws. I .. I wanted to go back and finish off the fight, but was forcibly removed, locked up and eventually rescued by Dr. Walker.

In due course I was faced with a prison commissioner and was in real danger of getting a recommendation for a flogging. It was clear to me that a flogging or a certification was what the Commissioner wanted. Dr. Walker stood firm: "*This* is not a case for punishment nor, at this stage, for certification. I believe, given *time*, Cranston will recover and settle down to do his sentence."

So I was taken back to hospital. But I made it plain that I wanted to 'face the music', take my punishment, and settle with those fellows so ready to attack me many-handed. My plea was ignored by Dr. Walker who said: "Whilst you are in *my* care, there is going to be *no* punishment."

Later, much later, Mr. Cousins the bandmaster came over to the hospital and said to me: "Nick, I bear you no ill-feeling. I understand just *why* you did what you did." And this magnificent *tolerance* from a prison officer I put on record as being only fair, we cons hardly ever allowing *any good* to be said of prison staff.

And so time marches on. I finish the *penal* part of the sentence and start the *preventive*, in those days vastly different to what it is today.

I'm allowed out of hospital, Dr. Walker taking the view that I'll get by more easily now the conditions of my jail-life are so different. I'm transferred to Portsmouth Jail, the holding station for P.D.s in those days. We have a special kind of clothing . . corduroys and Norfolk jacket, reasonably fitting shoes, comfortable underwear . . a cook of our own . . other privileges . . *unique* in those *spartan penal days*. The life of men in Portsmouth Prison is rather relaxed, not too regulated. Access to the yards is allowed any time during daylight hours . . access to the baths is *free* and unregulated. *All* this, and much besides, characterises the life of the P.D.s.

I must again say: This is not intended to be an old lag's tale, nor is it a whining prison indictment. In the nature of things *prison must be a dreadful place* and the life of a prisoner, no matter *what* privileges are allowed, must be an enslavement, a crushing destructive thing which produces either an *institutionalised robot* or a bitter, angry, deprived man . . never ever accepting this unnatural jail life. This angry rejection of jail life has nothing to do with *guilt* or *innocence*. *Jail* is *jail* whether one is a guilty man or an innocent man. For the rest I would say: whatever my reactions to the penal laws, I do not blame *them* nor do I blame their *administrators* for mine own self-induced follies and their consequences. I got myself into jail and exposed myself to *all* that jail life means.

I wasn't long at Portsmouth Prison before I again lapsed into violence. I was involved with a screw, struck him with a chair and was immediately returned to the Island. This time, unknown to me, my cards were well and truly *marked*. I arrived at Parkhurst Hospital hand-cuffed to two screws and preceded by an unsavoury report of *unpredictable behaviour*, fits of violence without rhyme or reason—or so it would seem.

At the desk in the Chief Officer's office is a tall, bespectacled, gold-braided man . . his face familiar. This gold-braided man looks at me saying: "I've seen *you* somewhere. Let me see . . oh . . I've got it. You are Rogers, you were with me in Leeds Prison when I was a Hospital Officer there. You are the man who turned his back on that Quarter Sessions Court, a brave, though *foolish*, thing to do. I've never forgotten it. All right, officers, take those cuffs off, you can go now. I'll look after this young man. He's had a tough time of it and I'll see he gets a fair deal here."

And so, once again, when I'm in real trouble, likely to have the book thrown at me, there is somebody to help me out. This was Jerry Slinger, Hospital Chief Officer. He saved me from serious lapses . . he saved me from that trip *back* to Broadmoor . . in fact, Mr. Slinger *saved my sanity*. His kindness . . his consideration . . his plea to the Senior Medical Officer that I should *not* be treated as a mental observation case, but allowed reasonable freedom in the hospital . . all this and much besides, that man did for me . . .

Finally I'm sent back to Portsmouth Jail . . the *war* breaks out, the war of 1939-1945 . . we P.D.s are evacuated to the Island Prison, placed in one wing on our own . . I am given a job, *Air Raid Precautions Orderly*, responsible for all fire-watching parties, late-night *refreshments*, responsible for the air raid emergency dressing station with the help of successive Hospital Officers.

The Island Jail in war-time was in some ways not a jail at all. Dr. Walker was gone for the duration of the war, so were many of the staff, even prisoners of yesterday were on active service. There was the day . . yes, broad daylight . . when Jerry machine-gunned the staff as they came out of their mess. Stray bullets found their way into the cells, through the windows, but there were *no casualties* among either screws or cons. The night when neighbouring Cowes was bombed *all night*, we could see the flares, hear the bombs and see the flames from the incendiary-bombing. In those days I had a portable gramophone, and at the height of the bombing I would put on dance records and out-dance Nijinsky, Lifar . . in fact, I would lose myself completely in the light fantastic solo . . .

Then there were the black-outs, when the cell doors were left unlocked, which means *all night card-parties* for the unleashed *cons*, and business as usual for the jail queers, who got more trade in the black-outs than they would ever have got in daylight. Most cons displayed contempt for the queers in daylight, but were not averse to visits in the black-out . . .

Me . . *me* . . I found this: *Given responsibility,* the feeling of doing something of *real value*, I temporarily *lost my hatred of jail life* . . and *lost myself* . . *in the war-effort.*

1942, just before Christmas, I'm free again, having taken my discharge from the Island. I return to *London*.

XII

AFTER A LAPSE of nearly eight years I return to London . . a changed London . . war-time London . . black-outs, bombing, rations. As usual, after getting *free again,* I lose *all* those tensions, *all* the nagging jail-cares, *all* the self-castigations. I'm *free* again and *who cares for the big bad wolf*? First I try for the Air Force . . even mention my clarinet-playing as a useful aid in the war-effort . . but unwisely reveal *where* I've been for the last few years. I am summarily rejected. I'm sorry about this, but decide to try for war-work. Probably I didn't try hard enough . . anyway I failed. Then I go after a job as night porter for a hotel. On revealing where I'd been during the *lost* years, I'm told: "Sorry, sorry, my fellow-directors would never approve your getting this job, though I . . I would like to give it to you." I'm now beginning to think it's *come home, Burglar Bill, you are not forgiven.*

I get angry with *me* . . the law . . and this cock-eyed world . . so I return to villainy. Back I go into the nearest hotel. Soon I'm in the money . . and *that* is the villain's downfall . . you forget *jail* . . the police . . the courts . . *all reality* . . you are lost in *fantasy* . . lost in a world of *false values.* Needs, appetites, natural functions, *all dammed up* by jail years of monastic living, find their way out—the money thieved proving the *passport* to satisfying all these clamouring *desires.*

So I'm on the way *back* and *don't know it.*

As I go on with this story, it gets increasingly *painful,* almost as if I am going to be *sick.* I look back . . I see what I've done . . I *know* what I *might* have done . . and as I've said, I feel like being *sick.*

If a man undertakes to write his story, it would be dishonest to *fake* the *truth.* So, however absurd . . foolish . . *immature* this life of mine appears, *it is my life,* and I must record it without fear, without favour.

London in war-time I found to be a gay, friendly place. Wherever I went people were friendly. My friends and neighbours were not in the villainy lark, but some of them were border-line cases . . whores . . head-waiters who would get you extra rations for a 'consideration' . . dealers who would buy *anything* of value without asking questions . .

Take my friend Ilse, a refugee from the Hitler purge: she's sitting there in the American Bar with another woman . . herself, *very chic* . . the other woman, *very plain.* I soon discover that Ilse, a kind of Ruritanian Princess, *still* sees herself as a Grande Dame who must never go out in public without her personal maid or companion . . hence this plainly-dressed woman . . she must not outshine her mistress . . .

Ilse had a flat in Belgravia, and I soon realised that she was a very choosy, very *high class whore.*

Isle was dark . . large, sparkling eyes . . hair which was long, thick and as *if illuminated.* Her skin was pale . . lips red . . her cheek-bones high. She looked like a woman straight out of a novel by Tolstoy.

I took Isle and her inseparable maid out to dinner, and *that red carpet went down* without my even *saying who she was.* Her style was self-assured, relaxed and yet faintly arrogant. Her way of speaking broken English, charmed everybody.

Later back home with Isle I discovered another old-fashioned Ruritanian custom . . not only did I have to make love to the mistress, but to the maid also, which was not entirely to my taste. It smacked too much of a cheap, cheap orgy . . you know . . *you fuck me* and *I fuck you* . . *all the family* having *such* a wonderful time. Funnily enough, though I am a bit of a tramp, a bit of a bastard in some ways, there are some things *I won't do* and this *maid* and *mistress* thing *I did not like.*

I called on Ilse one morning at about 10 a.m. I did not then know the custom of the smart world . . *never, never get up before noon* . . or *midnight* . . .

The maid didn't want Ilse disturbed . . asked me to call later. *Me* . . *me* I wouldn't *wait till later.* I walk into the bedroom and there is *Ilse* . . *furious.* "How dare you call on me *at this hour of the day*?"

Ilse was sitting up in bed . . her long dark hair wild and tangled . . her eyes flashing . . her teeth white and fit to tear me to pieces . . and her full, red-tipped breasts overflowing. "Get out of here. I'm not fit to be seen at this time of the day." *Me* . . a mere plebeian, vulgar and untamed . . I was angry too. "Who do *you* think you are? The Queen of *Sheba*? Why shouldn't I call on you at this hour?"

At this time of my life . . the late thirties, early forties . . I carried a swagger-stick, an antique stick with a hand-carved wolf-head. On leaving Ilse's flat in frustrated rage and anger, I had to go down a glass-enclosed stair-way, and on the way down I spitefully, wilfully *smashed every one of those glass panes with* my stick, hearing Ilse's voice screaming: "The *madman*, the beastly *madman, he breaks my beautiful glass . . .*"

On getting into the street, I cooled off and felt foolish. I rang Ilse to apologise, but was told: "*Go to hell, you mad Englishman!*" and that was the last time I ever saw or heard of my Ruritanian Princess.

At this stage I was staying at a place in Marylebone, very nice, very 'period' . . all around me famous places . . famous people . . Canuto's for food . . Regent's Park for swans and pretty maids, with their perambulated children of the *gods*, the wealthy *gods* who dwelt in *marble halls*, the halls of Marylebone and Regent's Park.

I was having a drink in Oddenino's when I notice this woman . . large in features, in body, in style . . a sort of wild woman of the French Revolution . . but retaining an aura of breeding and refinement. I got to know her . . she was called *Jeanne* . . and was one of the Free French (there were lots of them in war-time London). She had a young daughter at school, and was paying for the fees with money she got from 'selective' prostitution. Jeanne I liked . . she could laugh . . she could dance . . and she was good at love-making. I admired her for risking the dreadful consequences of her trade for the sake of her daughter.

As it was war-time and nobody knew how long they would be alive, what with nightly *bombing*, Jeanne and I, as with others at that time, lived for the passing moment. No one to my knowledge thought of moral issues. Certainly, I must confess, I did not at that time ever think of the *final accounting*. I thieved, I revelled in riotous living, I acted as if it was my *last moment on earth* and as *if that was all there was to it*.

The bombs were coming down, sirens were sounding . . . Jeanne and I were in this restaurant and she says to me: "Look, my dear, we must go. My dog, le Général" (yes, that was its name) "will be in *fits* . . the bombing will *keel him*."

Jeanne and I leave the restaurant, go round the corner. The

black-out is on . . the search-lights are busy . . bombs are crashing . . old familiar places nothing but a mess of ruin. Air-raid wardens with helmets on are warning: "Get under cover, stay off the streets." Here we are . . this is the street . . in the door . . up the stairs . . in this room . . and *there* . . *there* . . is le *Général* . . *sound asleep* . . dreaming, no doubt, of lady Générals . . . I look at Jeanne, look at the dog which she thought would be '*keeled*' by the bombing noises, if not by the bomb itself, and we both laughed.

All this time I'm going off on visits to the country, coming back loaded to sell the gear to that ever-ready buyer and putting the cash proceeds right down the drain, the 'drain' of restaurants . . clubs . . whores . . and all concerned with London's entertainment business. In those days it never occurred to me that some of the money could have been used in aiding people in distress, all the homeless, friendless folk drifting around in London Town.

I go down to the Hampshire coast, book in at a Bournemouth hotel as Captain Spencer of Intelligence. Choosing *that* branch of the Services stopped all inquisitive questions what with the posters all warning: *Don't talk too freely about your war work.*

I'm sitting there having dinner . . the band is playing . . there are a few couples dancing . . all very blasé . . all very bored . . or so it seemed. I've always noticed when eating out in one of England's posh eating-places, that the people there seem to be taking their pleasures very, very sadly. *Me* . . *me* . . I rejoice at all opportunities for eating, drinking, and talking to charming women or interesting men. For that matter, the *most* interesting people I've found in these places have often been the *waiters*, especially the wine waiters . . very knowledgeable men.

"Captain Spencer, pardon me, but wouldn't you like to join a party? Christmas is not the time for solitude." I look up . . it's the dapper hotel manager, worried about me being alone.

"I don't know any of these people and I don't care to intrude."

"Let me introduce you to those people over there, very nice people."

They were a middle-aged man, his wife, his daughter and two friends.

I join the party . . we talk . . *nobody* wants *any* details from *me* as my Army duties forbid too much Army talk. I dance with the daughter . . very *cool* . . very *detached* . . but not so nice as Jeanne or Princess Ilse.

One of the women is showing around a very valuable gold vanity-case, a present from her ever-loving husband. I look at this bauble and I think: What an extravagance. *That* melted down and turned into cash would feed quite a lot of people. I privately decide that bauble is for *me*.

The next day is Sunday . . fine, cold, crisp air . . a lovely winter's day . . good for a walk down there on the promenade. This couple has the idea too . . I see them going out after lunch. Their suite of rooms is on my floor. I note the door-key has been carelessly left in the lock. I open the door, go straight to the dressing-table, open a drawer and *there*, believe it or not, is the gold vanity-case in a luxurious black-velvet container. Also, a jewel-case so *full* of gear . . tom-foolery . . that the lid can't be properly fastened. I mutter a thank you to the gods for this luck, empty everything into a large handkerchief, stuff it all into my pocket and walk out of the room, down the stairs and out of that hotel. I'm so excited, so pleased at this extraordinary *luck* that I forget to collect my bag or pay my bill . . the *unforgivable, unpardonable sin*.

By taxi, then train . . a slow-moving war-time train . . I reach London, all blacked out ready for the night's *bombing*. Back in London I go to the Café Royal, straight through to the restaurant, avoiding the crowded café. I order lobster and hock, and have a good meal. I then drop in at the American Bar of the Piccadilly Hotel, see Jeanne, have a drink or two and take Jeanne home with me to my lovely Marylebone balcony-flat.

I'm taking my things off, emptying pockets, and the gear from Bournemouth scatters all over the floor. Jeanne, with popping eyes, gets down on her knees helping me to pick it all up.

"Good God, what magnificent jewellery! And *this*, what a lovely thing!" I put this stuff on the table, start examining it and roughly value it at about six thousand pounds. Jeanne, looking at this gear spread out on the table, says: "Neal" (my business name was Captain Spencer, but the name I normally used then was Neal Grayson), "Neal, I can help you get a good price for that stuff. I know a dealer in jewellery." *Me* . . *me* . . self-sufficient as usual, cocky, on top of the world, I say: "Thank you, I can manage quite well without your help." In the final event I *failed to manage quite well,* as I shall reveal later in this story.

The next morning I go out *walking on air* . . after all I'm loaded with nearly six thousand pounds' worth of gear and I'm on the way to sell it. I am going to a big dealer in St. James's Street. I'd already done a small bit of business with this man . . he was the buyer for his firm and asked no questions.

I'm in the taxi, passing this shop near Piccadilly Circus, and in the window is this sign: "We buy *gold*. We give *good prices*." I stop the taxi, thinking: That vanity-case could be sold here as *gold*, not at the other place as an *article*. I enter the shop, ask: "Will you buy this case as *gold* on the scales? My wife and I need some ready money?"

"Certainly, Sir, but as we are busy getting the windows dressed for the day, would you come back later?"

I agree to come back later and go for a coffee in a nearby café. When I return I'm confronted by *two gentlemen*, obviously *police* who have been tipped off by the shop-keeper. I take one look at these fellows, swipe them with my walking-stick and dash for the street . . across the Circus . . through Lyons' Corner House . . down by Leicester Square . . through a pub . . over the counter . . out the back way into Lisle Street. By now nearly *dead* with fatigue and followed by the *pack*, police, taxi-men, passers-by, publicans and barmen, I'm done . . I'm done.

So I'm in again. The police are puzzled . . no villainy has been reported for the metropolitan area. Who am I? Where does this gear come from? I say *nothing* other than claim that the jewellery and the vanity-case are mine or my wife's. I'm locked up . . same old detention room in Savile Row where they locked me up way back in 1928 when Molly was around, when I . . I was a younger man.

I'm thinking: If I had let Jeanne handle this business, as she offered to do, I would *now* be *free* . . . The door opens. "Captain Spencer, you are badly wanted in Bournemouth. We have been on the phone to the *Yard*, and we intend to hold you for the Bournemouth police, who are now on the way to pick you up."

The *big-time villain* is now no longer the *big time,* just a mug, a fool who couldn't even guard against the *oldest trap* in the business. "Come back later please."—*This* has caught countless villains, and yet over and over again they *do go back later* . . .

I'm in the lock-up at Bournemouth. The coppers, funnily

enough, are treating me with respect. I'm fed well, get 'smokes', and am given fresh air in the small courtyard at the back of the cells. Eventually I am committed for trial at Hampshire Quarter Sessions and transported to Winchester Prison.

By now, years after my first taste of prison, I tend to go along with it as if it were a sleep-walking act. Not that I'm unaware of the set-up, the cold, formal handling of a *human being* as if he were a lifeless *article*, a *package* to be *labelled, passed on, held for ultimate delivery*. Yes, I feel all this, but from experience has come a sort of *self-protecting manner* which gets me through.

I take my trial, plead *guilty* to being in possession of the jewellery and the vanity-case. I note that the woman from whom I took all this gear is loaded with expensive baubles. It seems that rich women learn no lessons from their habitual *exhibition* of fancy gear which so easily leads to its being snatched . . almost as if they *couldn't care less*.

"Neal Grayson, you are convicted of stealing jewellery to the value of six thousand pounds or so. You are a *pest*. You will go to prison for seven years, *plus* a further period of two years, residue of a previous sentence."

So here we go again : thirty-nine years of age, just been out of prison long enough to qualify for *another bit*, just *long enough* to see *what a wonderful place* this old world is. A *sniff* of *freedom* and *back I go*, almost as *if I liked prison*, as *if I had planned to get back* just in time for the Easter holidays.

XIII

WAY BACK IN my so-young days, down there in solitary, I used to have a dream that *one day* I would be with the top *villains* in *Dartmoor Prison.* Jesus, what a *dream*! *No glory, no memorable act* such as saving a child from an early death or neglect, *criminal neglect* . . no . . no . . just to be in that prison *labelled one of us, one of the chaps, a villain.*

Here I was, at Dartmoor Prison at last. Madame Tussaud's Chamber of Horrors was a *sunlit kindergarten* by comparison. Unknown to me, Dartmoor, like the Island way back in 1928, was in a state of near mutiny . . all the men under rigid control . . *no talking . . don't turn your head when on parade . . don't carry any fag-papers or any tobacco in your pockets . . do that cell task . . get a move on* . . . The screws were dolled up like Hitler's killers . . boots . . leggings buttoned up . . tight-waisted jackets . . breeches . . and the *stick* ready for action. Down below, the 'tea-garden' (as solitary was ironically known), was packed to capacity, and beatings were a *daily occurrence.* In short, the screws were having a *field day.* For some time previous to my arrival at 'the Moor', the men had been getting a little bit out of hand, a few of them taking liberties. There had been some gang-warfare, screws had been attacked, and the *heads* had decided to stop the rot. When the heads in English prisons decide to stop the rot, they go to extremes. *All* restraint goes . . the screws are given a *free hand.* Those screws who were pushed around when the discipline was lax, now very naturally aim to get their *own back.* So there are applied *Hitler tactics*: "*Bash them. Don't talk to them,* just *bash them.*"

In putting all this on record, let me say in fairness to the screws and the heads: at one time in Dartmoor's history a relaxed discipline was the rule; the men could do almost *anything they liked* and as a result, the worst kind of villain took liberties. Prisoners were beaten up for not settling gambling-debts, their pay was taken from them by the *strong-arm mob.* Some of the screws, fairly decent fellows, were *shit on.* So it was only natural that the screws and heads should call a halt.

But, as I've said, just as the con had taken liberties before, so *now* the less scrupulous of the *staff* had a field day. I arrived in the midst of it all, and, with my reputation for *opposition*, for *intransigence*, for being a no-good *bastard*, the screws soon picked on me, though I had *not* taken *any liberties* .. in fact this was my first time *ever* at Dartmoor.

I'm in that peter .. walking up and down .. it's cold .. the gas-lights are flickering up and down. The light is separated from you in that cell by a piece of thick glass in the wall. There is a peculiar smell which penetrates *everything* .. walls .. ventilators .. cracks in the door .. a smell of rotten animal flesh .. a compound of body-sweat .. dirt .. piss .. and .. the home-made gas. *Me* .. I'm very restless, asking myself: *What do I do about all this*? I wasn't to blame for the liberties taken by some of my fellow-cons. *Why* .. *why* should I suffer? In walking up and down in a jail peter, a man can talk to himself without even being aware of it. Next morning on unlock I'm told to pack my kit up. At that time of the morning, with several screws all round you and all the men still locked up, this means *you are 'cased'*—you don't know *what* your offence is .. just *pack that kit up* .. *keep your mouth shut* .. and, when going down those stairs, hold on to the rail for you are likely to be *helped* down those stairs by one of the more vindictive members of your *escort*.

"Grayson, you are charged with *talking in your cell* and *causing a disturbance*. What have you to say, Grayson?" *Me* .. *me* .. I'm *dumb*.

I look at that screw .. I think: *You bastard*. I tell the Governor: *"Nothing to say"*.

"Three days' *No. 1 diet*. Seven days' *loss of remission* and *one month's loss of stage privileges*."

"About turn, quick march, get moving."

In I go .. the old familiar scene .. a *punishment cell* .. I enter *almost gaily*. *This* .. *this* is a *sanctuary* .. a hide-out from *all* these bloody people.

It's winter-time .. stone-cold .. and *water running down those damp walls* .. the floor *wet* and *slithery*. I serve out this bit of un-merited 'chokey', resolved that if I'm ever cased again in Dartmoor, it's going to be for *something* .. *no more liberties* are going to be taken with *me*.

Punishment finished .. I go upstairs, back to the old peter. They put me in the laundry .. I like it .. you can do your own washing. First I have to see *somebody*, the Deputy Governor, number one *strong arm*. I'm in the Deputy Governor's office . . he is tough and *looks like a craggy mass of hard rock* . . *No* human expression . . *no* sign of any awareness of my being other than a bloody nuisance, a *prisoner* . . .

"Well, what do you want?"

"I've just come out of chokey . . three days' solitary . . bread and water . . loss of remission . . *all* for *nothing* . . for talking to myself. I want to say this: *If any of your screws ever again* cases me for *nothing*, I'll kill the bastard when I come up from chokey."

This man looks at me . . looks at the record lying on the desk in front of him . . glances over to the door where the screw stands, all ready for any emergency . . and says to me: "Grayson, my staff sometimes make mistakes. I don't think you will ever again be troubled. Yes, I suppose you *could carry out this threat*, but as I've said, you won't be troubled again."

I leave that office a bit puzzled. I expect to be thrown out and put back in chokey. Threats are not usually passed over.

"Grayson, there is a vacancy in the *Duchy*, the staff club and mess down in the village. Will you take it?" This request comes from the Chief Officer, and the job is the *plum job* of Dartmoor . . you go out beyond the walls, down there in the village.

This offer of a job in the Duchy is a surprise to me. To put *me* out there on a 'trusty' job just takes my breath away. But I agree to take it . . I join the party . . about six inmates, six of us cons *all* hand-picked. You go out of the gate every morning at 5.30 a.m. . . you march down the village street . . and right there on the Square is the Duchy, a former hotel, now a club and mess for Dartmoor's prison staff, mostly bachelors.

We Duchy workers are split up into waiters, cleaners and one cook, and the whole party is under the supervision of a prison screw. This particular screw is a man whose mission is, it seems: *Work those bastard cons to the death*. He never stops bullying. *No* work is ever to his satisfaction and he just *never* lays off. I'm thinking: Just *my* luck, a wonderful job *ruined* by this bastard. I get restless . . get brooding . . I notice that when the Duchy Superintendent goes out for a duck-shoot, which he does quite often, he leaves a shot-gun just inside the kitchen-door . . where I, as a cleaner, can reach it. I resolve that if this screw continues his bullying, I'll get the gun, blow his guts out and scarper. But, being plagued with a conscience, I decide to *warn* the Deputy

Governor and the Chief first, particularly as they had *trusted me* to go out there . . .

So I tell them what is going on in the Duchy, explaining that all I want is to be left alone, to do my work in peace and not be bullied all day long. I say: "You have put me out there. It's a trusty job and I don't really want to let you down by hurting this screw or by scarpering." I'm told: "All right, Grayson, you carry on. We will talk to this officer." There is a legend in jail circles that if a con says he is going to do something desperate, you can talk him out of it by using *diplomacy*. This is a *false view*: *diplomacy* only works for a brief time. If there is *no* redress of a con's grievance and the con is a determined kind of fellow, then his threat will be carried out.

There is *no* change in this screw's behaviour. If anything, it grows worse. I decide to scarper when this screw bully is on duty. I decide to leave the gun-business because if I get away when this screw is on duty, it will mean *suspension* for him, maybe even the *sack* . . and *that* should teach the bastard a *lesson*.

It is Sunday afternoon, a fine mid-summer day . . the Duchy is *all* quiet . . lunches have been served . . the place cleaned up . . and our screw is out there, talking to the cook. I go into the dining hall . . it's empty . . windows are *wide open*. Out there is a sleepy village square . . nobody about . . a few clickings and cluckings of grub-seeking hens . . a bark or two from straying dogs . . an English village on a Sunday afternoon. I step over the window-sill and I'm right there on the village square . . *nobody about* . . *all quiet*. I'm dressed in prison overalls, prison shirt, prison shoes, but I might have been *invisible* for all the attention given to me. I look right and left, see a turning to the right. I walk leisurely along, appearing to be just strolling . . a bit of summer air, mine only care, mine only wish. Down there is a row of cottages . . front-gardens a blaze of colour . . and *not a sign of life*, almost as if the whole village was *asleep*. I go in this gate, down the path look in the windows . . *no sign of a living soul*, not even a dog . . down the side-path to the back-yard . . here is a tool-shed and in it a *bicycle* . . a woman's bicycle. The back door is *open* . . I go into the kitchen, walking very softly. *No* sound of *anything*. I look in the other rooms . . *nobody* . . *all out* . . for a Sunday stroll probably. In here . . a bedroom . . a wardrobe . . on top a *Sten gun* . . in the wardrobe a Home Guard's *uniform* . . *a cap* with the H.G. badge . . on the arm of the jacket *three stripes*.

I think *What luck . . what luck . . .* I get my clothes off, change into the uniform . . a *perfect fit* except for the *chest . . I can't fasten the chest buttons*. I put the cap on, grab the Sten gun and sling it over my shoulder, thinking: This could be a *frightener* for anyone trying to *stop* me. I go out, wheel the bike up the path, go through the gate seeing *no one*, mount the bike . . . and *go . . go . . go . . .*

I soon discover this is the main road although not much more than a path, really, to Plymouth, fifteen miles away. I don't have to pedal, just free-wheel down. I'm *singing* for *joy* . . the *air* . . the green moorland *all* round me . . the sense of *liberation* . . I could *fly*. Then up this road, this narrow road, come a man, a woman . . and a perambulator. I think: Christ, a screw and his wife and child out for a Sunday walk. Will they recognise me? I start pedalling just in case.

"Good afternoon, Sarge," says this fellow as I pass on the bike . . *me*, I say: "Good afternoon," . . . *they haven't recognised me*, I breathe again, take it easy. *Swish, swish* . . a car passes me on its way down to Plymouth . . it's *loaded with screws* . . and the Duchy's Alsatian dog. I say: Whew, they don't know this uniform has been nicked. I'm *missed*, but they don't yet know of my change of clothing. *I sing again*, thanking all the gods for my *luck*.

XIV

I'M NOW REACHING Plymouth's suburbs . . a lorry comes from a side-turning . . stops . . I ditch the bike, scramble on the back of the lorry, stick my thumb up to the driver . . he nods and we drive on. The lorry again slows up to a stop . . I jump off, wave a thank you, and look round . . I've got to get rid of this uniform . . by now the owner may have got home and reported his loss. Over there is a semi-detached house . . *no sign of occupation* . . the garage is *locked* . . there is no sign of *smoke* from the chimney-stacks. I go up the path . . ring the bell . . get no reply . . go round to the back . . ring the bell . . no reply . . I think: These people are away for the day. I break a window-pane . . put my hand in . . turn the catch . . open the window and climb in. The house is empty, but has every sign of being lived in . . food . . clothes . . dressing-table fittings. I go into the kitchen, drop the Sten gun and look in the fridge for something to eat and drink. Then I find the main bedroom, and *believe it or not*, on the chair are a sports jacket, flannel trousers and underneath a pair of light shoes. I open a drawer . . in there are a change of shirt, socks, and *of all the luck five* . . *five* single pound-notes . . it's as *if the house owners had expected me* and had left my expenses to help me out of Plymouth, not to mention the change of clothing. I now begin to think: *Something* . . *somebody* is *on my side*. Maybe even *God* has *no time for the prison lark*.

All the clothes fitted except the shoes. I pack the Home-Guard uniform in a suitcase, the cap and the Sten gun, too . . I stuff the five pounds in my pocket . . and, grabbing the suitcase, I leave the house by the front door, hoping I'll not be confronted by the *owners* or seen by neighbours. Near the house is a building-site . . it's deserted being Sunday afternoon . . so over I go and plant that suitcase.

I'm in Plymouth . . it's early evening now, getting dark, near black-out time. I notice a café not yet lit-up . . I go in and order a coffee . . ask casually when the last bus goes to Exeter? There is much excitement I notice . . somebody has got away from Dartmoor Prison . . he's *still at large*. The talk amuses me . . I . . I just listen.

The bus is about to leave . . I get aboard, go up on top . . I can see the countryside from there . . also, I can see if any police cars are about . . .

The bus grinds to a stop . . this is not a normal stopping place . . helmeted *police* are coming up those stairs . . I think: *This is it* . . "*Identifications*, identity cards, please." Police are coming my way . . I haven't got a *card* . . I make believe, to reach for the card in my pocket . . and am told: *"That's all right, Sir."* The policeman moves on. I breathe freely. What a close shave! Clearly, though the hunt is on, they don't yet know of my latest change of clothing.

I say to the fellow sitting beside me: *"What is going on?"*

"Oh, don't you know? A convict has got away from Dartmoor, but *he will never get out of the Duchy*, the Duchy of Cornwall. *They always get caught*." *Me* . . *me* . . *f*or two pins I would throw that bastard out of this window for his apparent *joy* at the thought of the con getting captured. His supreme confidence in this happening eventually made me smile. Yes, I thought, you bastard, *this convict* will upset *all* your calculations. But for all that I was conscious of the amazing *good luck I was enjoying*.

It's getting dark now . . the black-out is on . . this could help me in evading the coppers.

Here is Exeter, war-time Exeter . . late evening . . black-out . . everybody off the streets except the police, the air-raid wardens and late home-goers. I decide to find a bed and room for the night. I'll call myself a reporter, on the jail-break assignment . . from Plymouth . . car broke down . . and the *last bus* to Plymouth has gone . . plausible enough. I'm in this street, looking for an ad for Bed and Breakfast, and I notice an American sailor seemingly doing the same.

"Are you looking for a night's lodging? *Me*, I've missed the last bus back to Plymouth and, noticing you squinting at the windows for rooms to let, I thought two of us might have better luck than one."

"Sure, sure. I missed that bus too. My ship is at Plymouth. Yes, let's join up."

So I lose myself in the company of this American sailor. We find a room, agree to share it, and we are shown upstairs. The landlady's last words were: "You boys can share this room and I'll only charge for one."

Once in the room, with the door closed, we get to know each other: *Me*, a reporter up at Exeter on an assignment . . there has been a jail-break from Dartmoor and I am on the trail . . . *He*, an ex-*sheriff* from California, in the Navy for the duration of the war . . attached to Naval Intelligence. We talk . . *he* of all those 'bastards' locked up in Folsom and San Quentin . . of the *delight* he always got from sending the 'so-and-sos' *up state* to be locked up. This sheriff did not like the *villain* at all. *Me*, I tell him just how keen I am to get this bloody escape-bastard rounded up . . what a scoop for me. All night long the ex-sheriff and I swopped yarns about the villainy world . . we got real friendly. He showed me all his family photographs in the wallet he carried in his pocket. "If you ever come to Californy," says he, "be sure to look us up."

In this world of *incredible* fantasy, the ex-sheriff and I spent the whole night talking. He had cigarettes and a flask of whisky, and I, a flow of absurdities to relate *all* about non-existent villains I had trailed around, the crime reporter par excellence.

Morning comes. I tell my friend I must get going. We shake hands and he says: "Buddy, I've *never* had such pleasure before. You are a wonderful guy. I'll be pleased to introduce you to my family if you ever come out to Californy."

I get over to the station, see the early morning editions of *all* the papers with the headline: *Convict Still at Large*. I buy me a ticket to London, and by a stroke of luck there is a train just going. At the barrier are several big, tough-looking coppers, one or two clearly recognisable plainclothesmen and the ticket-collector. There is a charming-looking woman fishing out her ticket from a hand-bag. I get close to her as she goes through, remarking to her: "Seems to be quite exciting here. *All* these police officers." We get through that barrier . . we get on board that train . . and naturally I try to find suitable seating for this charming woman and myself, too.

I'm thinking: *What luck* . . what luck! The train starts and it can't move fast enough for me. I look through those windows and watch those coppers . . .

And so we travel to London. It is a slow war-time train, stopping at *all* stations . . any *stop* could be my *last* . . I still have no identity card. The woman with whom I did the trip to

London is smart . . country-style sensible clothing . . *good quality* . . but *no extravagance*. We talked, *she* about her war-work . . a small farm in Devon . . committee-meetings in London . . a *beautiful* daughter . . *see* . . look at this photograph . . out in America . . "She will be a *film star* some day," says her adoring mother — *me*, oh just a reporter down here on that jail-break. She, bless her, says: "I would escape too if they sent me there. It must be a *dreadful place*." By the time we reached London I was *wishing* I was a *legitimate citizen*. I'd then have been able to cultivate this charming woman and even meet that talented daughter . . .

This is London, war-time London, and *it is still swinging*. I get out of the station, having said goodbye to my country-woman, and *I smell that wonderful London air* . . a compound of *petrol* . . *dogs* . . *women* . . and *massed humanity* . . *all* . . *bursting with energy*. I walk on air . . *nothing under my feet* but *freedom* . . *freedom is my sustainer* . . .

I haven't much money left . . must change these clothes . . must find a hide-out. *I must do some villainy* . . how else do I get by?

I see a newspaper kiosk: "Daring Escape from Dartmoor . . Convict Still at Large." I buy a newspaper and read: "No Sign of Grayson . . Amazing Disappearance . . Thought to be *Out of the Country*".

I go off into the 'sticks', Richmond, Kew. I'm looking here and there, casing the luxury flats all round me. I go in this door, ring a bell . . it's answered . . I make believe it's the *wrong flat* . . go away . . in another door . . ring that bell.

"Yes?"

"I'm looking for a Mrs. Smith. I think this is the wrong flat, I'm so sorry."

"Oh, just a minute, won't you come in? I may be able to help you find your friend." Well, this is a stopper. Still I go in. "Please come in here. Sit down and I'll get you a drink."

I sit down, look around. *What a magnificent room*, just like an advert from *House and Garden*. A row of photographs *all* of a bemedalled Air Force officer . . flowers . . ash-trays . . rugs . . an original water-colour or two . . a small piece of African wood-carving . . .

"I was just going out for a game of darts down at our local. Since my husband has been away I've been going to the local quite a lot." This from my hostess, a tall, striking-looking woman with a carriage and figure fit for a queen. We both forget my quest for Mrs. *Smith.* Clearly this woman is desperately *lonely* . . .

I'm asked quite casually about my war-work. I answer: "Merchant Navy. I'm on leave for a week or two. My ship is being overhauled in dock. I'm out here at Richmond trying to find a shipmate's wife as I have a message from him. He's in hospital." A plausible yarn . . it does nobody *any harm* . . and it accounts for that *bell-ringing.*

My hostess tells me all about her wonderful husband who has been on active service since the beginning of the war . . an air-man of *distinction*, I gather. Having finished my drink, I excuse myself, saying I must find my mate's wife. I'm invited to call again one day. "Perhaps we could have a game of darts, eh?" I promise and take my leave, going back to this casing lark with a *heavy heart* . . *wishing* . . *wishing* . . once again . . I *was not a villain* on the run from the Moor.

I'm coming out from this block of flats down the drive when, with a *roar* and a *scream* of *tyre-skidding*, a car drives right in front of me. Police . . police . . jump out of the car and surround me. I look at these fellows as if I'm a bit surprised.

"What's it all about?" I ask.

A big uniformed man, silver *all* over him, a policeman of *high rank*, says: "Excuse me, Sir. Have you an identity card? What's your business here?" *Me* . . *me* . . I pretend utter astonishment. "Can't a man go visiting without being bothered by police?"

It soon comes out that the police have been summoned by a busybody flat-owner who has seen me from his window going *in* and *out* of the neighbouring flats and, having a dirty mind, suspected *me* of being a sort of *thief* on the prowl. I affect anger . . I demand to *see* this *slanderer* . . I threaten to have *him summonsed* for *slander*. The police, meanwhile, are getting rather nervous about making a blunder . . after all I *might be an honest citizen*. I'm asked, rather apologetically, if I would please tell them just *what* my business is right *here*? "You see, Sir, we must report back so, for the record, what's your business?"

I say: "I'm looking for a woman I saw last night in a West End restaurant. She gave me her name and address, but omitted to give me the flat number. That's why I keep going in and out of these flats. I'm trying to find her place."

The big, silver-plated one touched his hat and said: "We

apologise for troubling you, Sir. *Good hunting.*" And with that he and his squad get back into the car and drive off. *Me . . me*, I breathe again and *get off that manor quickly . . .*

Months later, when I've been captured by West End police, the Richmond police learn who it was they allowed to escape them, and they send me a message: *"If we had known it was you, you would never have got away, you bastard."*

Meanwhile I've got to earn some money and get an identity card. I go into this Knightsbridge place, force a door and find a well-appointed flat. In the bedroom there is a uniform . . gold braid on sleeves and collar . . a smart cap . . lots of other clothing . . *all* trousers . . *much too long* for me, but I can soon get them altered. I find a suitcase and pack the gear. In a desk I find a passport and a Reuter's Press-card for a Mr. Desmond Tigh, War Correspondent attached to the Admiralty. *This* find is just what the doctor ordered.

I get me a small bedsitter somewhere in Marylebone. The suitcase is *my* passport to high-class hotels. Real leather suitcases are *always* taken as a sign of affluence by the hotel and boarding-house fraternity. I go to a small tailoring-shop to have the trousers altered and then proceed to get me some money.

I walk into a hotel, up the stairs . . into a bedroom. In the wardrobe is *another* uniform (an Army officer's), and a belt and gun-holster. I take the gun, a Belgian automatic, put it in my pocket and look around. I find a gold cigarette-case and cuff-links. I am satisfied so I get out . . I've got my *money's worth.*

I quickly sell the cigarette-case and the cufflinks. I'm *in the money* and *that*, however immoral it may be, is a very, very satisfactory state of things . . . I'm not a small-arms expert, but being on the run, I think this gun *might* be a stopper: with its aid I *may* get away. *Also*, I must confess, it *did* occur to me that if I was forced to use that gun, the doing so would mean the *Death Sentence* and *that,* I then believed, would *be better than going back to jail.* I examine the gun. Yes, it's loaded. I fix the safety catch and put it back in my pocket. It fits snug and tight in my hip-pocket.

I'm eating in this restaurant when I see a woman, dark, good-looking but just a wee bit too fat for *my* taste. On the other hand a sex-starved con on the run can't be too choosy.

"Can I join you? I am alone on leave and would like some company." The woman looks up, smiles and says: "By all means, join me. I, too, like company." Thus I meet a war-widow, living at a smart Kensington address. I introduce myself as Desmond Tigh, War Correspondent. I rather think this woman's name was no more *hers* than the name I gave was *mine*. In fact she later confessed to me that she was 'on the game', but was careful *whom* she took home. As for *me*, the Press was 'carrying' my photo every day, and though it was a *bad* photo, it *was* me. It was good enough for this woman to learn of my identity which she pretended to admire. I move in with her, find she is not so good in bed as she is in a restaurant and, being *my* sort of person, I tell her: "You are as *cold* as a piece of fish on that ice-slab and I . . I am going to find somebody a little warmer." She affects *amusement*, tells me to go and find 'something' and then come back and give her the *good news* . . .

I'm just leaving a restaurant when I see this lovely little blonde standing at a bus stop . . a leather-handbag in her hand . . no hat . . nice summer frock . . good shoes . . her hair shining in the sun . . a glorious blonde. I go up to her and say: "Has anyone ever told you how wonderful you are?" This girl looks at me and says: "For two pins, I'd give you a smack right across the face for daring to talk to me." Then she *laughed*, saying: "On second thoughts, I must thank you for a nice compliment." So I meet the nicest, *hottest*, little woman I'd ever known . . . Hazel is a ward sister in a big South London hospital. At the time we met, she was going back to work, but I ask her to come and have a *second lunch*. We go back into the restaurant, order something to drink and talk to each other as if we had known each other for years. Hazel is worried about Matron, she is a *Tartar*. I say: "Phone the Matron, tell her you are unavoidably delayed. You and I must find a place to live." And that is exactly what we do, Hazel completely forgetting her hospital responsibilities, enjoying this war-time *adventure* as if it is the thrill of her life. I help Hazel take all her things from her own flat, and she and I move in. We spend that night . . the following day . . and the next night in bed . . lovin' . . lovin' . . lovin'. There is an air raid the first night, but Hazel and I just calmly carry on. The next day both Hazel and I are a bit tired. We just talk. We go out for a walk, do some shopping, and then Hazel remembers she has not reported back to the hospital. She nearly panics, but we concoct a plausible story and Hazel goes back to work. *Me,* I return to the widow's place where I've left some of my gear.

"So the *conquering hero returns,* eh?" I tell her I've found a *red hot momma* and I'm going to join her in our own little place. My widow, the perfect actress, says to me: "Why don't you and I have a last little dinner together, a sort of *farewell* dinner?" I accept her proposal, phone a restaurant and order a meal for two . . flowers and wine . . for that night. Then, collecting my bits and pieces, I go on to my new place. I'm going out later and I notice there is no one in the office. Quickly, without any calculation and *forgetting* that I've installed Hazel in this very house, I get in the office and the cash box is full of 'oners', pound-notes, a veritable *parcel* of them or so it seems. I grab the lot and without further thought I leave the house.

Looking back on this episode, I must put it on record that this was the meanest thing I've *ever done*. In going for that cash, I failed to realise what a terrible shock it would be to Hazel, returning to find I'd left her, to find I *was just a cheap bastard*, a *petty thief*, leaving *her* to answer the inevitable police questions. I'll never forgive myself for this dreadful mean act. At the time . . jail-breaker on the run . . I just didn't think of *ultimate consequences*, either to *me* or to others.

I find a new hide-out, change my clothes and go to keep that farewell dinner appointment. I'm waiting outside this restaurant. My guest is late . . ah there she is . . we sit down, look at the menu. There are police about . . plainclothesmen asking for identity cards, a common practice during the war years. It suddenly occurs to me that, having changed clothes before coming out, I've forgotten to bring the Desmond Tigh Press-card, though I had put the automatic pistol in my pocket.

"Have you your identity card, Sir?" I look up, feel this pocket, that pocket, appear to be worried.

"I'm so sorry, it looks as if I've left my papers at home."

"There is a car outside, Sir. We can easily run you round to get your papers. This is a routine check, but as you know, we must see everybody's papers." I get up, suspecting nothing, ask my guest to excuse me for a few minutes.

I produce the Desmond Tigh Press-card with my photograph on it, also his passport again with my photograph on it. The senior police officer seems satisfied, but the other officer is obviously *not* satisfied. He goes into a huddle with his superior, then: "I'm sorry, Sir, but though this looks all right, I must ask for the regulation identity card, too." I . . I am now getting a bit bothered, even suspicious. Do they *know* anything? Is this really a *routine quest*?

"Look, officers, I am Desmond Tigh, you see the Press-card: War Correspondent on leave. I've mislaid the ordinary civilian identity card. I had no use for it. The Press-card was usually enough. You saw that woman down there in the restaurant, well, she is not my wife and I'll be very embarrassed if you start making unnecessary trouble about this. Please let me return to my friend." Again the superior officer seems satisfied. "All right Sir, we will run you back in the car, but take my advice: carry that identity card with you in future." I sigh with relief, but then that other officer, this 'doubting Thomas', goes into *another* huddle, taking something from his pocket and showing it to his superior. *Me*, I am thinking: This is a *trap*, that bastard suspects something.

"Sir," says the senior officer, "I'm sorry, but on second thoughts, I must insist on your coming to headquarters with us. My colleague tells me you are very like a man we are looking for." I suddenly see *red*. I take the pistol from my pocket, press the safety-catch down and, stepping right up to the doubting-Thomas, stick the gun in his stomach, pull that trigger, saying: *"You doubting bastard."* There is confusion . . shouting . . the doubter throws his hands up . . screams blue murder . . the other officer falls back . . and I . . I keep pressing that trigger . . desperate . . angry . . *scared*. That gun *won't go off* . . it's clear there is something wrong with the gun . . these officers quickly realise the situation and jump me . . I'm disarmed . . thrown on the floor and held there. The door opens . . others come in . . and as I lie there . . I'm beaten . . kicked . . and am made all but unconscious. I only vaguely understand what's going on. I feel the blows, the kicks, but the overwhelming thought is: *This . . this is the end*, and I wish for death . . in fact, at one point, I *think I am dying*. The beating was the worst I'd ever had.

They get me into a police cell . . I'm examined by the police surgeon . . my head is stitched-up and I'm given a drink of some kind. The Judas hole is opened . . I see part of a face and eye . . I hear this voice: "Neal Grayson, never trust a woman. It was the woman you were eating with who tipped us off. She phoned us on her way to meet you. It's a pity you used the gun. It was a good jail-break. We admire you for that, but never use a gun, Neal, we police don't like it."

In due course I'm charged with using a gun, a loaded gun, with intent to escape lawful custody. As I am a convicted man, I am sent to Wandsworth Prison and there, as a *maximum security prisoner,* held for trial. Later, the police in my case, the arresting officers, come to see me. They confess to having got very angry, but after all, their lives were in danger. Still, they regretted setting about me. I could have been charged with attempting to murder a police officer, but in view of all, all the facts, the police agreed to the lesser charge of 'using a gun to escape lawful custody'. There were several charges of house-breaking, stealing jewellery, and of course I was charged with stealing that gun, too. It proved to be the property of a high-ranking Belgian officer.

I was in the cell, awaiting one of the preliminary magistrate's examinations, and I was told: "A solicitor to see you, Grayson." And there was Wally Silverman, an old jail-friend. Wally was a brilliant law-man, a qualified solicitor's clerk, but he had this itch for the *show-off* life . . he would persistently get valuables on false pretences . . then sell them and go to town as a lush *playboy*. Like me Wally was not very clever at beating the rap, so after a bit he landed up in jail. On getting out from his *last* jail sentence, Wally was helped by good friends to re-establish himself: he got a job as solicitor's clerk . . with a prominent legal firm and *now*, seeing my case in the Press, he'd come along to help me, *free of charge*.

Thanks to Wally I got Hemmerde K.C. as my Counsel and he was a very fine man. My defence for the attempted shooting was: Dartmoor Prison was a dreadful place, considered by me to be nothing more than a *graveyard* for the *living*. Faced with imminent capture and inevitable return to the dreaded Moor, I lost my head and in desperation tried to shoot my way out, preferring to *risk death by hanging* to going *back* to Dartmoor Prison. My defence was given wide publicity and ultimately led to most of the cons being moved *away*. However, because of the alleged *need* for *more accommodation* in prisons, after a while this jail, this graveyard, was again fully used and, so far as I know, will stay open . . till the Public *demand that it be closed*.

I took my trial at the Old Bailey. Sir Gerald Dodson was my judge. There was a lot of Press coverage—I suppose people wanted a change from war-news. My story went out far and wide, the story of the man who would *rather die* by *hanging* than go *back to Dartmoor*.

I won't dramatise this situation. I *now* know that my absurdities were puerile. Sure, sure, jail *was* a terrible place, but so were the battlefields terrible places, and . . I . . I . . 'qualified' for Dartmoor. I got another nine years, the previous sentence being quashed, and I was returned to Wandsworth for later transfer *back* to **Dartmoor.**

XV

I'M LOCKED UP in Wandsworth except for a few hours a day in the mail-bag shop. In my peter I brood . . all the excitement of the scarper, all the thrill of the melodrama, the shoot-up, all the absurdities, can now be weighed up in a cold Special-Watch cell. I don't like this idea of returning to Dartmoor. I hated the place . . all those unnecessary restrictions . . the *all-pervading stench* . . the never ending *rain . . fog . . dampness* . . and the *screws' intimidation*. Across from me was the Condemned Cell, and *always* in coming in from the shop under heavy escort, I'd *wish I were in that cell.*

I'm in the shop one day, and over there, I hear a fellow-inmate say: "I wish I were at the Moor. It's a better nick than this fucking place." At the side of the shop is a cutting-up bench . . knives lying about . . I get up off my stool . . grab one of these knives . . go over to this *Moor-lover* . . grab his hair . . pull back the head . . and *stab* . . *stab* . . his throat . . saying: *"Go back to Dartmoor*, you bastard, *but it will be in your coffin*." The blood spurts all over me . . the man struggles . . screams . . and . . I . . I . . am jumped on . . carted off . . stripped . . thrown into the cell . . warned by the screws: "*Be sure you don't start with us, Grayson.*" *Me*, I was ready to start anything.

I was obsessed with *fear*, fear of returning to Dartmoor. I hoped this man would die; then they could hang me. The man recovered, but it was a very narrow escape: his carotid artery was nearly reached by the knife. I was tried by the visiting magistrates—for some reason the prison authorities didn't want to send me out for trial. I'm given the maximum sentence possible: 1 year's *loss* of remission, 1 year's *loss* of Stage Privileges, 56 days' Close Confinement, 42 days' No. 2 diet and 15 days' No. 1 diet. Except for lukewarm porridge at mid-day on the No. 2 diet, it was a *cold water diet,* and funnily enough, it was *that* which really *hurt*; not the starvation, not the solitary, just that bloody cold water . . .

I finished the punishment on New Year's Day, 1945. They came for me that *same day*, hand-cuffed me to a screw and, with two other screws, I was taken back to Dartmoor. In the train those screws relaxed, talked freely, shared their sandwiches and tea with me and acted in every way as if they were *gentlemen born*. I lose myself for the time being in this friendly climate.

The train slows up . . this is Tavistock . . next stop is Dartmoor . . the screws begin to tidy up . . I have the cuffs on again . . after all, it would never do to let the tough Dartmoor Mob even suspect a screw of having a heart . . the Moor's screws would mock any such softness.

It's bitterly cold. The moors are barren and utterly lifeless. The whole countryside is wrapped up in blankets of snow and down there, as we drive along in the bus, we can see those jail-houses standing up like frozen *gravestones* . . locked and barred and walled around as if to keep the *dead* from escaping. Looking down, I felt scared.

Much to my surprise, *no* rough stuff was tried on at my arrival. I was received without malice or hostility, shown into a chokey cell down in the notorious tea-garden . . and, though that peter was not really fit for a dog, at least there was no 'heavy stuff'. It was cold and damp . . it was quiet . . in fact, you could *hear* that quietness . . it was a speciality of the famous Dartmoor *treatment* . . the idea being that silence, *all*-pervading *silence*, could drive you nuts . . . It was worse than Broadmoor.

"Grayson, glad to see you back. I note you have brought your own toothbrush."

"Chief, he didn't think we would trust him with one."

"Well, we are taking no more chances with you. Special Watch and the small shop where the staff can watch you."

So, I'm back where I started. There is a rumour going round that the Moor is being closed down. In the meantime I'm stuck in that shop right under the screws' eyes. The work is carpentry, but for some reason it doesn't really interest me—chiefly, I think, because it is compulsory . . .

I'm up on the landing waiting to go to labour, standing on my door-step, when down below I see a marching file of men. Among them is George whom I had known in Parkhurst . . he had been serving a 'lifer' . . was then fit . . well . . and very much alive intellectually . . he had been a Cook's courier at one time, had taken his discharge on licence, and gone back to some kind of petty larceny for which he got another five years. So there he is, 'ticket' on a life-sentence plus five years. I look at him . . he's greying . . shoulders sagging . . feet dragging . . inward-turning . . *lost*. George was later again let out on ticket, and that time he *dropped down dead in the street*. I believe it was the lifer and the subsequent five years and his personal *self-disgust* at lapsing into villainy that *killed him*. He was dying that morning I saw him going to work in Dartmoor Prison, but neither he nor I realised it. I'm sorry about George . . .

The day comes when the rumour proves true: we cons are off to the Island, Parkhurst Prison, and there is *joy in the land, rejoicing*.

I get back to the Island. The weather, the conditions, the staff, the whole *human* climate, have changed considerably since I was there last. But it is still just another jail . . milder than Dartmoor, but *still* a *jail*. My experience is proving to me that no matter *what* the conditions of jail, I will resist it, fight it, hate it. And yet, I must confess, I am a very long way off full inner conviction that the villainy-thing is not for me . . .

I'm in the laundry as a starter, but get in 'bother' with the screw. I go down below . . do my punishment . . get back to the old angry state of mind . . come up . . more trouble . . more punishment. Finally, as the prison staff are fed up with handling me, I'm put in hospital, given a job over there as orderly. I live in the emergency ward on my own . . keep it clean and ready for use.

At this time there are many big-time operators in Parkhurst. They rate as a sort of jail-hero and I meet quite a few of them, all remarkably intelligent and having a kind of 'principle'—some things they will not do. Today the average villain is an unprincipled *bastard* . . he will do anything, having no regard whatever for his neighbour and despising any screw or governor soft enough to treat him as if he were *human*.

This is the year of grace, 1945, War's End, *peace* on earth . . but *me*, I'm still a wild, irresponsible *mug*, still wedded to this thing called *villainy* . . . For a time, because I am rarely searched by staff and because I have the advantage of a hospital job allowing me to go around the jail with the medicine basket, I act as banker to 'the *mob*', the big-time operators. I arrange the passing out of mail, deal with the incoming snout (tobacco) and I hold on to any money not yet handed to the screw concerned. This banker lark is surprising really as I myself am a very lone wolf, certainly *not* a mobster. But there it was, these fellows trusted me to do their business and it pleased *me* to *beat that rap*. After all, the judge *didn't intend me to have any sort of luxuries* so by doing this service for the mob, *I proved that judge to be powerless*. In that jail, so far as I was concerned, the judge could stuff himself.

I'm in bother with a new screw from tough Durham Prison. He is going to put this bastard called *Nick—me*—in his place. We have an argument . . I threaten to put it on him . . he says: "Go ahead," and starts to reach for his stick . . I am rolling my sleeves up, ready for a scrap, when I *remember* that in my pocket are nine one-pound-notes, which belong to that mob. If there is a fight, I'm sure to be taken down below where they'll find the money. So *I roll my sleeves down* and *walk away* . . *walk away* . . .

As I walk away from that screw, I hear him say: "*That*, Grayson, was the finest, wisest thing you've ever done . . to walk away from trouble."

The screw *never cased* me, and, funnily enough, *never, never* bothered *me* again. As for the mob, they were *jubilant*: now they *knew* that *'mad bastard' Nick* was to be *trusted* . . *he would never let himself be caught with their gear*. From then on *business* for me was *good* . . .

During these years on the Island, from 1945 till end of sentence, I was a very stormy petrel . . I often exploded into unreasonable *anger* . . did a lot of punishment, but was always returned to the hospital. In fact the M.O. of that day, a Dr. Mathewson, often sent for me to his office, talked to me, shared his cigarettes with me and prescribed *tranquillisers* in an effort to curb that violence, *me* always saying: "The *only* way to cure me is *stop putting me in prison*." Strange to relate, he thought I had had *too much imprisonment*. But if I said to him: "O.K. O.K., then why not write to the Home Secretary and tell him so?" he would reply: "I can only write in that way if I'm *invited to do so* by the Home Secretary."

In my leisure time I did a lot of reading . . mostly books of depth and power. I avoided *make-believe* . . yet *my own life was make-believe*. I was lost in *fantasy* and *did not know it* . . .

One day there was a telegram for me: "*Am coming to see you tomorrow*" it was signed by a reporter from the *News of the World*.

"Yes, Grayson, we are interested in your story. It is a good story, in fact I think it has *film possibilities*." *All* this and *more* besides came from that reporter but *no written contract* . . just a verbal agreement to take my story on my release. I return to my peter, thinking for the *first* time *ever*, it *might be possible to pack up* this *villainy lark*. After all, I could get a fair sum of money for the story. So, until sentence-end I *dreamed* of *finishing with that villainy thing*. I even *planned what I would do with the money*: I'd buy myself into a *good restaurant business*. My knowledge of food, wine and the luxury life could pay off. Also I *saw* myself as a *genial host*, a *good* maître d'hôtel.

I finish my time. Except for that six weeks on the run from the Moor, I had now done exactly nine years in jail since they gave me my time in that Hampshire Court for the Bournemouth job.

XVI

1952 AND *I'M free.* I go straight to the *News of the World* in Bouverie Street, acting as if that *saga* of mine was already on that *front page.* I leap up the steps . . go to the porter's cubicle . . tell him I am expected . . go up on the lift . . in that waiting-room . . only to be told that this reporter is away.

This was the *first premonitory shock* . . I had expected to find *that red carpet down* . . after all, this man had come *all* the way to the Island just to buy my story. "I don't know when he will be back, but if you will *sign* this *retainer,* we will give you five pounds to tide you over for a few days. But *don't go elsewhere with your story.*" I sign.

Come Monday morning, I'm up at the *News of the World* offices and the man is there. "Sorry, very sorry, but since I saw you on the Island, we have had a change of policy here and we can't take your story. In any case, the space which *might* have been given to you is being used for Wally Silverman's *story.* He is in trouble again and, him being on bail, we've taken his story." *Me* . . *me,* I'm *sunk* . . *all* those *dreams* . . *dead* . . *dead.* "Oh, I think we might do a small *photographic feature* on *you* : the first *luxury bath,* the *first luxury meal,* the *first look at the flowers in* St. James's Park, the *first look at* Trafalgar Square and those pigeons, all after nine years in *jail.* This, Mr. Grayson, Mr. Carasov, *might* give you a few pounds to go on with." *Me* . . *me,* I fall for this offer. After all, I am penniless. I sign again, get another fifteen pounds and go out on this ridiculous *exhibition.* Lunch at the Cheshire Cheese . . *flash* . . in St. James's Park . . *flash* . . I look at those yellow daffodils . . *flash* . . then Trafalgar Square and the pigeons . . *flash* . . *flash* . . And so for a mess of pottage I have *sold all the newspaper rights to my story.* I did not know at that time, that this deal with the *News of the World* would *rule out any kind of deal* with the rest of London's Press—the *news value* of my story was cancelled out by this photographic feature. I think: *What luck,* Wally Silverman is *going into jail* again and *can't use money there* . . *me* coming *out* where money *can be used, don't get it.* They give me the paltry sum of fifteen pounds plus five pounds.

I then went round *all* Fleet Street and everywhere I went the answer was the same: "Sorry, Mr. Carasov, if you had come to us before that *News of the World* feature went out, we would have taken the whole of your story."

I get feeling that old anger again. It strikes me *no* luck is coming my way. Nevertheless I don't break down just there and then . . I go after a job as a kitchen porter at the Westminster Hospital . . not *much* of a job, but I go after it.

I see the Personnel Officer. I tell him frankly where I have been during the last nine years. He does not believe you can get nine years in prison just for stealing a jewel-case of gear. I tell this Personnel Officer something more of my past, concealing *nothing.* He expresses sympathy and says: "You can have the job, but *I have no intention of keeping you in the kitchen.* You mentioned *music,* clarinet-playing. Do you think you could organise the staff dances here, make up a small band and handle entertainments generally?" I am bowled over by this generous offer. This *prospect* of *music-making makes me gasp.* What a break! I'm thinking: *To hell* with the *News of the World, this will do for me.* I'm told to start work the very next day.

I turn up at the hospital full of joy and enthusiasm, and am told that the Personnel Officer wishes to see me before I start work. I go up those stairs *full* of *foreboding. I knew* this wonderful break was *not for me.*

"I'm sorry, Mr. Carasov, you can't start work *here.* I had to inform the Security Officer of your appointment, and *he* says: 'I won't take the responsibility of that man, Carasov, being employed *here.*' " So I am sacked even *before I start . . .*

There is an *explosion* in my *brain* . . I go straight back to my bedsitter . . pack that bag . . and take a taxi to a posh hotel, intending to go back in style to that villainy lark. And *fuck* the *News of the World* . . and *fuck* that *security officer too.*

1952 . . just finished nine years in jail . . yes, I qualified for the bird . . yes, I had tried to gun those officers just doing their duty . . but . . I . . I am *still* a *man* . . I am *still* susceptible to *love* and *hate* . . *heat* and *cold* . . and *I had planned to finish with that villainy lark.* For me a newspaper offer would have been an *open door* to a *new life.* Then I get a *second chance* of a *new life* and *this too* was denied me. O.K. O.K., I should have been a *hero* . . I should have *laughed* . . *laughed* . . and started *humbly in the gutter,* climbed *all the way* to those *stars. Yes, yes, that's what I should have done* . . but I failed . . failed once again to see that *light* . . .

I book in to a West End Hotel in my *own name.* In my bag are *all* my worldly belongings, even *letters* addressed to me at Parkhurst Prison. Everything pointed to the fact that at that time *I was temporarily insane. No* thief . . no *experienced* hotel thief would go to a hotel intending to *rob* and *sign in in his own name,* nor would he carry incriminating letters sent to a prison address in his bag. *All* this I didn't know then . . I'm now looking back and seeing all this. I now *know* that the *News of the World* fiasco and the Westminster Hospital fiasco *together* had *temporarily knocked me off that normal balance* and left me at the mercy of a state of desperation and *fantasy* which led me into the most dreadful *crime* I'd so far committed.

1952 . . the year in which I reach the lowest point in my criminal career . . the year in which my descent into Hell was an actual *experience.*

All my dreams of finishing with that villainy thing were smashed to smithereens. I had experienced what seemed to me a kind of treachery. And living in a jail-world *fantasy* for years had not helped me to a *clear vision* or a sense of proportion.

So here I am in this hotel . . angry . . frustrated . . desperate. *All* I want is some jewellery . . some cash . . then I can *lose myself* in a flight from a world which *does not want any part of me.*

I see this woman and I note she is wearing a ring with a fine diamond . . she is alone and going up on the lift. I've been trying to find a room with the key left in the lock. I've been watching the porter's desk . . maybe he will go away for a moment . . then I can take one of those keys. So far I've had no luck, and everywhere I show myself . . on those corridors, up and down those stairs . . I've bumped into a floor-valet, a chambermaid or a floor-waiter. This is jolting my nerves. I am sure that these people must be getting suspicious . . they will be tipping off the management . . and *that* could be disaster . . police . . detention for enquiries . . . I try a door . . it opens . . but the room is not occupied . . I try another door . . it is locked . . and there is that damned valet again. He gives me a questioning look: "Can I help you, Sir?"

"No . . no thank you. I . . I seem to have got on the wrong floor." Jesus, more of this will drive me *nuts*. I *must* disappear. If that chambermaid sees me again she will report me. At *that* moment I see the woman with the diamond ring going into her room. *Me* . . I'm scared of being seen again by staff so, without *any* plot or *plan*, I go straight to this door . . knock . . the door opens . . I mumble something about the phone . . I enter the room . . close the door . . I've no actual plan . . I must just get off that corridor and grab anything of value.

"What do you want? Get out of this room," the woman says and reaches for the phone. I *panic*. I am scared of being found there . . and in one red, searing flash of anger . . hatred . . fear . I knock the woman down on to her divan . . grab her throat . . and . . press . . press . . thinking: *God* . . *God* . . I don't want to do this but I must. *I never want to be caught again by the police.* That can mean *prison* and *I would rather die than go back to prison*. The woman falls away from me . . I think she is dead . . I'm sorry . . sorry . . but . . desperate. I take the ring, some Traveller's Cheques . . and, covering the woman's face with a pillow, I leave.

I leave that room in a kind of daze, thinking: Christ, I have killed that woman. I'm sorry . . sorry . . but *now* if I am caught I will die . . they must hang me and *that is better than prison* . . *that will end it all*. I return to my room . . look around . . still in a sort of daze . . sit down for a minute . . then go downstairs . . past the porter's desk . . straight into the street. There is a drain opening in the gutter . . I throw the Traveller's Cheques down there . . and, in a kind of sleep-walk, I find my way to a fellow who once told me to come to him if I had any gear for sale.

He is looking at the ring. "Jesus, Nick, has this come from *that hotel*? It's *all* in the *Press* . . this ring is *red hot* . . I won't be able to sell it for some time . . 'ere you are, twenty-five quid . . I'll probably have to *give it away*. *Me* . . *me*, I couldn't care less. I just want to get away from there, *anywhere*, just lose myself. I'm not thinking very clearly . . I believe I'm now wanted for *murder*. I think it won't be long before they get me. *All* my things are left in the hotel, even *letters* sent to *me* when I was in Parkhurst Prison, and my *own name* in the hotel register. I feel the world is rocking. I see a sign in a window: *Our sherry is good sherry*. I enter . . it's a brightly lit pub . . talk . . laughter. I say: "A glass of your *good* sherry, please." Then I ask: "Have you any Sobranie cigarettes?"

"No, sir, we don't stock Sobranie."

Then a strange voice interrupts: "Excuse me, I don't smoke Sobranie but I do smoke Piccadilly . . will you have one?" I look over in the direction of the voice and I see a tall, fair, slim, gaily-dressed woman. She wears a red swagger-coat, black shoes and handbag and her hair shines in the pub's light.

"I thank you," I say. I go over and take a cigarette.

"Won't you have a drink with me?" the lady asks . . and so I meet Elizabeth, ex-teacher, ex-librarian, now a housewife with two children . . separated from her husband . . having a drink before going home after an afternoon's shopping.

Of course I didn't learn *all* this right there and then. For the moment she just looks at me and says: "Tell me, have you been ill lately? You look rather tensed-up, as if you were recovering slowly from some kind of shock."

I say: "I've just killed a woman in a hotel, maybe that's *why* I look so strange and tensed-up."

Liz looks at me, smiles and says: "Nonsense, *you are not a killer*. You are a newspaper-man on some assignment . . you are just joking about the killing."

I tell Liz the whole pitiful story as if I'd known her all my life. She listens *spellbound*, then says: "*Nick*, I don't approve of murder or stealing. Let's *hope* this woman isn't *really dead*."

In the meantime I am learning something of Liz . . she has had a very unhappy married life . . were it not for the children, she would have left her husband years ago. By now it's getting late. Liz says: "Let's go for a walk in the park. I want to know just what you are going to do. *What would you like to do*?" We leave the pub . . cross the street . . into the park. I tell her: "This woman may *die*. That means a hanging job for *me*. So . . as I've had *no* free-world *life* for the last nine years, no womenfolk, no *real good food*, no *wine* and *no* free-world entertainment . . *this* is what I would like: A nice meal with wine, shared with a woman, a *good show* and plenty of gay music . . then I'd like to *make love all night* with the same woman." After all, *this* could be my *last night in the free world* . . she looks at me, saying: "I will have that meal with you. We will try and see a show, but as for *loving*: I am not promiscuous, Nick, nor am I a prude, but let's leave the loving for the moment. I'll have to think about that.

Also, if I don't go home tonight, the children will worry . . though I *can* phone our housekeeper and, I suppose, talk to the children on the phone. *Now*, where do we eat? I've been out of the eating-world for a few years, but I remember a favourite place of mine was in Hampstead."

I took Liz to this restaurant . . candle-lit, quiet, and smelling of good cooking . . the service was unobtrusive and she and I talked . . talked . . talked.

As we came out of the restaurant, she says: "Nick, I *will* stay the night with you, but first I must phone the housekeeper and the children, telling them I'm staying the night with friends. Also, you must assure me that we won't go to any shady sort of place."

We find a phone-box . . Liz and I squeeze into it . . . All the time I'm listening to Liz talking lovingly, gently, to her children . . I'm feeling rather *sick* . . so *sick* . . this charming woman . . her home-life . . her children . . and *me* . . *me* . . out of it all. *This* could be my last night in the free world . . and is that woman *dead*?

We step out of the phone-box, call a taxi and I give the address of a small but good hotel which I remember from days gone by. On the way to the hotel Liz takes my hand, saying: "Don't worry, Nick. *Tonight is ours*."

Liz and I book in, go upstairs, order some wine to be sent up, and look around. It's not bad. It wasn't the Savoy or a private home of our own, but it was clean, nicely furnished and had a bed fit for a royal bridal couple. When I said this, Liz laughed and laughed. Again we talk . . I hear all about her life . . she met this man . . she was young . . thought it would be nice to be rich and independent . . they married. For the sake of her children and their education, she tolerated her husband . . lived with him for eleven years. Then, when the children were at good schools, she got a separation. She went back to work as a librarian and got a housekeeper to care for the house-chores and look after the children. For some time before she met me Liz had been getting depressed and she was inclined to *drink that depression away*. She said it was grand meeting me, but dreadful to do so after I had done this hotel thing. If only she had met me *before* I had gone there . . .

We go to bed. For a time our loving was quiet and tentative . . two people getting to know each other . . rather shy . . .

That night with Liz was unlike any other night I'd ever spent with a woman. It was like seeing the sunrise for the *last time ever* . . it was like hearing the joyful voice of a child for the *last time ever* . . everything we did . . touching . . caressing . . holding . . even the final act of coitus, that grand volcanic eruption, that cosmic convulsion, we tried to hold back. It could have been the *last* experience of the kind for *me*. All the time Liz and I were making love there was this *fear* that we might never ever meet again after that night. Liz and I got very close that night.

Next morning we look at the newspapers: "American lady still unconscious," the report stated, "but otherwise *unhurt*. The police are looking for a man known to them, for questioning." Liz and I were so happy . . the woman *was alive*! Still, it meant jail for me if or when they caught me, and this thought made me very sad . . chiefly because it would mean separation from Liz to whom I was greatly drawn.

Before leaving the hotel, Liz and I discuss the situation. She said: "No more *stealing*, no more *violence*. You must disappear into the country and lie low. I will get my divorce . . we will marry . . and you and I, Nick, will find a *new* life somewhere in the world." Liz opened her handbag, took out a roll of notes, saying: "Take this money. There's about seventy pounds which will keep you for a time. Later we can meet and I'll let you have some more money. Then one day when all has blown over we will go away."

I tell Liz I can't take money from her: "I've got a few pounds left from what that fellow gave me for the ring. Maybe I can make him give me some more. The papers said that the value of the ring and the Traveller's Cheques was believed to be about two thousand pounds. All right, so I threw the cheques away, but the ring must be worth more than twenty-five pounds."

"Nick, forget the ring," Liz replies.. "Take this money . . I have plenty more. Go into the country. Here is a phone number which will always find me."

In the end I take some of this money from Liz, privately resolving to do one more piece of villainy so that I can pay her back. The rest of the money I'd use to pay my share of our run-away expenses . . . I take my leave of Liz and get a bus from Victoria to Midhurst, Sussex, where I knew there to be a good hotel. At this place I can probably get all the gear I want . . *this* time without *any violence*.

While I wait for the bus, I get another paper: "The woman has recovered.. no serious injury.. the police are seeking a *known criminal*, believed to be only recently released from prison." I'm wondering if anybody will see the connection between a nine-year term in prison and an explosion into violence when that man is confronted with a return to *prison*?

At this time.. just after that hotel affair, when I am a wanted man on the way to my hide-out.. I didn't really think things out. I knew deep down inside the inner-core of my being that this violence of mine on a defenceless woman was *not the action of the real Victor Carasov*.. it was the action of an ex-prisoner.. *scared*.. *scared* of ever going *back* to that prison.. it was the action of a panic-struck, frustrated man.. an angry man, too. *All* this I *felt*, but it was years and years before I actually began to see the *inevitability* of what I was doing. You sow the wind..you *reap* the *whirlwind*... You plant thorns.. you *get* thorns. First you steal.. then one day you get violent.. then you kill.. though you may *plan* none of this...

I buy a small bag.. get a few things.. shirts, socks, brushes, shaving-gear, etcetera. I arrive at Midhurst, book into my hotel in the name of a well-known Fleet Street man. I am accepted as a welcome guest... At this hotel I am so completely accepted by staff and guests that I just *can't* rob anybody.. you can't rob your own kind. It never occurred to me that if my fellow-guests had known I.. I was a character suspected of a cowardly attack on a defenceless woman, they would have ganged up on me without scruple.

I'm now getting down to the last pound-note. I don't want to return to Liz empty-handed.. I don't want to rob these friendly people either... So I get out into the countryside.. look around for a temporarily unoccupied house.. I see a place which looks all right.. no smoke from the chimneys.. all locked-up.. I try the door-bell front and back.. *no answer*.. I note postal packages on the back door-step.. assume the occupants are away for the Easter weekend.. this is Good Friday.

It is easy to get in this house.. you smash the glass-pane.. put your hand in.. open the door.. go upstairs.. in there is a beautifully furnished bedroom.. windows overlooking the front lawn.. a tallboy.. a dressing-table. I open the window, and proceed to look for valuables. I am putting odds and ends in my pockets..rings, brooches, pins..when I hear a gate clang shut . . look out the window . . see a woman come up that path . . . This must be the housekeeper . . she has a shopping-bag in her hand. *Me . . me* . . I am thinking: *this* time I am hurting *nobody*. I will not wait for the woman to come in. I note that she is making for the back-door. I get on the window-sill . . drop down, hoping I'll not get hurt . . I land on the soft lawn-grass . . can hear a woman's voice shouting: *"Help, help, burglars!"* (She must have spotted that broken pane.) I dash over the lawn . . through the gate . . across the road . . over a fence . . into a stretch of woodland. *What bad luck*, I think to myself. Still, I've got away and I have not hurt that woman. I come out on another road . . walk down there . . see an inn where I ask if they will phone for a taxi, as I have hurt my foot. I wait outside the inn. Down the road comes a car . . I think it is my taxi, but *no . . no* . . it is *not* my taxi . . it is a *police-car* . . and sitting there on the front seat looking right down at me is the woman from the house I have robbed. She is pointing at me and screaming: *"That's him. That's him. I saw him jump from the window."* The police-car comes down that driveway like a bullet from a gun . . an arrow from a bow . . and I am *trapped . . trapped.*

This was the old familiar pattern: you break that Law: you make that slip . . and you are trapped. I'm captured, taken to the lock-up, *identified* by this woman and searched. The stolen gear is found . . and . . like a play staged by the *gods* in comes the *avenger*, a senior police officer. He identifies me as the notorious *Victor Carasov*, suspected of committing a serious offence at a West End hotel in London. This man says: "Drop that charge. Hold this man in the cells, he is wanted by Scotland Yard." Back there in the all-too-familiar police-cell, I don't even look at the graffiti . . I don't even look at the barred window . . I'm looking *back*, to London, the scene of the terrible Hotel Affair, to Liz whom I have now *lost* for *ever*. My mind is in a turmoil . . it looks as if the *gods* . . as if *Almighty God* . . is in on this round-up. I am well and truly *done*.

I stay the night at the local lock-up. In the morning: *"Two gentlemen to see you, Sir."* Yes, even those words repeat the pattern of my recurrent arrests. It seems I'm not just a *criminal*, but a *fool*, too. I can't even beat the rap . . .

I'm taken back to London by car. The police seem to be very sorry for me . . I'm invited to tell them all about it . . I am *not* a wide boy, not even a clever villain. I *talk* . . the police say they will help me all they can . . .

After the preliminary Magistrates' Court proceedings . . my plea is *insanity* at the time of this crime . . I am remanded to Brixton Prison. The following day is Sunday . . *no visits allowed* . . but I am told that a visitor . . has called at the prison and left a message: "Tell Victor I won't leave him and I'll be in to see him tomorrow." Liz had left me a parcel of food, a half-bottle of wine and a note.

It soon comes home to me that the Press are having a field day with this affair, the American lady getting a big write-up: little old lady, American Visitor . . surely *this country must be made safe for visiting Americans*? As for *me*, the Press gave me a real going over: *No-good bastard . . unfit to be at large* . . the *law* should *make an example of this vicious criminal* . . .

No one in that Press World asked *why* this man suddenly did this violent thing? He had *never* done this before and, if he had *intended* it, why did he register in his own name?

I realised that my plea of *insanity* could be *misconstrued* by the 'gentlemen' of the Press, so I dropped that plea, agreed to the charge of *robbery*. But I refused to plead *guilty* to the charge of *violence*, saying that *it* was not the *real* Victor Carasov who committed the *violence*. *That* was done by an *ex-prisoner* . . *frantic* . . *desperate* . . *afraid of returning to prison* . . .

Because I had no funds I accepted free legal aid. The solicitors concerned aimed at an *unopposed trial*: I must plead *guilty to everything, I must not antagonise* the *court*. The barrister didn't see me *once* during *all* the preliminary proceedings . . he would send a junior to stand in for him. I was advised to plead *guilty to everything*. I say: "*No, no,* I'm not guilty of this violence-thing. *That was not* the real *me*." Clearly, they all thought I was a real bastard . . and finally, at my trial at the *Old Bailey*: "I am sorry, my lud, I'm afraid I can say *nothing* in this man's favour. His crime is a very unsavoury one . . perhaps he suffered some kind of black-out. *That's all I can say* . . ."

"Victor Carasov, you are charged with a very serious crime . . robbery with violence. Have you anything to say before I pass sentence?"

"I am guilty of the robbery, but *not* of the violence. That was not committed by the *real Victor Carasov*."

"Tut . . tut . . you can't divide your plea like this. You'd better go down below and discuss this with your defending Counsel." I go down below. My Counsel: "Plead *guilty to the lot*, otherwise you will antagonise the Court." I go upstairs and say: "On advice, *I plead guilty*."

"Victor Carasov, the last time you appeared in this Court, you were sentenced to nine years. As *that* doesn't appear to have done you any good, I now sentence you to twelve years . . twelve years' imprisonment." *Me* . . *me* . . I say: "Thank you," and I go down below.

XVII

I NOW ARRIVE at a very crucial period in my life, a kind of cross-roads though I did not then know it. I had reached my forty-eighth year, had wasted all those years in jail and out there in the free world. I had learnt no lessons . . I had had brief moments of near-madness . . and now, to top it all, I had nearly killed a defenceless old woman. I *knew* it was not really *me* who had done this thing . . yet *it was I* . . and the world would *laugh* at any attempt on *my* part to explain all this in terms of *insanity* . . in fact, I could not proceed with this plea. I took the rap . . I swallowed that *pill* . . and I *still taste that thing* in my inner being after all the years between.

Let it be clearly said by me : I do *not* wish to *excuse* any act of mine in the name of *insanity*. I was conscious of *all* my actions, even at that moment of *violence* . . and yet I say it was not *me* . . .

To go on with this story : I'm walking up and down in my peter wondering *how you correct the uncorrectable* when the door opens. I can see a head and shoulder.

"Carasov, I hope you don't mind but I've noticed how depressed you are. Here is a book . . read it . . it may help you." I recognised this voice. It was the Church Army Chaplain. Obviously he didn't care to come right into my cell . . after all . . I . . I . . was dangerous . . hadn't I attacked a defenceless old woman? I hesitated to take the book, thinking that it was probably some religious thing, but an inner compulsion induced me to take that book. The door closed and I was alone, again. I look at the title of this book : *Release* . . *Release* . . by Starr Daily, published by Arthur James, Ltd. I open the book, see some quotes from the *Psalms* and throw it down, thinking : To hell with the *Psalms*. Then I walk up and down again. But there's that book on the floor . . I kick it away . . then, almost as if I had heard a voice saying : *Pick it up* . . *pick it up*, I *take it up* and start to read. This fellow, Starr Daily, was an American ex-convict who'd done time for safe-breaking. *Now he was claiming to have seen the light* and, with the aid of the New

Testament and the story of Christ, he claimed to have kicked the villainy-thing right down the stairs. *Me . . me* . . I throw the book away again . . *shit* . . *shit,* I say. I walk up and down . . see the book on the floor . . pick it up . . read it at *one go* from beginning to end. I look out of that barred window and say: "O.K., *God,* if Starr Daily could do all this in America, I . . I can do it in England, but in *my* fashion, *not his*." I wasn't prepared to go all the way, religiously speaking.

So I go the Starr Daily way. He took the orthodox path, using the Old and New Testaments . . I took a personal path, more suited to my way of thinking but still on the right track.

My first Starr Daily effort was to write to the publisher of the Starr Daily books as I was not sure that Starr Daily was a *real person* . . his story had elements of the *incredible.* In due course Mr. Arthur James, the publisher of *all* the Starr Daily books, came to see me at Wandsworth Prison. Mr. James was an impressive man . . tall . . heavily built . . a massive head containing a fine brain . . his heart too was big and warm and generous.

"Yes, Carasov, if you can stay the course, you *may* do in England what Starr Daily has done in America." Arthur James said much more about Daily . . his *reality* . . . his writing . . his work for ex-prisoners. Finally Mr. James departed, promising to keep in touch with me. That promise was kept until he died. His death was a very personal sorrow to me: I'd lost a good friend.

During those early days at Wandsworth, at the start of the twelve-year sentence, I thought a lot, read a lot and for the first time in my life I prayed a lot, too.

Now I come to a very personal thing in my life: *what is loosely called religion.* I had had early experience of a brand of religion which put me off for a very long time. But as I grew up, as I had experiences which just *couldn't* be given commonplace explanations, I was becoming increasingly aware of the *invisible forces* of the *universe.* Not that I had any deep . . deep convictions about all this . . it was rather a vague personally felt thing, disturbing but not yet a *restrainer,* not yet a *discipline* on my life-long wildness.

Time passed. I read *all* the Starr Daily books . . I read bits and pieces of the Bible . . I was in touch . . with several people out there whose business it was to serve their *God,* a *Christian God.*

I was Special Watch on account of previous jail-breaks, which meant much restriction, daily searches, etcetera. I applied to the

Governor, 'tough' Governor Laughton, to take me off this Special Watch thing. After two refusals, I ask him for the third time. I say: "Before you say no this time, Governor, may I say *why* you should take me off Special Watch?" Governor Laughton looked at me, then at the Chief . . finally he says: "Well, what is the reason, Carasov?"

I answer: "The man asking you *now* to come off Special Watch is not the man you put on that restriction. I have changed. I am no longer a security risk."

"Chief, take Carasov *off* Special Watch," he replied. *That* was my first ever contact with the much maligned Governor Laughton. I later discovered him to be a man of courage, a man of character, a man of human, if limited, understanding.

I'm now transferred to Dartmoor Prison, a place I always dreaded, a place from which I had escaped. I had even risked *hanging* rather than . . go back to it. This time I do not fear Dartmoor . . nor do I particularly look forward to it.

As I have said so often in this story, I'm *not* writing a prison documentary. I don't wish to emphasise unduly . . the prison aspects of my story. I broke the Law . . the law put me in prison . . when in prison, I continue to grow, to develop into what I am right now . . so, except to show that line of growth in the environment of prison, I'll not have much to say about it.

Since my first visit to Dartmoor things had changed considerably in the inner life of the jail. There was more *tolerance* from staff . . less *violence* from the inmates . . a more relaxed climate . . still a *prison*, but less harsh, less directly brutal. For a time I find a kind of peace in my reading, my talk to *God*, my letters to friends and from friends.

I did not know it at the time, but I wasn't really ready for this thing called *religion* . . I wasn't quite ready for *God*. I fell away from the Starr Daily course . . I fell away from rationality . . I got lost down there . . old angers, old resentments . . all mixed up with the deadly Dartmoor weather . . moisture . . down those walls . . cold damp floors . . the essentially *deprived* life of a prisoner . . *all* this caught up with me . . I forgot *God* . . I forgot Arthur James . . I forgot my intention . . my *quest* for *freedom, liberation*. In short, I was not yet ready for the essential changes which must take place before that villainy thing is *out*.

I come near another breakdown . . I move on to other jails . .

Birmingham . . Canterbury . . Maidstone . . trouble *all* the way . . violence . . near-violence . . bitter thoughts . . angry thoughts . . foolish thoughts. Finally I meet a prison governor who shows the most remarkable kind of tolerance. This man, Governor Ffinch, actually talked to me as if we were *brothers*. To start with Governor Ffinch didn't like me at all. We were at loggerheads. I defied him and his staff, but little by little this patient, tolerant man won me over to a kind of guarded acceptance of his kindness, his truly Christian charity . . .

I must now pause for a moment or two to let you see just *how* I arrived at this point in my life when I was still *unaware* of the persistent *self-destruction* my own behaviour was bringing upon me.

There had been moments of clear vision in the years since the London hotel affair . . I had been getting dissatisfied with *myself*, my way of life. I had even started thinking of a *new* kind of life, a near Christian life. But it seemed as though something more was needed in my life to bring me to a *deep, abiding conviction* that *villainy* was *not* for *me*.

So, though I responded to Governor Ffinch's kindness and his very *real* concern for my welfare, I wasn't really *ready* for the last act of my foolish life. *That* didn't come until I got me yet another of these long terms of imprisonment.

I had nearly finished my time at Maidstone when Governor Ffinch asked me whether I would like to go to the hostel at Pentonville. This was a reference to a scheme for long-term prisoners: there was a residential hostel within the walls of Pentonville Prison, from which the prisoners went out for daily work in the free world, and got a decent wage for it too. *Me*, I didn't want it. I just wanted to finish my time, then go free. After a while I'm persuaded by Governor Ffinch, against my own judgment, to go to the hostel.

I did not want this thing: it came at the end of a long term of years in prison . . I felt angry and frustrated at having been kept in jail for nearly eight years . . and *now, tired . . weary . . bitter . . sour*, the account with Society all but paid in full, I felt this was not *real rehabilitation*. Rehabilitation . . to be effective . . should come *before* the jail-rot sets in. After the first four or five years jail begins to have its deadly killing effect. By the time a man gets to the end of a term of eight years, he is either *unfit to go out* or *unwilling to work* for an *honest living*. He thinks: The bastards have made me do all my bird bar a few months . . *fuck* them, I'll finish my bit and *help myself*. Usually this means *back to villainy* . . .

The hostel was in the prison grounds. It was just like a well-appointed working-man's residential club . . but under prison administration . . .

My first job was impossible . . lifting and carrying very heavy rolls of paper in a sort of factory not far from the prison. I had a dispute with a foreman and I was *sacked*. I was in danger of being sent straight back to prison to finish my time, having been sacked from the job found for me by the prison authorities. But I returned to Pentonville, reported the facts and asked if I could be trusted to go out and find my own job. I was given permission . . and that *same day* I get me a job . . warehouse porter in a big North London store. This work, like the paper factory work, was too heavy for me, so I saw the General Manager, Mr. Parnell, a fine, intelligent, understanding man. He put me up in the carpet department as a *carpet salesman* . . .

I like this place . . bright . . cheerful . . busy.

The lift stops. Out steps my *first* customer . . a woman, a small boy and a smaller dog. I go forward and, with a sweeping gesture of my arm, indicating the whole carpet display, I say to the little boy: "Want a pretty carpet for Mum, Son?" and he says: "*Yes* . . *yes* . . *yes*." I talk to the dog . . he wags his tail . . I talk to the woman and . . she . . *she* buys a carpet . . . So . . I make friends . . woman . . child . . dog . . and I *sell that carpet*.

There is a canteen for staff . . women on one side, men on the other. *Me* . . *me* . . I prefer to join the *ladies* . . I've seen and lived with *enough* men in jail . . *I much prefer the ladies*. I'm enjoying myself. *This* is *freedom* . . you work for a living . . you meet people . . *you are free*.

On coming out of the canteen, I am confronted with a delegation of salesmen . . they want to know *why* I sat with the ladies. Didn't I know this . . was simply *not done*? I answer: "Gentlemen, if you had spent as much time as I have with *men* . . *under duress* . . *all together in one solid lump* . . stinking to heaven of *concentrated maleness* . . you would *not* want to *see* . . *smell* . . *taste* . . another man . . as *long as you live*." I walked away. Later, some time later, I noticed that the *men*, the *gentlemen*, were *sitting with the ladies* in the canteen.

It's evening . . I've finished work . . and the hostel rules permit us the evening *out* till ten o'clock. I see this girl . . small . . shapely . . attractive. She smiles . . her name is Betty: "*Bett*, if you like." She lives near, asks me to come on up.

Of course Bett is a whore on the make. However, when she learns I am a sort of villain on licence, she accepts me on *reduced terms*. I get to know this little woman: she's got a kid that her mother looks after in the country . . though a whore, she likes sex . . so do I (after umpteen years in jail a man is *bound to like sex*).

Years before I got out on the hostel scheme, I had met Mr. Victor Gollancz. He thought I had a story in my life and had encouraged me to write it, but up till then I had written *nothing*. One day on my afternoon off, I called on Mr. Gollancz. I asked him whether, if I started on that story, he would give me something in advance of royalties. He replied: "Mr. Carasov, if you were *Montgomery himself* . . or *Churchill* . . and asked for an advance *before the story was written, I would say no*." Mr. Gollancz then reached for the phone, spoke a few words and said: "Mr. Carasov, go round to this address." (He gave me an address . . in Blackfriars.) "It's Mr. Frank Betts, Literary Agent. He will help you with this story of yours."

Mr. Betts was tall, distinguished and *authoritative*. He had a modern office . . *all* amenities, including very pretty *typists*. He gave me five pounds and the promise of a *contract*. He also introduced me to a journalist with whom I could collaborate.

We start on this story . . I'm *not* happy about it: The journalist's approach to the story is *cold . . scientific*.

Mr. *Gollancz*, Mr. *Betts* and *the journalist* were very well-intentioned men . . Mr. *Betts* was *generosity itself* . . *the journalist* most able trying, no doubt, to make *his* kind of story of *my* life . . Mr. Gollancz was kind, helpful, encouraging . . a great man in many ways. *But me . . me I was not yet ready for that story. It should not* have been written by *anyone* but *myself*. I did not *know* this then . . I did not *realise* the *inner war* that was still going on in my wild soul . . I was very, very *divided* within myself . . hence the antagonism, the recurrent explosions, the arguments . . . In this disintegrated inner state of mind I failed to appreciate the *value* . . of Mr. Gollancz' and Mr. Betts' interest in me . . *All* this was *no anchor* for my *wild condition*.

So comes the day I am off for the weekend . . the pass says Maidstone, but I am in London visiting *Bett* . . I climb those stairs . . put the key in the lock . . the door opens . . the whole place is in *total darkness* . . I step back, *puzzled* . . what's going on? I hear a voice . . Bett's voice: "It's all right, *Nick*, it's all right. *It's only two gentlemen: come in.*"

Christ, *"two gentlemen"*, the *law* . . they must have found out I am *not where the pass says I should be* . . *I panic* . . I drop the key . . run down the stairs . . I . . *run out on the hostel scheme* . . I've *panicked.*

And I am on this *downward path* again. Everything has gone west . . hostel scheme . . the story-writing scheme . . I'm on the run . . a *wanted man* . . a bloody fool. I've got nothing but what I stand up in, very little money . . Christmas is a *week off* . . everybody's *home* for *Christmas* . . but me . . *muggins* . . a nutter.

I meet a fellow in a café. He says: "I want some *lolly* for Christmas. Are you game for a bit of *villainy*?" This was a tempting thing. I was in just the mood for *temptation* . . it was just the situation for villainy . . *villainy* for *fools* . . .

We screw a house out in Suburbia . . *old silver*. We drink sherry . . we eat biscuits . . we leave that house. Later a *buyer*, a *fence*, says that the stuff is *hot* and he will have to melt it down. He offers me a tenner. I look at this bastard . . I'm thinking: *Same old crap* . . *same old price*. But, *trapped in circumstance* . . *in my own folly*, I take the tenner, give my mate five and go to an all-night café. I sit and listen to the talk . . it's *mostly* about the *joys* of *Christmas* . . .

By morning I've recovered from that *panic* . . by morning I'm *sane* . . *rational.* I get on the phone and ring up one or *two* friends . . one, Dr. Boag, a good man, a very good man. I tell him some of the facts and say: "If the prison commissioners will permit me to spend the Christmas weekend with you, I'll go *back to prison. I don't want to commit any more villainy.*" I tell Dr. Boag that I'm in a fix and have panicked, but *don't wish to sink any deeper*. Dr. Boag asks me to come back to the phone-box in an hour's time. When the hour is up, the Doctor rings back to tell me that I can stay with him until New Year's Day.

I get a tube-train out to North London . . and there I'm met by Dr. Boag who takes me home and introduces me to his wife,

Isobel, also to a friend and her children. I'm given a small room which is mine for a few days of *freedom* .. and .. I settle down .. to the *first at home Christmas* and *New Year* I'd had for many, many years.

The Boags are kindness itself .. their friend is rather nice and the children too. It is a beautiful home .. spacious .. warm .. comfortable .. the food is delicious .. the friendly talk is *good* .. everything very *peaceful*, very *quiet*. My *private* thoughts were *mixed* .. I liked this *home life*, but *I was going back to jail* .. *and I was afraid* ...

Monday arrives .. *black Monday*. For a moment or two I come near *panic* .. I come near *that impulse to run* .. *run* .. *run* .. before it's too late. But *no* .. *no*, I don't run. We arrive at the jail .. the gate opens .. I enter .. it *closes* with the old familiar *clang*. I'm back in jail .. in disgrace. The *law* has caught up with me again .. *"Two gentlemen to see you, Sir"*. Fingerprints on *that* wine-glass .. on *that* sherry-bottle .. I'm *guilty* .. *no excuse* .. I take my trial at the London Sessions. They give me *another three* years, to be *added* to the twelve years I was still serving. I return to Dartmoor .. I *lose* the confidence of friends .. I lose that contract with Agent Frank Betts .. *I nearly lose myself* sinking into depression and self-contempt ...

I get a letter from the *other* friend I had "out there", a Mrs. Phillis Wood, a Quaker lady, a woman of great compassion, a woman *always* thinking of *others* .. *others* in pain .. in distress. In the letter Phillis Wood tells me of a girl paralysed from the waist down .. *Ruth*. I tell some of the lads in Dartmoor Prison all about this child and her *helplessness*. We plan a campaign, a Christmas *fund* for Ruth .. *toys* .. *sweets* .. a *doll* and *cradle* .. the *lot*. We get the governor, the chaplain, the staff, *everybody interested* in Ruth. Finally, we dispatch this bumper parcel.

Later, on a brief end-of-sentence leave period, I visited *Ruth*. She seemed to be rather taller than I expected, very mature looking .. a big, over-developed body .. but her *face* .. her *face* was beautiful .. not classic beauty, a *beauty of innocence* .. lovely *clear skin* .. fair hair .. *bright, bright, shining, laughing eyes*. Ruth couldn't speak except by *signs* .. a flicker of *eyes* .. a movement of *lips*. She tried to say thank you for the toys. Clearly she *loved* those toys.

I understood that was Ruth was *incurable* but I thought she should be in a hospital like the Mayo Clinic in the U.S.A. I offered to run a Press campaign for Ruth but her foster-mother was not keen on the idea. She said: "I don't want *any publicity* for Ruth" . . my shining-bright *Ruth* . . I was sad, so sad . . there was so little I could *do* for this child. I returned to prison, told the lads all about it and *thanked* them for the toys. Later I heard that Ruth had died.

XVIII

IT IS NOW nearing the end of 1962 and I am about to go free again after a period of ten years in jail . . except for eight weeks or so on the hostel scheme for which I wasn't really prepared.

I am now fifty-eight years of age. I have travelled a long way in jail . . out of jail . . still no anchorage . . still no inner conviction that the villainy thing is not for me. But I *was trying* to earn a living. I had no *definite plan* for the honest-thing, but there *was* a tendency *away* from that *villainy-lark*. I had no *home-town,* no *compass-point*, but I tried *job* after *job*.

I started off reasonably well. For the first time ever I got adequate help from the welfare people, though this, I believe, was due to a friend of mine who had put some money in the hands of these people, to use for me on release from jail.

My rent was paid for several weeks . . even clothes were supplied, though these were second-hand. A job was found for me . . hospital porter in an old out-of-date place. There were no lifts . . the work was too heavy for me so I proposed to the welfare people that I found my own work. My first job was as a theatre attendant in a Newsreel Theatre in Leicester Square. The Men's Rooms were infested with *queers* whom I . . I . . was expected to clear out. This job was distasteful . . I am *no moral welfare expert* . . so I walk out on that job.

There was no difficulty for me, *ever* . . in finding a job . . though it must be said . . I was not too 'choosy' in the work I sought . . for *me* . . this 'job-seeking' was a *great adventure* . . always . . I got *fun* . . even *joy* . . in seeking work . . yes . . losing the job, too . . was *fun* . . .

My next job was at a London theatre . . doorman . . front-of-the house brass-cleaning . . collect those tickets . . open those doors. I had a girl-friend, Bridget, who wanted to see the show so I sneak her in. Though in uniform, I join Bridget in the stalls, sit down with her and enjoy the show. Comes the end of the show, I leave with my girl and there is the *manager* . . larger than life and *twice* as *nasty*. He is *purple-faced* with rage. "*How dare you go into the show* when *on duty* and in *uniform*?" I . . I . . am *sacked.* I didn't even know enough to *ask, demand* a week's notice or a week's money in lieu.

Before going on to my *next* job, let me talk about *Bridget.* I had been very lonely since coming out of jail. There were *two* friends, it's true, both Quakers, both kind and helpful. On occasion they would even give me a meal or put me up for a weekend or, as in the case of Dr. *Boag*, pay my rent during a break between jobs. But I needed *more* than rent-money. I needed *love* . . a woman to talk to . . a woman that I could *eat with* . . *walk* with . . yes, *sleep* with, too.

Funnily enough, though I had no religion, no orthodox faith, I *did* have a kind of *belief* in *forces of the universe* which I believed to be *essentially good* and on the side of *humanity.* I'd *pray* . . sort of *talk* to *God* . . ask for a woman whom I could love . . maybe a woman . . who could love *me.*

I'm out there looking at the frontage of a large West London teaching hospital when I see a small, trim, neatly-uniformed woman. I think: She must be a nurse . . it's an answer to prayer . . I want a woman to love, and *I do love nurses.* Here is a *woman* who is *also* a *nurse.* And *that* was how and where I met *Bridget, my little Irish woman with a* heart of *gold* and the greatest *appetite* for *sex* of *any woman I had ever met up till then.*

The first time I saw *Bridget* I was plagued with a dreadful head-cold. I went right up to this little nurse and said: "Can you do anything for my cold?"

She looked at me, saying: "I'm not a nurse. I'm only a domestic worker, but I will help you get rid of your cold."

She cured my cold with the aid of *hot water* and *honey*, a home-cure known to all simple Irish folk (Bridget came from Donegal and was *proud* of it).

This woman had a heart of gold and a great sense of *comradeship.* Bridget *shared everything* . . her life-story . . her work-story . . her love-life . . even her savings . . she unhesitatingly shared with me.

Quickly she and I got together almost as *man*-and-*wife.* I had a small bedsitter in Streatham, not far from the Common.

There Bridget and I set up housekeeping, she living at a hostel; but joining me as often as her work-duties permitted.

We would go out shopping . . or *eating* and *drinking.* Bridget's favourite drink was a concoction known as *Double X.*

And *she* would natter on, yes and *sing*, too, whenever the opportunity knocked, which it often did in Bridget's chosen pub. After a night out Bridget and I would return to my bedsitter and, after a glass or two of *my* favourite drink, which was Hock or Burgundy, and a couple of sandwiches, me and Bridget would start the *business* of the *night* . . a *bath* . . a hug or two . . and *then to bed* for an *all-night love-session.*

Don't get me wrong about *love-sessions.* I am not thinking of the *great romantic thing.* That I can't record, that I know nothing of. I am no Richard Burton nor Valentino. By ordinary standards, for ordinary men and women, the *affair Bridget* and I had was *wonderful.*

This little woman from Ireland was separated from her husband and had a little girl whom she loved. This woman, whom you would *pass by* in the street, had a terrific *capacity* for *loving.* She would work on the *love-act* as a musician would work on that piano. The chords my Bridget found in that love-thing were *unbelievable.* I was no *innocent* . . I had bedded down my fair share of women-folk . . but for the *basic plan* for *loving,* I bow to my Irish colleen . . . At the ejaculation-point with Bridget I would *shout* with *joy.* I . . I would *storm that fortress.*

Back to my run of jobs: I am sacked from the theatre and Bridget and I go home laughingly discussing the latest misadventure. (I was to have quite a lot of misadventures before I chucked it all up and in anger and near-despair returned to that villainy thing.)

We go to a pub in the Strand. *Me,* I don't like it . . it *smells,* it *stinks* . . it's *noisy* . . it's crowded . . and I . . I . . want Bridget *alone.* But she is gregariousness itself . . she chatters, she laughs, she sings—out of tune, of course—but this is Bridget . . and, for the time being, I find in this woman something of the comradeship between man and woman I so desperately need.

Bridget has no intellectually slanted mind . . she is just a very ordinary woman . . practical, world-wise, house-wifely and intensely concerned with how to make the most of that love-thing which, for me . . woman-starved in jail for years . . is something very good indeed.

I go to an agent for domestics. I ask if there is any work for a man-servant, hotel or private service?

"What have you done in this line?" they ask me. I choose to

lie. The days of telling the truth about my past are ended . . at least for the time being . . so I say: "I have been in and out of hotel service and private service for some years now but I have been laid-up by illness and I've not been working for some time." I am referred to a luxury block of flats in Curzon Street where a second head-porter is required. I go along and so impress the head-porter that he engages me on the spot. I'm fitted with a gorgeous uniform . . so *magnificent* I don't care to change into private clothes when my work is done. *I look like a general* in some mid-European country . . dominated by *my magnificence* . . .

One Sunday when I am on duty, acting as head-porter, a group of people arrive including a famous film-actress who is visiting London for the première of a film in which she had starred. I see the party upstairs, get the luggage up, go downstairs . . the bell rings from No. 1 suite, that occupied by the film-star. Up I go and there I see my film-star in *all* her *glory*. I am not an over-zealous film-fan, but I *am* an admirer of *all* women, especially attractive women . . and this woman was *very* attractive. "Oh *portaire*. Please, please, get me something to eat and to drink. I am *starveeng* . . *starveeng*." I explain that service is not possible in the flats on Sunday, but say: "I will go out into the market and get what I can for you." For this woman I would rob Fortnum and Mason. I get cheese, brown bread, butter, tomatoes and a bottle of *good* vin ordinaire. The entrance-hall is quite empty when I get back . . no staff . . no guests. I leap up those stairs . . *no lift* for *me* . . ring the bell . . am admitted . . told: "Come in, *portaire*, not that I believe you *are* a *portaire*."

The food is taken from me . . I'm told to sit down and take off that damned silly uniform. I unbutton my gold-braided jacket but assume that gesture will be enough to mark the informality of the occasion. I look at my film-star. She is rather small, slim, pale-faced and dark-haired. Quite *unfashionable* in dress but lithe, *alive*. Her *hands* are *clean* and free of *all garnishings, no varnish* on those nails, no *rings* on those *fingers*. Her voice *soft* and *musical* . . .

For a brief *eternity* . . a moment of *stopped time* . . she and I are a pair of *old friends*. She tells me all about her picture, shows me the script . . she asks me who I really am. I tell her something of my story . . I tell her one day I will write it. I am promised a photograph later. In the meantime I remember, in spite of her doubts, I *am* a *"portaire"*, so I button up that jacket, wish my star "Goodnight" and . . *float* . . float . . down those stairs . . and . . *bang* . . *bang* . . into *reality* . . . The head-porter has returned from his day out, and, it seems, has been *waiting* for an *hour*.

"Where the hell have you been? What right have you to leave the hall?" *Me* . . *me*, I don't like his *tone* . . it is reminiscent of *Dartmoor Prison screws* . . I *explode* into *anger* . . threaten to strike him . . he reaches for the phone . . *police* . . *police* . . I recover from *anger* and *laugh* . . it's *my last laugh there* . . I am *again sacked* . . I lose my job . . I lose *my star* . . but I *don't* lose my *sense* of *humour* . . I just *laugh*, thinking how much *Bridget* will enjoy *this story*. *Me* . . I'll get another job . . .

In the meantime Bridget gives up her job at the hospital . . and goes into a hotel as a chamber-maid. This job has its attractions for Bridget: she meets *all* the world's *headliners* . . from Danny Kaye to Sophie Tucker . . and as perks she often got left-over American cigarettes, cosmetics, chocolates, foreign coinage and liquor galore.

My next job was with the Metropolitan Police Catering Service as a trainee steward. On the tube-train one day I met a young girl who told me her father was a police sergeant and she was in the Police Catering Service. She gave me the name of the Catering Service Personnel Officer, a woman whom I later rang up. I was invited to come along for an interview.

The Personnel Officer was a charming woman whom I *liked* very much. *She* said: "You, Mr. Carasov, are *ideal* for this *service*. You will go a *long way*, but, as a mere formality, I *must* ask for at *least two references*." *Me* . . *me* . . I've got *no references*, but to get the job, which I 'fancied' very much, I *lied*, saying that I'd never really worked for a living, having been a kind of free-lance writer. As for references, would private references do? Say the names of two good friends of mine, both Quakers and in the world of Quaker activities? My charming personnel officer, who *really* wanted me to start work, phoned up my friends and they said: "*Victor is a dependable person* and we would like you to give him a job."

So I start as a trainee-steward in the police canteens. Putney . . Notting Hill Gate . . and Battersea . . I am serving the cops, *plainclothed* and *uniformed*. I like these fellows . . they are cheerful, friendly and intelligent . . I serve beer, tea, breakfasts and luncheons. Sometimes I help in the cooking.

I'm serving at the Putney canteen, *singing* as I *work*.

"Here, you, where do you get that voice from?" someone says. "You want to come to our choir practice out at Chelsea Police Barracks. You could easily get into the Choir." *Me* . . I have *visions* of myself, singing in the *Metropolitan Police Choir* and playing the clarinet in the M.P. *Band*.

Alas, alas, dreams are flimsy stuff. I *did* attend a choir rehearsal, I *did* propose to offer myself as a clarinettist and *I did intend to make this service my service*. It would make a wonderful story: "From the *jails* of *England* as an *old lag* to the *exclusive clubs* of *England's finest cops*."

But one day I am getting breakfast ready for the Notting Hill Gate Police canteen when I'm told: "Somebody to see you from the Yard, Mr. Carasov. *Two gentlemen to see you* . . ." I go *cold* . . that frying-pan in my hand seems to go *cold*, too. Apparently the form filled in by my Personnel Officer and forwarded to head office was checked by the Yard . . and my *undisguised* name . . *Carasov . . . rung that bell*. Hence the early morning call right here in *this canteen*. Put that frying-pan away. *You are sacked*. So ends my *magnificent* project to serve Her Majesty's Police.

Being *sacked* was getting quite commonplace and I was getting a bit rattled. It seemed that either my ungovernable temperament or that past of mine . . was always to betray me. However I still persisted in this chosen course of *trying* to fit in as a *legitimate citizen*, laughable though this may have been.

Bridget and I celebrate my latest sacking by going out for a drink, a meal, a song and a dance. Later, as usual, we make love *all* night . . *me* getting up next morning . . *rejuvenated* and *refreshed*. I see Bridget off to work and I go job-seeking, back to that agent.

A bar-help, lounge-waiter and cellarman. *All* in one piece . . is wanted at a famous country club. I go out to this club, a neo-Georgian country house set in fine grounds. I meet the steward, am taken on and shown my living quarters. I have a nice room . . bath . . radio . . *all* situated over the stables, away from the club. My job? To help in the bar . . replenish stock . . wait in the period-piece lounge . . and, for parties, out there on the balcony.

I began to *forget* my losses, my past . . even my tentative thoughts re the *writing lark* .. were forgotten. The job was *good* .. the people I served were *great* .. *all film people*. I talked to these folk and got on remarkably well. I was quite frank and uninhibited, and forgot that I was supposed to be *an honourable citizen*. They even thought a film-actor could be found to play the part of Niki Carasov .. *in a film* ...

The scene is *set* .. here I am, right in the heart of the *film-world* .. in a club patronised by film people. I have met and talked to many of these people .. *all* of whom .. like .. like .. *this saga of mine* ... You would think: Nick has *got it made*. That *villainy thing* is *out* ... Well, well, it just didn't go like *that*.

It's early morning .. I am cleaning the entrance-hall .. on the table I see some note-paper .. I want some paper for noting bar-stocks .. I take a sheet of paper .. and I hear: "*Put that paper back. That is for guest use* and *you* are *not* a *guest*!" I look up .. it's the Steward .. who has already expressed *displeasure* at my presumption in talking to guests as if I .. I .. was a *guest, too*.

I go up to this man .. grab him by the front of his jacket, and say: "Are you a *bloody screw* from *Dartmoor* or somewhere?" He screams *blue murder* and blurts out: *"You are sacked! Get out!" Me* .. *me* .. I get out and, sick to death of all *this bloody crap, all these sackings, I go back to villainy* ... *But before* doing so, I have my *last meal* with Bridget .. my *last* night out with Bridget and my *last night of love-making* with Bridget, telling her *nothing*, only that I am *sacked* once again.

I've *no* savings, one week's wages only in lieu of *notice*, but as usual Bridget tells me: "Don't worry, Nick. I have a few pounds saved up. We will use that till you get another job." I don't like taking Bridget's money, but I privately resolve *one day* I will pay her back. Needless to say, I have *never yet paid Bridget back*, neither *cash*, nor *love*, both of which she gave to me so *freely*, so *lovingly*.

Funnily enough, after a defeat, a *sacking*, there was *always fun* and *laughter*, even though it was all mixed with anger and near-*despair*.

During this period I was still thinking about making something out of my story. I wrote to several people about the possibility of a collaboration. John Creasey replied that he found the idea very interesting, but he was going away for two years and so couldn't be of any help to me. Edgar Lustgarten, the writer and radio specialist in notorious crimes and *criminals* said he had all the copy he needed. I wrote to Lionel Bart and suggested the idea of a film or musical comedy on the lines of the *Carry on Nurse* .. *Sailor* .. *Screw* .. *laughing* at the jail scene instead of weeping. He thought it was a good idea, but for the next two, three or four years he was fully committed. Tony Richardson, the film-man, suggested I send him a script.

Eventually I went to the *News of the World*, in spite of my previous experience with them. I was told by several sub-editors that my story was *good* but the Editor said *No*.

I contact Michael Dove of the *Daily Express*, who puts me in touch with a man who is part of an agency-set-up for the writing-lark. He does nothing finally because I .. I was *not* at the time *ready to write my own saga. It was not written*.

I've privately decided to chuck all this *legitimate stuff*. I've had enough sackings. Also *independence* is calling, and I have not yet learnt that independence can be had *without villainy* and without *servility* to *arrogant employers*. I arrange with Bridget to have a bang-up dinner and night out even though I've very little money to do it with.

I left my bedsitter, took *all* my possessions in one good bag, and booked in at a very good hotel near Leicester Square where I knew *discretion* was the *password*. I pick Bridget up and I tell her that I am taking her to a *top* hotel because this could be our *last* night out for some time. We arrive, go up to my private suite, and having unpacked, bathed, had a little 'love', we go down to dinner. Bridget, being a humble chambermaid accustomed to *giving service*, relished this ceremonial-thing as *no queen could ever do*. I sign a bill for the meal and give a pound note. Bridget misses nothing and, with her usual generosity, slips me *all* her available cash, which was now about six pounds. We go upstairs .. undress .. bathe .. get back to bed .. Bridget showing me her *great big breasts* which she never tires of asking me to *suck*, as if I was a *baby* in *need of nourishment*. After our third or fourth round we stop, have a cigarette, a glass of wine, a *talk*. Bridget tells me *all* about her daughter, whom I would meet one day. She also speaks of possibilities for herself, her child and me. She gives me a *ring*, a *Cladagh ring*.

The morning after our night-out I see Bridget off to work. She asks me never, ever, to part with that Cladagh ring, as it was a kind of family heirloom which had been passed down from generation to generation. I have never parted with that ring nor ever will. I have not forgotten Bridget .. kind and warm-hearted .. generous .. full of real femininity .. and a *natural appetite* for *shared sex*. With Bridget sex was not *dirty* .. it was a wonderful, stimulating, life-giving thing. I owe Bridget very much indeed, not just *cash*, but respect and affection, too.

I wave Bridget a *last goodbye,* and from *that* day to *this*, I've *never* seen or heard of Bridget again.

After leaving Dartmoor Prison I was a very lonely man .. in spite of Bridget and in spite of the possession of two *good friends* who never *failed* to help out with the rent when I was out of work. All this was giving me much unease .. I preferred *independence*. I soon stopped going to the welfare people .. in any case, it was clear to me that they wanted *no part of me* .. my work record was very bad .. also, I suspect the money originally ear-marked for me was exhausted.

I wasn't sleeping very well. I'd go out into the streets at nights and wander along the Embankment .. *dream* .. *dream* .. whilst looking at the old river and its opposite bank. I'd stop off at any all-night joint, drink coffee and look around at my neighbours. I'd wonder what they did for a *living*. I'd talk to them, hoping to find someone who would ask me *home* with them. Sometimes I'd invite a girl home with *me*. I'd take her up those stairs, let her in my hide-out, then tell her all about my *absurdities*. Invariably she would say: "*Why don't you write your own story*?"

There was the night .. early-morning rather .. when I'm walking home and I see this very pretty girl .. red *hat*, red *coat*, red *shoes* .. lovely young face .. pale, thin, tired, but very young.

"What are *you* doing out at this time of the night?" I ask her.

"Nowhere to sleep," she says.

"Come home with me. My place ain't so hot, but you are welcome."

This girl comes home with me. I switch the fire on, put the kettle on, tell the girl to take off her hat and coat, and sit down in front of the fire. I make some Horlicks, offer the girl a cigarette. She seems shy .. finally I learn her story .. she is older than I thought .. nineteen .. she was an ex-dancer but, because of drugs, nobody would employ her. She did not want to go on the game and lived on hand-outs and doctors' drug prescriptions.

I liked this girl Rita. I was sorry for her, but she wanted *no pity, no sympathy* . . just *drugs*. I proposed to make love to Rita. *She* doesn't mind *but I must not look at her legs*. She undresses rather *shyly*, seeming to *hide* her *bare legs*. I soon know *why*: her legs are *all pock-marked* with *needle-points*. She seemed to be *ashamed* of this.

Rita is *no Salome, no* world's greatest female. In fact she confesses to me that *loving* is not important for her . . *drugs are her love*. I let Rita out . . the sun's up and she wants to go.

Weeks later I am in another bedsitter in Victoria. It's on the ground floor with windows overlooking the street. It's *snowing* . . and out there, believe it or not, *is Rita*. I go to the door . . let her in . . ask her how she knew I was here. She says: "I didn't. I've nowhere to sleep. I was just wandering in the streets and looking in windows when I saw you."

"Take those things off," I say, "and get into bed. You'll be warm, there." I've two beds and Rita chooses the bed I am *not* using. *Me* . . *me* . . for some foolish reason I am angry because she doesn't choose *my* bed, so I tell her to get into the other bed. Rita refuses, saying: "I don't want *any loving*, just *sleep*." *Me* . . *me*, the *bastard*, I say: "If you don't get into *my* bed, you can get *out*!" Rita put her things on and got out, back there in the *night* and the *snow*.

I never saw Rita again. For the record I confess that I will *never forgive myself* for this behaviour, for turning Rita out in the snow.

XIX

I RETURN TO my life of villainy. I go back to my old digs in South Kensington. I still have the key to the front door and know where the pass-keys are kept. With them I enter several rooms, collect pieces of jewellery, some old gold bracelets and leave the house. Then I go down to the South Coast, where I sell the gear to a *robbing bastard* and go to *Wales*. It's early summer and a *holiday* was my very present *need*. For years I'd *not seen* the *sea* . . for years I'd *not smelled the sea* . . for years I'd *been dead* . . .

I loved the Welsh scene . . the *sea* . . the *hills* . . the *people*. I meet a girl, a shop-girl as pretty as a piece of delicate *porcelain*, but I don't stay long enough to get to know her. I'm restless, uneasy . . this *illusion* of *freedom* is *not the real thing* . . this beating the rap is *all balls* . . *all crap* . . *self-deceiving*. A successful steal always gives this illusion of *freedom*, but the truth is: *no thief can be free*.

I have a few pounds left. I go to Liverpool where I get a modest flat . . two rooms and use of a bath, which to me is essential. The house is out in Parkland. One side of the street is *very* respectable, the other side *not* respectable at all.

I am not a habitué of pubs, but occasionally I'll go in, have a rum and lime and look around. Maybe I'll find that *great romance*. I am in a pub one day when a woman addresses me: "Gee! Long time since I saw *you*. Just got back from a trip?" The woman is *no* raving beauty . . plain of feature . . comfortable figure . . dark . . friendly . . warm. Clearly this woman has *mistaken* me for an old friend. I don't bother to un-deceive her. We have a drink or two. I learn her name is *Mary* . . she lives nearby, in fact opposite, on my side of the street. Mary is a *widow*, having killed her husband by *accident*. They got into an argument . . he attempted to *strike* Mary . . she was cutting up food and when she raised the knife to scare the man, he fell *on the knife* and *died*. Mary was tried for *manslaughter* but after a terrible ordeal in jail on remand, she was *acquitted*. She was *now* living alone with her two children in a worn-out one-room bedsitter which she kept as *clean* and as *comfortable* as strength and very little money permitted.

I visited Mary. I saw her pitiable living-conditions, admired her *courage*, her *cheerfulness*, her homely, down-to-earth *honesty*. We made love behind a screen which separated *her* bed from that of the children. There was a dog, too, small and very *bad-tempered*. Funnily enough, he *did not like me*.

Mary told me that the following day being Sunday, she would have the *only hot dinner* in the week. To make this really good Mary sometimes had to rob her *own gas-meter*. This I couldn't believe, I thought such things had gone out with Charles Dickens. I was invited to Sunday dinner. A real home-cooked meal and a *family* to eat with . . this was a *rare occurrence* for *me*.

On Sunday morning I seek out the nearest general store. Fruit, vegetables, canned goods I buy . . *everything* that can go into a Sunday dinner except fresh *meat* which was unobtainable . . brussels sprouts, spinach, lovely potatoes, big oranges, a bottle of fruit-juice, and the *largest packages* of *ice-cream* I could get. *Loaded*, I make my way to Mary's place. There she is, as large as life and twice as wonderful . . the mother, the housewife, the cheerful welcoming hostess, right there in front of an old beaten-up cooker. I can smell things *heavenly* . . *roasting meat*. I hand over my shopping-bag, and go out for a walk in a park nearby. I go through those wrought-iron gates into the main path-way . . shrubbery all round me . . flowers . . trees . . children's voices . . *this* is *life* . . *everything* around me *growing* . . *growing* for *joy* . . .

I return to Mary. Dinner is all laid out, a place for *me*, the place of *honour* so Mary said, places for the children and *another place*. I ask Mary who the place is for. "Oh *that*, that's for my old pensioner. He lives upstairs, Nick. Poor fellow, he can't afford a Sunday dinner . . so I always invite him down to join us." I nearly weep at this woman's kindness. I excuse myself, dash over to my place, get a sports-jacket out of the wardrobe, put a pair of socks, a handkerchief and a packet of cigarettes in the pockets, and return to Mary telling her the things are for her pensioner if he will accept them. Mary goes out and when she comes back there, in all his glory, wearing my jacket, using my handkerchief and smoking one of my cigarettes, was the old pensioner, stammering out: *"Thank you . . thank you."*

Mary and her dinner-party sit down. The meal had a sort of sacredness, a kind of *ceremonial solemnity*. To me this was the family, *united* in real community feeling. The meal finished, Mary gets up, goes to the door and calls: "Johnnie, Jim, Anne." I hear clattering feet, children's voices . . in the open door come children . . bright, hopeful faces . . lovely smiles. Mary cuts up *all* the oranges, *all* the ice-cream, and then to each child she gives a piece of ice-cream and a piece of orange. With a pat on each child's head, she sends them back to their mothers. *Me . . me*, I'm thinking: *Straight out of* Charles Dickens.

The next day I return to Mary's room, hoping to have her to myself for a while. But there at the table was a man in his shirt-sleeves, a typical working-class man of the house . . no tie . . braces on display . . feet slipper-shod . . and reading the Sunday paper! I take *one* look at this man of the house, curse and swear, and *walk out*. Mary follows me, saying: *"Nick, Nick,* what's wrong? Don't go away. That's my brother-in-law . . he married my sister, but since her death he comes here about once a week." I tell Mary I do not want to know her precious brother-in-law, who seems to *own the place*. She says: "As a matter of fact, Nick, my brother-in-law and me *may be getting married*." For one brief moment I felt *murderous* . . I . . I . . God forgive me . . had had thoughts of marrying Mary *myself*. I was powerfully drawn to this simple, kind woman. I left Mary then, and from that day to this I've never seen her again.

I return to my flat . . my heart is heavy . . my mind *aflame*. In some mysterious fashion, contrary to *all reason*, to *all* so-called *rationality* . . in spite of my being *nothing* but a thief, a jailbird with *no place in the scheme* of *things* . . I have been actually dreaming of *marrying* Mary . . then comes the awakening. I go out for a walk uptown . . in Lewis's store I see a *typewriter, shining bright* . . I take it, put it under my arm and *walk* out of the shop. I've no thought of what I am going to do with that typewriter. I have *never ever* done this before.

"Excuse me." There is a hand on my shoulder . . a man . . "Please, will you come back to the shop with me?" I look at this man and I *freeze* . . I *go stone cold* . . I'm puzzled. What have I done this *for*? Then I nearly *panic*: I'm in it *again* and for *shop-lifting*. I'm *ashamed* . . I'm *afraid* . . I'm *sick*.

We return to that shop . . I'm taken to an office . . questioned. The police are sent for . . I'm arrested . . taken to the lock-up . . Dale Street it was, as I learn later . . Dale Street, where I went over forty years before on my first crime ever, if you discount the boyish bicycle-theft which landed me in Reform School way back in 1915, when I was eleven years of age.

I am in a state of near-shock. I really *don't know what I took that typewriter* for . . *me* . . *me* . . a jewel-thief . . pictures, objets-d'art, bric-a-brac, and *now* a petty shop-lifter. I go to Walton Prison on remand. I haven't been in this jail for forty years. This experience of my *beginnings* in *crime*, in *jail-life*, nearly finished me off. I know Walton Prison was *not* what I knew in the years 1920 and 1921 . . *not the grim, dreadful, murderous thing it was* then . . but for all that *memory* caught up with me, and I was *terrified*.

I plead guilty at my trial, and get *six months. I might* have got *six years* or *more*, as a *habitual thief*, but I was spared that ordeal for the time being. I did not realise that this was *a warning, the writing on that wall.*

I do the six months with remission, the *shortest sentence* I have ever done since way back, before 1935.

I have an impulse to go to Mary, but that dream was over, so I return to London. There I meet one friend who still believes in *me*. She introduces me to a *psychiatrist* who *warns me* that I'm in *great danger*, very accident prone, liable to fall very easily. She wants me to go away . . hitch-hike . . write a book . . suggests I let her see my writing from time to time. *Me* . . *me* . . *crazy* . . *nuts* . . *lost* . . I go into *another store* . . this time it's *chocolates, cake*. I am arrested and the police say: "You are a sick man, Carasov. This pilfering is *not you*. It's out of character, you must get treatment." I'm remanded for a medical report and get *probation* for the *first time in my life*. I am obliged to *go for treatment*, but I'm *overjoyed* . . I feel *liberated*. I go to Maudsley Hospital, am interviewed and advised to attend there for treatment. The doctors say that I *need* their help, but I am not so sure . . I prefer to *help myself*. But I agree to attend this hospital as an Out-Patient . . .

Then one day I go into this food-shop . . I actually *buy* some food . . but I *take a piece of cheese* wrapped up in *shining bright paper* without paying for it. I am arrested . . *another shop-lifting act*. I break down completely . . *sob* . . *sob* . . *can't* understand it at all . . go back to prison for *six months* . . come out again . . renew probation . . promise to renew treatment . . intend to *do so* . . .

I am not too keen on national assistance, so I get me a job as *dish-washer* at Boodle's Club in St. James's Street. It is heavy work down there in the basement . . great big *copper pots* . . piles of plates . . but there's a *bath* for the tired *servitor*, right *there*, outside the washing-up place. I've finished for the night and, at about 9.30 p.m., I get into the bath leaving the door *open* to let the steam out. Some girl or woman still on duty sees my *male body* . . *screams* . . *screams* . . *me*, I get out of the bath, close the door, *laughing*. Ain't she *ever seen* a *man* before? Next day I am politely requested to keep the door closed when *bathing*.

Boodle's was a *museum piece* . . *silver candelabra* . . *paintings galore* . . . *me*, I want no part of nicking this gear. I see the silver man locking up his *silver* . . I am tempted to clean out this *silver* . . but . . *no* . . I am reaching a *point of no departure*. I am caught between the *old* and the *new*. I haven't recovered from that shock of the *shop pilfering*, and I am *against* any further villainy.

Boodle's are *extending* the premises and will be needing a residential valet shortly: would I take the job? *Yes* . . *yes* . . I visualise *me* as the *best valet* Boodle's have ever had. I go home for the night, and there a letter awaits me. I look at the post-mark . . *Yorkshire*? The letter is from a *widow* living at Horley Junction near Wakefield. She has read about me in the Press . . apparently a prisoner leaving Dartmoor Prison went to the *Daily Express* and told that paper all about the effort I made to get an interest, a *helpful* interest, in the life of a paralysed girl. The paper contrasted my reputation . . *hard* . . *tough* . . with this *gentleness* in taking trouble over a handicapped child. The widow has read this report and thinks I . . I am a kind of hero, a noble fellow. She *invites me to* come up there to meet her and her family. I haven't been working for very long and have no savings, but I want to visit this widow. What a wonderful invitation! Not many people in the whole world will invite a bastard like me to meet them and their family. I go to the *only* long-standing friend I have at that time (except for one other whom I didn't care to seek out). I ask this friend to lend me the return fare to the place named in the letter so that during a weekend off work I can go and see this kind widow. The friend says: "Victor, isn't it time *you stood on your own feet*? I . . I have *no* money to give you." Looking at this 'friend', I'm thinking: It's a *loan* I am seeking, to be paid back out of earnings. I'm *not* cadging. This is supposed to be a *friend* . . .

I get angry, *unreasonable*, bitter, *defiant*. I say: "Sure, *sure*. I'll *stand on my own feet*. To hell with *you* and your bloody *friendship*." I forget Maudsley Hospital and my *need* for *treatment* . . I forget the *prospect* at Boodle's Club . . and in one wild, angry move I return to *villainy*. Strangely enough the chosen *villainy* is right into the so-called *big time* . . *jewellery* . . *tomfoolery* . . *pictures* . . *silver* . . . and the *all-obliterating gay time* . . good food . . good wine . . good women. Everything of moment, of real *significance*, of real *value*, I throw away. So unknown to *me* at that *fatal moment*, I head for yet another of those interminable *life-sentences* . . never called a life-sentence in Her Majesty's courts, but in effect . . *more* . . *more* than *any lifer* would be required to serve.

XX

WE ARE NOW in the year 1963. Since leaving Dartmoor Prison I've worked for a living and *enjoyed doing so* . . it was good fun, even *joy* sometimes . . I've met *people* . . lovin' some of them . . I've sunk right down there into petty shop-lifting . . done two *'sixers'* . . been recommended for treatment . . and now I've *lost myself again*: 1963 and I am lost in *fantasy*, lost in *anger*, lost in *folly*. I am fifty-nine years of age and have spent forty of these years in *jail* and Reform School, yet I have not attained what is called *wisdom*. I love *life* . . *people* . . the whole pulsing, vibrating *world* . . . and yet I'm *acting* as if I were a *lunatic* . . . *protest* . . *rebellion* . . the drop-out *act*. O.K., *this* would, *might*, be regrettable but *why, why*? Why this villainy-thing? Why do I repeatedly *war* on the supposedly *opulent* police-protected society? Why this *lone, lone war*, knowing as I do the dreadful self-destructive *price* of it all?

All this and more I think of *now*, 1969, sitting here typing this story of life-long absurdity, life-long *waste* . . waste of the *years* . . waste of *power* . . *vitality* . . *creative force*. I still don't know the *answer*. *All I do* know is this: so far as I am able the villainy-thing is *out* . . *out* . . *out*.

To resume the story: I go back to villainy. I have no special plan . . just go where the money is . . "Help yourself, plenty where *that* came from". I'm *lucky* . . lots of gear comes my way, some of it so lovely I keep it for me, decorating *my* home, my *temporary theft-bought home*. I collect *old clocks* . . I love to hear the clocks *ticking* . . *ticking* . . *they* are *talking* . . *talking to me* in that lonely pad. I collect *pictures* . . I stand and *stare* at their *rare beauty* . . the other gear I'd practically *give away*, having *no commercial sense* and knowing that there is *lots more where that came from*.

I go down to the coast . . breathe that ozonic air, that *free* air . . I look at the sea stretching away to that far *horizon*. I feel I'm on *top* of the world. As for girls . . women . . dogs . . buses . .

taxis . . trains . . I *love them all* . . this is *life* . . *life* . . *freedom* . . *freedom* . . .

I go to Eastbourne, that fine old resort for the people of taste and wealth. I get me a ground-floor flat . . living-room, bedroom, bathroom, and kitchenette and hallway, furnished tastefully with collector's pieces. This to *me* is *home* . . contrasting with the old jail-peter . . which has been my home for interminable years. I go out for the evening . . I'm alone, know nobody, but my state of mind is *gay* . . I feel good. I . . I am *free* . . that street is *mine* . . that shop-front, that window-display is *mine*. Outside that shop is a notice-board: *vacancies* for *work* . . for *lodgings*. I see a little woman . . quite *undistinguished* with blinking eyes . . trying to read the notice-board . . clearly her sight is *not* good. "Can I help you to read the thing?" I ask. "What is it you want to know?"

The little woman turns, blinks at me and says: "I'm looking for a room to let." Thus I meet Celia. Celia, is unassuming, undemanding, humorous and very *lonely*. She lives alone and joins her family once a week for dinner. I take Celia to an eating-place . . bless her . . she doesn't want *caviar* and *Campari* . . She is very very abstemious . . doesn't drink or smoke . . but she likes sweets . . . I was getting to like this little lonely woman . . .

From time to time I go out villainy-bent . . take the gear to a fellow in Brighton calling himself a dealer, an *art dealer*. He is a bastard . . mean . . calculating . . *false*. He invariably says that the gear I bring him is too hot to handle, and I, impatient to get back to my little Celia, answer: "O.K. give me a fair price, let me get out of here." His fair price is bare-faced *robbery* . . .

I return to Eastbourne, take Celia to a dance-hall . . it is a *gala* night . . we dance . . dance . . dance . . we laugh . . Later I take her home with me. *She* has *misgivings* . . we get in bed . . she is very shy . . can't look me in the face. I ask her to put that thing in there . . . She . . . she . . recoils as if it was a dangerous *snake* . . . Later I convince her that it is *not* a *snake* but a very charming little thing. Afterwards Celia gets to *liking it*.

The day came when circumstances beyond my control forced me to leave Eastbourne. *This* I regretted. I was performing in a private house, looking for gear, when I heard the front-door open. I froze right there in the bedroom . . recovered quickly . . fixed the door . . went to the window . . I heard someone screaming for *police*. They must have discovered that the back door had been forced. I dropped that gear all packed-up in a suit-case and *leapt* through the window (mercifully a ground-floor window). I was in a large garden with a wall facing towards the sea beyond. I jumped the wall and *ran* . . *ran* . . *all* the time hearing those *screams* . . *police* . . *police* . . .

I get on to a nearby road with a row of houses, beautiful houses. I go up the path to one of the houses . . ring the bell . . *no answer* . . ring again . . no answer . . smash the glass-panel . . put my hand in . . turn the lock . . . and . . I'm *safe* . . *safe*. I look around . . nice furnishings . . portable television . . leather bag. I quickly pack it with any valuables I can find . . not noticing that there are already in the bag some *documents*. As I've no hat or coat and may have been seen leaving that other house, I take a smart hat and a well-fitting coat. Then I grab television set and bag and get *out*. I go straight to a telephone box and dial for a taxi. When it comes, I ask for the station . . get out there . . change taxis . . go to my place . . pack my clothes . . other gear . . and leave resolving to come back one day for my little Celia.

I go to Brighton . . get a flat in Hove, right near the sea . . I could *hear* the sea, and sometimes by stretching my neck I could *see* it, too.

I felt *good*. The south-coast air did me a lot of good. I began to relax. I'd walk . . walk . . all along the water-front, from Hove or Portslade to Rottingdean. I'd *sing* . . *sing*. One day on the promenade I was stopped and asked: "Do you *sing* at the Hippodrome? I'd like your *autograph*." *Me* . . *me*, I just laugh and go on *singing* . . *singing* for *joy* . . joy of *life* . . of *freedom*.

I settle in at Hove, sell the television set for next to nothing as usual . . the *robber buyer* pretending the set was *red hot*. The documents which I didn't at first see in that bag turned out to be *war office* . . *top secret*. I promptly put them in the post returning them to the owner, a *top war office army officer*. Funnily enough, when later I stood trial for this robbery amongst others, I got *not one word of thanks* for this honourable behaviour; that I could have flogged them to a *foreign power* was not even mentioned . . so much for *principles* which even I, a *thief*, demonstrated . . .

At Brighton I had a woman friend called Sue whom I'd known way back in 1959. She was a *drunk*, dead drunk most of the time. She was intelligent, cockily *independent* . . slim . . dark . . good-looking . . and she walked like a queen. She had been married three times and had four children, three boys and one girl. The boys I met and liked very much. Sue fascinated me: she cared for those children, in fact was *devoted* to them. She saw to their schooling and their clothing. The girl lived with Sue's mother, but the boys lived with Sue.

I'd go to bed with Sue, lovin' her as best I could, but she was either drunk and *couldn't* care . . or cold and *didn't* care. One night Sue said to me: "Nick, you haven't *satisfied me*." I was *thunderstruck*. I didn't know she even knew I was performing. I got angry . . put my clothes on . . was going *away* . . then I had second thoughts . . came back, and *satisfied her* . . .

This Sue bothered me. I liked her style . . she was cocky in a delightful sort of way . . very honest and forthright . . she was a good and amusing talker . . was food-wise . . wine-wise . . was equally at home eating fish and chips or delicately savouring that Royal Sturgeon . . *but* she wouldn't *stop* drinking and was hardly ever *sober*. When she *was* sober, she always had a hang-over (except that once when she said I did not *satisfy her*). I tried to wean her from the drink thing. I even had notions of asking her to come away with me, children and all . . . Finally, however, I found her at a local club *dead* drunk and havering about the *heavy mob*, her name for the local squad-police responsible for raids on clubs and other places, coming to their notice as *undesirable*. I tried persuasion . . I tried cajoling. Then I walked out and from that day *Sue* was no longer in my blood.

I paid a flying-visit to Eastbourne and took Celia out. We went to a very nice small hotel and registered as man and wife. That night, my *last* with Celia though I did not know it at the time, we bathed together. Then went to bed and made love . . Celia, as usual, was not too *demonstrative* but clearly she enjoyed the experience. Next morning we had breakfast . . a nice breakfast for two . . an 'at *home*' breakfast . . cornflakes . . cream . . hot toast . . marmalade . . eggs . . bacon . . coffee. All this is very commonplace to the *permanently free* and fairly *opulent*, but to *me this meal had* a kind of *dignity*, a kind of *personal worth* and *meaning* . . .

I say goodbye to *Celia*, give her a few pounds . . and go my way, alone again.

Before leaving the Eastbourne area I look around for possible loot. I find a house in its own grounds . . it's good to look at . . I go up that path, intending to ring the bell, but when I touch the door, it *swings open*. I step in, wondering why the door is unlatched. I hear an old old querulous voice, a woman's: "Is that you, doctor? Please come up." I guess the door had been left open for the doctor . . I look up and there is a dear old woman, straight out of Galsworthy, leaning over the first-floor banister. Obviously her sight must be bad, as she mistakes *me* for the *doctor*. Nothing daunted, I go up the stairs. The old woman beckons me into a nearby room.

I enter the room and my old lady is seated in a chair in front of a glowing fire. "The drops are on the mantelpiece, Doctor," she says and I realise the drops must be for her sight. I pick the bottle up and administer those drops just like a professional. The old lady thanks me and I leave the room (but not before I have taken a look at all the period stuff in the room . . china . . pictures . . clocks . . silver). I turn away . . I *can't* rob this old dear. I'm going down the stairs . . the walls are lined with very fine pictures . . some genuine, some reproductions . . I see a Franz Hals, a copy but *good*, I take it as a *souvenir* . . put it under my arm . . and walk out.

I move from Hove to Portslade near the sea. I get me a small suite of rooms in a private house kept by a Victorian old lady, *very very respectable*. The house belongs to her daughter, who lives in another house in Hove. I meet my landlady. She is very gracious, playfully so, very nice . . until I talk of *two sheets* a *week* instead of *one*, until I talk of an *improved hot-water system* in the bathroom. Then my gracious one explodes into *vulgarity* . . and I leave this cursed woman's bloody house.

I go back to Hove, get me a ground-floor room in a period house, all Georgian . . the entrance-hall is marble and gilt-mirrored. I soon discover all the guests are period-pieces too, except for *one* woman . . large . . genial . . smokes *cigars* . . and, I suspect, a *lesbian*. We talk sometimes . . she is a *mid-European* who came to England because "There ees more *leeberty* in thees, your country." As usual with me on meeting almost any female, I want to bed her down, but she says: "*Meester . . Meester . . I . . I . . am not like that* at *all*." Yes, she was a lesbian and not my kind of female.

At this time I am posing as a dealer in objets d'art, not making any money, merely accounting for my interest in *all* things *beautiful*. I meet a widow, *full* of *money* I gather. She has a set of lovely *pearls* which need cleaning. She asks *me* to get them cleaned for her, which I do, not even *thinking* of *knocking them off*. It amuses me to do this legitimate business. I like the idea of being trusted with the pearls. I arrange with a local jeweller to do the cleaning. I am *accepted* by the jeweller as a bona-fide dealer. This woman insists on *watching* the cleaning being done as she did not *trust* that jeweller. Afterwards I hear from the jeweller that *madame*, this bloody woman of *wealth*, wasn't too keen on *paying the bill* . . saying it was far too much. Me . . me, I am *disgusted* !

I go out for the evening. I eat where the food is *good*, at a famous oyster restaurant. There I see a charming waitress. I date her, later, and meet her as she comes out of work. We go for a drink. She asks me to buy some whisky and cigarettes, a most expensive brand. Then she takes me home to a fine modern flat outside Brighton. She is called Diana and is Irish. She has ideas of one day having her *own* business, a guest house perhaps.

Diana was the poet's *dream* of an Irish girl or woman . . she was pale . . had jet-black hair . . lovely *dark, passionate eyes* . . a figure that was very very *provocative*. I soon discovered that this woman, Diana, had some secret sorrow and she drank, drank to drown the sorrow, champagne being her choice. We drank champagne even in the early morning. One or two days after meeting Diana I suggest it's about time we had some lovin'. She asks me : "Would you marry me ?"

I . . I say : "Yes, when ?"

"Thursday . . Thursday," says Diana. I agree. In the meantime, Diana tells me, I must call on her mother. I do so and she asks me : "Didn't Diana *tell* you ?"

"Tell *me* ? Tell me what ?"

"She's *already married*, separated but *still married*." I am furious . . I've been to a jeweller and got an engagement ring . . a wedding ring on *order*. I've sought a friend of mine, the maître-d'hôtel of a well-known hotel, to be my best man and to arrange all the wedding-feasting. And now . . now I have to cancel all the arrangements.

Eventually I saw the funny side of it all, became reconciled to Diana, and went to a party at Diana's mother's place. I supplied *all* the drinks and expensive sandwiches. We sang Irish folk-songs and the whole party got wildly drunk, myself doing the light-fantastic, dancing on chairs, tables, all over the place. It was a *crazy* party but I loved every bit of it . . *crying* . . *weeping* at the sad Irish songs . . the *laments* . . and *laughing* . . *laughing* at the irresistible *humour* of the comic Irish situation . . .

Now my money is running short . . I decide to move on, along the south coast . . I stop at Bognor. What decided me to stop off at *that* place, to this day *I know not*.

All hotels are *full up*, but while I'm talking to a hotel-manager, asking if he can't fix me up *somewhere* in his crowded hotel, I hear this voice, a woman's voice, a very nice voice saying: "I can fix you up for a few days. I have a small room at present *vacant*."

Thus I meet yet another of these *eternal females* with whom I *always* have some kind of rapport, some kind of life more or less intimate, but *never* of permanent value nor capable of dissuading me from my chosen course of *villainy*—though that might have come from Liz had I not *already* been *trapped* and *held* in that jail-sentence of twelve years.

My landlady is very good-looking, a smart turn-out, married with two children and a husband . . working in London five days a week. I move into this woman's house. I am very attracted to her, but she goes out playing golf all day. In my travels I pick up quite a lot of gear, and I give a piece I like to my landlady as she has expressed *admiration* of it. She thinks I am a *dealer*.

I burgle a nearby house, take away pictures and china. I carry it over to the place I'm living in. My landlady sees the gear. (I have been to a sale, I tell her.) She fancies a picture . . it will fit in with her living-room style of furnishing. I give her the picture. Meantime I don't try anything on with this woman.

My landlady's husband will be returning for the weekend and her son will soon be home from school so I move on. However, I am still *addicted* to *Bognor, respectable Victorian Bognor*. I don't realise that, in *all* my beach-wear *glory*, offering pictures for sale, clocks to be valued, I am *bound* to arouse suspicion in the minds of these convention-ridden people who won't even go to the pee-house without an *overcoat on* and *that* in *mid-summer*! I find fresh digs. This landlady is dignified, stately and *guaranteed above reproach*. I do some more villainy, pick up some *devastating perfume*, and give it to my landlady, telling her it was bought at a sale with other things. In my room at this new hide-out I have put pictures on the wall . . clocks over there . . candelabra here . . and I walk around, looking at all this beauty . . crazy, of course, but that was *me*: *drunk* with the *illusion* of *freedom*, with the *illusion* of *independence*. Having some more money, I change into light sports' clothes and . . go over to Brighton.

All this time I'm living as if this was the *real thing*, not dreaming that under my feet was a very thin crust of *good earth*, that I was treading very, very dangerous ground. *Lost, trapped,* I sing . . dance . . make love . . behave as if the angels were protecting me.

After leaving Brighton I stop off at a small fishing-port between Brighton and Hove and Bognor. I liked the place, with its houses almost in the sea. I get talking to a man about the possibility of accommodation. Down the street, coming our way, are a tall man and a young girl. The fellow talking to me says: "Excuse me, but that is my brother-in-law. He's on holiday staying with us. *He's in the Prison Service*." I say: "I . . I . . don't think I'll stay here after all," and taking *one look* at this Prison Service fellow, I beat it *quick*! Strange . . strange . . *that* was the *writing on the wall*, if I had *only realised it*. I was very very near giving that kind of fellow some *employment*, but *I did not know it then*.

I go on my way to Bognor, arriving at my temporary home, feeling very *good* . . after all, I was free. I arrive at my lodgings, and there in the hallway is the landlady, a great big *Edwardian smile* all over her face. "Oh, good morning. There are *two gentlemen to see you, Sir*. I showed them into your room." '*Two gentlemen*'—Christ! Christ! Those words . . . I nearly panic, but decide I'll face the music. I enter my room and there they are, sitting in my most comfortable chairs, *admiring* the *pictures* on the *wall*. As I step in that room, I'm greeted with: "Good morning, Sir, we are police officers investigating a robbery in a local house and we think you might be able to help in our enquiries." *Me . . me*, I just stand there. "We have a car outside. If you care to come quietly, we can go without fuss. The Inspector would like to see you." Inwardly I'm *dead . . dead*, but I appear calm enough. We leave the house, enter the car and drive off. I see the landlady peeping through the *window*.

XXI

I'M TAKEN TO the police-centre in Bognor and charged with burglary, in a Bognor house, of pictures, china, a period clock .. some of these things were actually in my possession at the digs where the police were waiting for me. I'm told: "Help us. Don't give us any trouble and we will help *you*." This meant I had to admit *everything*, fight nothing, and go with the police in *all* their efforts to *convict*. "We know who you really are," they say. "We know of *all* your activities along the South Coast, but help us to recover the gear and we will endeavour to get you off very lightly .. maybe three years .. maybe probation again." I'm helpless, stunned, bewildered. I know the danger is considerable: I have no real friends, only a few pounds left of all my 'earnings' .. then there is this thing right down there below my heart .. *cold fear*. I agree to help the police, sign *everything, twenty-four counts* .. all for burglary or house-breaking .. items to the value of six thousand pounds. I'm told: "Don't worry, Victor, only one charge will be preferred, all others 'taken into consideration'." I'm *mesmerised*, completely *hood-winked*. I sign *everything*. There have been *no* warrants for my arrest. A *similarity* of *method* in the burglaries was the *clue* for police.

I'm treated as an *important* person .. fed well .. allowed the remnant of my cigars .. allowed the use of the radio found in my possession. I am kept in the lock-up for some days before my *public appearance* at the Magistrates' Court. Little by little there is a formidable *indictment* against me. I am interviewed by many other top police, all of whom are delighted with this easy capture, this easy *conviction* .. *self* .. *self*-conviction. Finally I am remanded to jail, Lewes Prison. I don't ask for legal aid, because I *trusted* the *police* to keep their word and get me a light sentence. I even plead guilty to charges they *could never prove*!

All this time I'm in a strange out-of-this-world condition, swinging from *deep depression* to *high excitement* .. flattered by all this police-attention, *sickened* at *mine own folly*. I write to Victor Gollancz from Lewes Prison. I write to Tom Tullett of the

Mirror. Both of these men have been interested in me in days gone by. I offer to write my story *before sentence*, thinking: If I succeed in this, there will be some security for me after sentence is done. The stuff I *write* is *awful, crazy crap* stemming from my disturbed condition of mind. Mr. Gollancz writes that *regretfully* he can't use this *fragmentary .. wild .. disordered stuff*. Tullett didn't even *reply*. Meantime I'm back in a *jail condition .. cells .. corridors .. gates .. bars*. It's true I have my *own clothes on*, even get some food from the *free world*, but those *gates* are about to *close on me again*. I get a visit from the television people .. they want my story and offer a *contract*. I am *elated*, thinking at *last* there may be *something* for me after release, some kind of security to keep me from the necessity for *thieving*. These TV people say: "We have heard *all* about you, for and *against*. We are *sure* there is a *story* in your life." Their contract claims *all* rights of every kind in my life .. it's book, paper, film, television rights in *return* for *what they choose to leave me*. I tear this damned phoney thing to bits, later enjoying *their discomfiture* when they learn the *sentence of the court*. I reflected then that there *wouldn't be any television* when I finished this lot. But I am getting ahead of myself. Meanwhile I turn up at the Magistrates' for the last time and am committed for trial at the Chichester quarter session court on September 22, 1963.

There are two possible judges for me .. one, they say, *good* .. the other *bad*. I get the *bad one* . . .

I return to Lewes Jail. There is a letter waiting for me: the Yorkshire widow has found me again and reproaches me for not coming to her after my release from Dartmoor Prison. "My home is still your welcome," she says, "if you get away with it at your trial."

Whilst at Lewes Jail, I'm lucky in that I get the *only* large-windowed cell on the landing .. it's normally reserved for T.B. cases. I'm in there one day when the door opens to admit a *woman* and a screw. I'm asked: "Do you want to see the Visiting Magistrate?" I don't like Visiting Magistrates, but this one looked very nice. I invite her into my room, take her to the window and point to the wall. On top of it are two little birds, obviously very much in love. I say: "Nature provides a *mate* for *birds*, but *not so* the *prison authorities .. no mate for me*." The woman *smiles* and goes out saying: "Maybe you will find that mate when you are free again."

It is after this that I see the TV people. When I get back to the wing after their visit, expecting a bumper parcel from these precious *television* men, I find they have left me, their *client*, their *potential money-maker,* a *lousy packet of cigarettes.* They were not even *good* cigarettes . . and . . that's why, together with their dubious, phoney talk, I tore up that bloody contract. These shits I never heard of again during the *rest* of my time in jail. They said they were friends of a man I knew, but where the dickens he picked up the bastards I know not nor do I care.

A word or two about this man: he was a very clever, intelligent youngster whom I met briefly in jail when he was serving a comparatively short sentence of corrective training. He came of good family, had a loving mother, but was a bit wild. I gathered he had learnt the trade of carpentering, but he was *ambitious* . . he was not staying in the *building trade.* He took up *photography* and to judge by his work which I saw some years ago now, he has good prospects. He was very generous, very kind and very helpful to me when he saw me for the first time after my release from jail. It was when I was on the door of the Newsreel Theatre in Leicester Square . . . He stops and stares, not *believing his eyes*! He comes over to me and we talk. He gives me his address which is round the corner quite close by. Later I call on him . . I am *welcomed*, fed, offered money if it is needed . . he even offers me some of his smart clothes till I could buy some of my own . . Later, much later, we go down to Trafalgar Square. I get those pigeons on my arms, shoulders, head, and he takes photographs. I lost him for a time after that, but in 1963, down there on the south coast, now in the *money*, I invited him to come down as my guest and, I'm glad to say, I entertained him right *royally.* Then I lost him again until, as I've said, those odd television people came to Lewes Prison mentioning his name. That's the last I heard of him.

So I get nearer and nearer to my *day* of *destiny.* I am *caged* but not yet cuffed, not yet 'chained' . . *jailed* but not yet *convicted.* The day of trial arrives . . I'm taken down to Chichester by car with two screws as my escort. I am hand-cuffed . . they are taking *no chances.*

In the cells down below the court are many men, *all* in a state of *suppressed excitement*: after all, whether or not they return to wife, family and freedom, *that day* will be decided. It will be decided by a man who will act *strictly according to the law* . . and the *law* is not only an *ass,* but sometimes *a mad vicious ass* as well.

—What are *you* in for, mate?

—So I says to this *copper*: come off it, mate, you knows *I couldn't have done it,* I was in bed with the missus.

—Last time I was 'ere it was Sir Jeremy . . 'e was a toff, lets me orf wiv a fine.

—Blimey, mate, if you get that *block* fellow, he'll knock *your* block off.

Me . . *me*, I am wishing I was *dead*, wishing I was *alone*, away from all this chatter . . wishing . . wishing . . .

Finally, at the end of that weary day with *all* the chatterers dealt with and the peter empty, I face the stark reality, the *end-product* of a failed *villain* . . a *fool* . . a *mug*.

A screw summons me. As I leave that peter to go upstairs, I see one of those coppers . . he is holding out to me a *ring*, a gold ring with a heart and two clasped hands on it, *Cladagh* ring, Bridget's gift to me. He's saying: "We've found out that you did not steal this ring so you can have it." I put that ring on my finger wondering whether I would ever see Bridget again.

I go upstairs, escorted by a screw on either side. The court is held in a barely-furnished room, rather like a school-room in a not very good school . . *sombre* . . silent except for rustling papers, an occasional cough and whispers. I notice the court is *empty* . . as if on purpose: *justice* must *not* be *seen* to be *done*. I see a reporter, a court official and the *inevitable policeman*, also my man, the 'artist' who had wheedled me into unprovable *admissions*, the police officer in charge of the case.

I'm directed into a *box*, a *coffin* standing on its *end*, with a very narrow seat, obviously not intended for *leisure* or *comfort*. On either side of me is a screw. I'm told to sit down. I look *up*: same old *theatre setting* . . same old crap . . a sort of throne with two lesser thrones one on either side . . a clock . . . I'm thinking: *Time* . . *time* . . how *long will it stop* for *me*?

The court is silenced . . people rise . . up there I note a man, expressionless except for a slight *sneer* as if he despised us all . . he looks like a farm-hand . . next to him is another man . . then a woman . . at least she is *dressed* as a *woman* . . but she has *no* sign of *gentleness*, of *pity* or *compassion* . . she might be the female *counterpart* of that *farm-hand*. Below these high and mighty thrones and their occupants is another man, also seeming to be without any flicker of *warmth* or *feeling*. He looks at me. "Victor Carasov, you are charged with various serious offences against property. Are you *guilty* or *not guilty*?" *Me,* I look at this man who *might* be asking if it's *wet* or *fine*, who *might* be asking *any frivolous question* instead of asking a *question* involving years . . years of *life* . . *my life* . . .

I look down to see if that policeman is around, the one who persuaded me to plead guilty. I see him . . he looks at me, as it were, *regretfully* . . as it were, with *pity* . . *pity* that I should be *such* a *mug*. Relying as I am on police promises, still trusting this fellow and his assurance that there would be only *one* charge to answer, *I plead guilty*. That means in effect that I am *now sentenced*. All that remains is for evidence to be given. The police give their evidence . . *bad* for *me* . . the Prosecution then recount my dreadful record, missing nothing that will do me the maximum harm. Very *slight* reference is made to the *recovery* of £2,400 worth of goods, allowing the court to infer that the recovery was due entirely to *police efficiency. No* reference is made to *my essential information* given to them under promise of *clemency* to come. As a final blow, the court is not even told of the treatment Maudsley Hospital doctors believe I need. However, there *is* a reference to my time in Broadmoor, obviously intended to make the court think I am a *very, very dangerous man,* Broadmoor being *notorious* as a holding-station for *vicious criminals*. (This is in fact untrue: many of Broadmoor's inmates are *totally harmless*.) Next the court asks if there is any more evidence. A Probation Officer gets up (a man I've never seen before) and *he* says: "I'm instructed to say that this man had an *army* of *friends* to help him when he last left jail . . he was given a chance by getting probation for his last offence." He omits to tell the court that my last offence was so petty they could hardly have given me *anything* more than probation. Also I was at that time considered *sick* and in need of psychiatric treatment.

On instructions from some unnamed authority, the Probation Officer ends by saying that I deserved *no mercy*. Mercy would be *wasted* on me . . .

My '*army*' of friends numbered *two* . . the 'help' given was *financial* only . . what I needed was *acceptance* . . *love* . . *affection*.

In *all* this evidence not *one* word is said in my *favour* . . no reference to the return of *top-secret papers* . . no reference to the old lady I treated with eye-drops . . no reference to my continued help to police after my arrest . . no reference to my *eagerness* to recover stolen property which I had *unwittingly* taken, not knowing of its *sentimental value*. Lastly no reference is made to my *disturbed condition*, all the way through from shop-lifting to attempting to sell pictures in the *open market*, all dolled-up in magnificent beach wear. In fact, let's face it: my papers are marked . . the order has come through: *no mercy here . . no mercy* for ***this one***.

I know now that, not withstanding my disturbed condition, I *had* let good friends down. I had perhaps even let down the judge who originally gave me *probation*, though I'm doubtful of the wisdom of that: enforced hospitalisation might have been best for me. Also I acknowledge full responsibility for my villainy . . *I did* merit *correction*. But for *all* that, I remained a man, very lonely, very disturbed, very *uneasy* at *mine own self-destructive course*. Whilst *guilty* I still felt that something . . something in my favour was sadly *absent*.

At this court, before sentence, I'm asked if I have anything to say. Me . . me I *explode* . . I denounce a prison system which had *failed*, over a period of *forty* years to *deflect me from my course* of *villainy* . . I denounce the unfavourable comments from a Probation Officer who has not even *met* me . . I tell of the repeated sackings from work, especially the job for the police catering service which I did *well*. Finally I say: "If over forty years in jail has not *stopped my return to villainy*, surely the court will see the *unwisdom* of sending me *back* to *prison*."

The court adjourns . . I *hope . . hope* . . for *clemency*. The court returns . . the sentence is read: "You, Victor Carasov, will go to *prison* for *twelve years*."

XXII

SO I START on that last lap of jail-journeyings, a long long lap, it's true. I could be seventy-two when this lap is completed . . long after man is supposed to be fit to manage his affairs. At the earliest I'll be sixty-eight unless . . unless that elusive thing, *luck* comes my way and the *unforgiving* prison commission recommends me for *parole* . . and *nothing* in this world is *more unlikely*.

After sentence I go down below to await that bus or police van to transport me and the others to our immediate destination . . some men to the Scrubs . . some back to the remand centre . . others, me included, to Wandsworth . . .

All this time I'm *bemused* . . *befuddled*. That crazy past of mine reveals itself on the screen of my inner self as if it were a television show. I think of Celia . . Elizabeth . . Bridget . . Mary . . Diana . . . I think of serving beer and food to the finest . . . I think of my little film-star . . . I think of that saga of mine which might have been written . . . *all* this I ponder as the bus moves along through country scenes . . old-world Sussex villages . . small towns. I see the people . . the shops . . an occasional dog . . the posters advertising things I'll *never get* . . not for at least eight years anyway, maybe twelve. As I see newsagents . . bookshops . . I reflect that's where my book should be on display.

We arrive outside that gate . . it opens . . we move in . . the gate closes . . another gate opens . . we move on . . it *closes*. This is it . . *Wandsworth* . . cold . . harsh . . hardly *human*. From now on I . . I am *nobody*, a mere *body*, a mere *parcel* at the mercy of *any prison official* concerned in handling *me* till jail-sentence ends. I'm no longer a free man. Everything's done for me and to me without even *consulting* me.

From time to time I have to remind the reader that this saga of mine is not *intended* to be an *indictment* of the *prison system*. If there is *any indictment* it's *me* who should bear the accusation: I am the villain of this piece. On the other hand I have had a *unique*, front-seat view of the prison scene . . from way back in 1920 (not to mention the reform school scene in 1915) right through till now, 1969. For over fifty years I have seen the prison scene grow and develop as I have grown and developed in those years. As I have *changed* in many ways, so has the prison system, and so has its *administration*. But just as I have still got much to change and *improve*, so, needless to say, has the prison system. So here is my dilemma: I wish to tell of *all* my experiences in and out of *jail* . . I must be *truthful*, but not biased . . not unfair . . above all, *not bitter* or *sour*. Yet *I am bitter* . . sometimes *sour* . . sometimes even *unwittingly unfair*. So please accept my assurance that whatever is said about this prison thing, the law thing, the *punishing thing*, I'll try to make it *true* but *fair* . . seeing *their* point of view as well as my *own*.

I'm here in Wandsworth Jail, a very tough place, but then the inmates are tough, too. Maybe the jail has to meet toughness with toughness. Be that as it may, this toughness seems to me to lack *perspective*. The Wandsworth regime makes *no discrimination* between one inmate and another, thus perpetrating *gross unfairness* and *cruelty* on harmless inmates who only want to be left in peace. For the rest . . food . . work . . general living conditions at Wandsworth are no better and no worse than in other *jails* . .

I remained at Wandsworth Prison for approximately fourteen months. During that time I touched depths of *self*-contempt, of utter *sickness* of heart . . of *mind* . . of *soul*. For years I had fought my way through the prison situation . . for years I had used every device known to the imprisoned to *beat* the *jailer*. Now time was catching up with me: I was getting older . . shortly I would be *dead* . . and that epitaph would say: "*Here lies nothing*. It *did* nothing, *said* nothing, *left* nothing before *passing on*." This I did not like. There were stirrings of what a cleric would call *conscience*. I was questioning my *right* to live the life I had been living. I was wondering: had I any moral right to *rob*, to *hurt* other people? Above all, had I any right to *misuse* this *brain* . . this *spirit* . . this *body*?

Three episodes stand out from my time in Wandsworth Prison:

I'm in my peter and they have just served supper. I have a letter to write which I want to go next morning. I haven't a pen so I ring the bell . . a screw comes: "*Well?* What do you want?"

"I need a pen to write a letter. The man next door has a ball-pen, will you ask him to lend it to me, please?"

"Do you mean to tell me that *all* you rang that bell for was to get a pen?" The screw then *banged* that door on me and the letter was not written *that* night.

I'm in the mailbags shop making tabs sitting at a table with about ten other men. A screw shouts: "Pack up and *stop talking*!" A kind of nutter on my table goes on talking. We get up from the table and file out of the shop. As those on our table reach the door, the screw asks each one of us for our number and cell-location. This means he's going to report *all* of us for the offence of talking. I don't like it: it's *gestapo* stuff. I stay behind and say to the screw: "Don't you think it's *unfair* to report *all* the men for *one* man's offence?"

This screw looks at me. He looks at the other screws in the shop. I thought he was going to strike me . . I was *ready*, but all he did was say: "Go on . . get *out*." I got out, joined the file of men. "*No talking. Button your jacket up. Get* a *move on*."

I'm back in my peter, glad to be in this hide-out, this temporary sanctuary. The next morning I expect to be reported, but no, the screw *must* have decided not to make that report.

On another occasion my door *opens* . . a screw says: "Pack your kit up. Go downstairs. We want this cell for another man." *Me* . . *me,* I hesitate: after all this peter is my *temporary home*. I've cleaned it up. "Come on, get going." I get going down to the *basement* . . *dirty* . . *gloomy* . . *smelly* . . *I* don't like it . . *more gestapo* stuff. I tell the principal officer of my grievance and he says: "Carasov, I remember *you* from the *past*. You are a *changed man*. Once upon a time you wouldn't have asked to see me. You would have started trouble-making. I'm sorry we had to move you . . I didn't realise that this new cell down here would be *dirty*. As soon as possible I will get you back up there in a *clean cell*." The next day I was sent back upstairs.

Finally, before leaving this *cold comfort station,* Wandsworth Prison, here is another story . . a good one . . a *human* one. I hear the key in the lock of my door . . the door opens and there is a *stranger* . . a tall, very large man, very fat. He's in free-world clothing, perfectly fitting his well-rounded body . . his clothes I note are of good quality . . "May I come in?" he asks. I reluctantly say "Yes". This man introduces himself . . he is a Quaker, an unofficial visitor to Wandsworth and Wormwood Scrubs *prisons*. He talks about this and that. *Me* . . *me,* I don't want to talk, especially with free-world people. That reminds me of *lost freedom, lost life*, free-world *life* . . .

My Quaker visitor leaves me, promising to call again . . before I leave Wandsworth Prison on the next stage of my jail-journey. This visitor, Basil Burton, came again and again, never obtruding upon my *inner life* yet being *well aware* of it. He brought books . . he brought papers . . he would sit there in *silence* on the occasions when I *could not speak* . . *lost* . . *lost,* as I often was, in my inner world. One day I'm told: "You are off to Parkhurst Prison, *tomorrow*" . . and I see Mr. Burton for the *last time.* He shakes my hand . . wishes me well. From *that* day to *this* I've not seen Mr. Burton, but for the *last six years* or so he has never failed to send me a weekly paper which I once said was a very very *human* paper, concerned with *ordinary folk* . . ordinary human folk doing *unadvertised* acts of simplicity and *goodness.* I've not forgotten this man Basil Burton, a *Quaker gentleman* . . .

Another Quaker, my old friend Mrs Phillis Taunton Wood, was a faithful correspondent during my stay in Wandsworth. She was an artist . . she painted wonderful sea-scapes . . horses . . birds. She was also a healer of things *spiritual,* in fact a *good woman.* I had on one or two occasions got her all *wrong,* and been momentarily *angry* but I was always able to *recover* myself.

At this time I again start thinking about the *writing lark.* So I write to Phillis Wood and ask her to find me a *real, live* writer with whom I could correspond . . someone who might help me in my efforts to write that story down. (It's only of recent months that it's come home to me that I *don't need any help* in this writing lark. For years I have failed to realise this, chiefly, I think, because *I didn't believe in my own powers* . . my *own creative powers.*) After a time Phillis Wood writes to me that she has found me a *writer,* a *real, live* writer . . a *woman* of great character . . talent . . *experience.* I don't *believe it*! Then I get a letter: "Your friend, Phillis Wood, tells me you want to know and write to a *real, live* writer. Well, I am a *writer,* real enough, and I think live enough! If you would like to write to me or have me visit you, please let me know. I'll be delighted to help you in any way I can." *This* is the manner in which I met the "woman of whom *Nottingham should be proud*" as was written of Miss Dorothy Fisk, writer, traveller, actress, a woman who has travelled *alone* right across the Siberian Steppes and brought up a family of four boys, too. This is Dorothy Fisk, my good and loyal friend. She came in at the start of my long long journey, and after over seven years of storms and stresses she is *still my friend.*

This little woman came to see me for the first time in November of 1964. She was small, pert and lively. She was no beauty, but she gave off a kind of *power*, a *capacity* for *doing things her* way. She was dressed in a well-fitting two-piece . . *tweedy* . . her shoes were for walking . . and her hat, a *cocky*, *saucy* little thing . . her handbag was for *use*, not *ornament*.

Dorothy and I very soon got to know each other. I talked thirteen to the dozen while she led me on by showing a *keen interest* in everything I *said*. The visit ended, *Wandsworth*-style, when thirty minutes were up. Dorothy promised to come again as *soon* as visits were permitted. We parted . . *me* . . *me*, I had never been so stimulated mentally by any other woman, I had known.

I return to the shop. Someone says: "Good visit, *Nick*?" I say: "Yes, *wonderful*, but I'll never see her again. Her kind ain't going to bother about *my* kind. Besides, it *would be too good to be true* for *her* to stay around." Time passes and I'm told I am off to Parkhurst the very next day. I panic: am I not going to see Dorothy Fisk again? I see the P.O. and ask if it is possible to have my friend, Dorothy Fisk, invited to come and see me *that* night. The P.O., much to my surprise, says: "Leave it to me." An hour or so later I'm *told* by the Welfare Officer that Miss Fisk is coming. And so she *does*. She drops everything to come and see me! She looks *great*, very very much *alive*. They put the red carpet down for Dorothy . . the visit is in the Solicitor's Room with the screw *outside* . . he can *see* but *not listen*. This *kindness* of the Wandsworth authorities in allowing me special facilities for our visit I appreciated. This was real humanity in what I considered an *inhuman sort* of *place*!

I move on to Parkhurst Prison. The familiar trip: bus, boat, bus, and there we are. *Gates* . . *gates* to be opened and *closed*. *This* is the *hallmark* of all Her Majesty's jails—an *opening gate* and *always* the *closing gate*. In fact, I recommend to the House of Heralds the following devices for jails: two gates with hand-cuffs and a lead-weighted baton superimposed . . *sinister* . . .

I'm not very long back here in Parkhurst before screws from way back are *actually shaking my hand* as if I were *one of them*. Indeed, the truth is that sometimes screws and cons resemble each other in behaviour in prison.

My stay at Parkhurst was *mercifully* short. During my time

there I heard stories, fairy-tales I thought they were, about a place called *Blundeston*, a *new look* prison: *No* bars except in the form of window-frames . . elsewhere . . the dining-halls, stairwells, front door . . all had delightful *ornamental bars* to *please* the *eye* as well as *hold that body* . . *no* walls, a *wire fence* only, topped with a tiddly-bit of *playful barbed-wire*. Inside this fairy-tale place were fitted rooms with central-heating . . hot and cold water . . well-appointed wash-houses with flush toilets . . bath-house with showers and baths, too . . *all* this wrapped up in an *unbelievably permissive system* within which the tired and poor old inmate could *do anything he liked* short of *murder*! Well, needless to say, I did *not believe* a *word* of *this*. In any case, I was out of the running: no one in their senses, their 'head-office' senses, would send me there.

However, just before Christmas in 1964, I am asked if I would like to go to Blundeston . . one man has dropped out on medical grounds. Me . . me, I am in two minds . . maybe this place was *too good to be true*. A screw *knowing me* from *way back* says: "Carasov, take this chance. Go *away* from here. If you stay here with *your sentence you will never 'do' it*."

I elect to go to Blundeston, and so begins a brand new chapter in my life as a prisoner. In Blundeston I experience things *good* and *bad* . . I meet people *good* and *bad* . . I touch *heights* and *depths* of great *meaning* in my life . . . *None* of these things, these experiences could have been mine in any other jail in the *world*, so far as I know.

I now enter upon the most *meaningful phase* of all my jail life. Things happen to me that I *never* dreamed of in my *wildest moments* of *fantasy*. I enter an *experimental area* of the penal scene. So far as I know, *nowhere* in England do they have *any place* to compare with this *permissive establishment*. It is *new* for staff . . *new* for the inmates.

At this point let me pause to indicate my state of mind. I'm getting on for 60 and have reached *depths* of *depression* bordering on *mania*. I am *sick* of *me* . . my follies . . my absurdities . . my *failure* . . failure even to be a *good* and *successful thief* . . . Yet in spite of all this, there are stirrings of *hope* . . *hope* that I *might* still retrieve *something* of this wasted life if I could get it down in *writing*. So many times I had come *near* doing just *that,* and *failed,* that I nearly got to thinking I'd *never* get it down. It is in this state of mind that I meet Dorothy Fisk. She says *without any reservation* : "*You,* Victor Carasov, have a story to write. *Write it* !"

On the way to Blundeston I travel with other men, some of whom have already been to Blundeston, and *all* without exception say : "A piece of *cyke*, Nick . . . Do what yer like . . . The screws call you by your first *name*." Here and there in this busload of cons, there was a *cautionary* note : "The place might not suit you, Nick, there's no privacy till night lock-up." Ah well, I'm thinking, *we will see.* I suppose I can always get back tc Parkhurst if I want to do so. The bus stops at Chelmsford Prison. We get out . . are led into the gym room . . fed, watered, and rested for an hour or so. The *talk* ? *All* about Blundeston, that *wonderful home*-from-*home*, that piece of *cake*, that piece of *delicious cyke* !

EPILOGUE

Notes selected from a Blundeston Diary
Spring, 1969

WHEN I FIRST thought of writing the Blundeston story . . I had intended to do so *after* release, thus providing a point in *distance* from the scene . . but, coming in and out of my peter, seeing the days go by, the grass changing colour, the trees changing shape, noting the song of that *bird* and listening to the prattle of the little ones . . *out there* in the Staff-quarters . . also, having that itch to get it down, the *real*, the *true*, I started out . . first with a *diary*. Realising *this* in my kind of hand-writing would be *undecipherable*, I got the typewriter to work . . and . . just bashed it out as the days marched on.

Lest it be thought that here, in Blundeston Jail, three hundred men are all engaged in reading, painting and fucking only, when in their peters, let me say: there are ball-games, music-making games, even a drama class. Also, for the social-minded, parties *galore* . . tea-parties, with some mini-skirted villagers in attendance, parties for the Alcoholics Anonymous . . for the Never Again Association (originally founded by *me* . . to encourage the *packing up* of the villainy thing) and . . *exhibitions galore* for the budding artist. I must say, there are talented men in this place: Bill Draine, first-rate painter of the Impressionist order . . then, the writing lark . . quite a few fellows here, budding Frank Normans and Brendan Behans. So . . my reader . . don't think I fail to see, in a balanced way, the many-sidedness of a Jail Community. But I must say, in all honesty, whatever the leisure-time activity of a prisoner . . and his work too . . he *is a captive, an involuntary, unwilling captive* . . and *all* he does is jail-conditioned. Jail conditions are *unnatural, false, bad* . . for the human being. In fact, do to a *dog* or a *cow* what you do to a *human being* in jail, and you'd have the League of Nations hollerin' for *justice*!

Before packing up this night, I'd invited a screw to come in and hear a reading of this story. He did so, and as he was leaving my peter he said, "That was *great* . . I like it very much . . I'll come again tomorrow if I may . . I'd like to hear some more."

* * *

I awake . . it's cold . . don't want to get up . . I hear those screws coming upstairs, whistling, nattering like old women . . I think: The bastards! They might well *whistle* . . full of good food . . good cheer . . home-life . . fucks *galore* . . children . . ever-loving wives!

The key goes in the door . . the screw moves on, with a "good morning" . . that I ignore . .

Out I go . . pot in hand . . oh yes, even *here*, in this *new look* establishment, 'pot-carrying' is still the rule . . . I empty the pot . . get out of this wash-house and W.C. *quickly* . . to escape the over-night *stench* . . and to avoid *seeing* these bastards coming out of their rat-holes . . pot in hand . . as if they loved the whole set-up.

Up to the kitchen . . grab my tea . . maybe, if lucky, a little corn-flakes . . maybe a slice of bread or toast . . back to the peter, look out of the window, note the sky, blue or grey, hear the birds' careless chatter. The grass down there is green . . the lake beyond the barbed-wire rather grey . . bordered by green rushes.

I finish my breakfast . . finish the morning chores . . go downstairs for my gate-pass . . decent screw on duty . . gives me that pass without argument . . almost as if *he* liked to see me getting the pass.

Before going out, I listen to the radio: "How I Start my Day" . . Sybil Thorndike . . I like her voice . . I met her once, many years ago, when I was a boy. Now she is much older, but very much the *Queen* . . a veritable *Queen of women*.

Out to work . . down the corridor . . the place *stinks*, over-night stench permeating the whole place . . no proper ventilation! I'm thinking: How lucky to be going *out there* . . beyond the gate . . on the driveway . . around and about the Staff Quarters . . brushing up . . cleaning up.

Over the yard . . note the spring air, fresh, cool, sweet. Through the first gate, the little one, then . . that big, fortified, double-strength Gate . . that Invulnerable Bar to Freedom! I hand in that pass . . and . . I am *out*!

Early in the morning, not many cars, as yet . . lawns . . *all* wet with dew . . trees, quiet, dignified, seeing everything but saying nothing. Here and there, bird-noises . . heard the *cuckoo* . . first time this year.

Get the barrow, broom, shovel . . brush the driveway. A car arrives . . Mrs. Norgate, a good-looking, intelligent woman . . office staff . . very nice woman . . *me* . . think: "I'll bet she is wonderful in *bed*!" I say to Mrs. Norgate "Let's have a *look at you* . . Fill my eyes with *glory*!" She laughs, saying, "Go away with you, Mr. Carasov!" Mounts the steps and disappears into the Administration Block . . *me* . . wishing . . wishing . .

I move on . . wondering: Will I see Lorraine? that little starry-eyed one? She is four . . very small . . has blue eyes . . tender blue eyes . . can be very sweet . . can be very *sour* . . and *temperamental*! Lorraine is the small daughter of a staff-member, whom I meet when I go down the Staff Quarters way. She often asks *me* to play with her . . which I do . . as a kind of brother . . elder brother . . sometimes as a kind of play-fellow, same age as herself! And sometimes . . I talk to Lorraine as to an *equal* . . *man* and *woman*! *This* clearly puzzles her . . and her puzzlement makes *me* . . *laugh*!

I do work, go around, note the Governor's wife cleaning the windows of her home. I like this woman . . she is quite plain . . just a house-wife amongst many other house-wives . . medium-height, full-breasted, nice legs, and a very friendly, kindly, warm-hearted manner! This woman, the Governor's wife, invites me to have a cup of coffee . . we talk about life in general, books, poets, places, people . . she is intelligent, down to earth, sympathetic . . I like her.

Finally, my work finished, I reluctantly return to the Prison . . I *avoid all contacts* . . won't talk unless *invited* . . won't *listen* . . except to an *adult, grown-up sound*, which I rarely *hear* inside this jail! I make for my peter . . *there*, behind that *door* . . I live my *own life*. I have books . . my Diary . . this beloved *typewriter* . . which I once *smashed in anger*! Because the writing I did . . *could not reach a publisher*, this being a *prison rule*. And I felt furious . . frustrated! Then, too, in my peter, I have the *radio* . . music, talks, a window of sound transformed into *mental pictures* . . pictures of the world out there . . and . . there is *me* . . my dreams, my hopes, my despairs.

As I crossed the yard on the way in I saw a man carrying another man in his arms! Around this scene, other men . . all jabbering away like frightened *monkeys*! It seems this was the *end-product* of a brawl, up there, in the Dormitory . . a knife, a 'chiv' had been used . . the man cut. His knuckles were *bleeding* . . . I'm thinking: What bastards . . they are transforming this *permissive establishment* into a King's Cross back-street slum . . can't even *fight* as men . . must carve 'em up, especially if it can be done *safely* . . without *detection*!

I have the midday meal . . a little soup, green stuff, a bit of meat, a piece of duff . . wonder: Any letters for *me*? Later . . I learn: *No letters*. Funnily enough, my experience of this *letter-lark* is that every now and again *all* correspondents stop writing *at the same time*, almost as if by *mutual arrangement*.

The afternoon work is a repeat of the morning's . . a little variation, perhaps, see Julie, David, other children . . as well as my starry-eyed one, Lorraine! The children and I play together, talk together, even share *sweets*.

I get back to my peter . . the day's work *done* . . .

*

Today was wet . . cold . . breezy. I had this reluctance to go out. I find, in here, no matter what the weather, this reluctance to leave my peter . . I just don't care to resume the day's sights and sounds peculiar to *prison*.

As I go out, I'm thinking: What a *dream* I had! There I was . . in a sort of basement, stone-floored, stone-walled, and with *strong* fortified *doors*, on every side! I see an open door, go in . . it's a kind of *rest-room*, table, chairs, a locker . . I hear someone coming. I hide. "It's all right, come out." Out I come, and *there* is a good-looking boy. *He* says: "What do you want?" "I'm looking for a job," I say. "Oh . . that's funny . . we could do with a *cleaner*." At that moment a man enters. The boy tells him I want a job. Another man comes in . . very tall, ungainly, his face *lop-sided*, eyes not in line! Nose where his mouth should be! *Me* . . feel nervous . . afraid of I know not what . . also . . a bit *sexy*!

I'm invited to go with this strange man into a sort of shop . . *through the window*, not the door! In there . . a strange collection of people . . *all lop-sided* . . eyes, noses, mouths, where they should not be. They seem to be lining up for something. I notice, amongst these freaks, some rather nice, *normal-looking women* . . I again get that nervous feeling, and . . the sexy one, too! I see the man sit at a table, with what I thought was a typewriter in front of him. Immediately, I say, "I can type," believing this might ensure a *job* for me. The man looks up.. saying: "This is *not* a typewriter.." Me.. look closer.. it's a sort of *tape-recorder*.. Again.. that *fear*.. *nervousness*.. *sexiness*! I come *awake*..

On the way to work.. I'm thinking of all this and reflecting: In actual fact.. I *was* seeking a job, in connection with *possible parole*! The work? It could be in a Hospital for the Handicapped.. and.. some of those Patients would be *malformed*! As for the stone floors, etc.. and *that sexiness* thing.. *that*.. was a part of the *jail-scene*.. with which I was all too familiar! The sex thing is with a prisoner *all the time*.. provided he is not impotent or a sweet-smelling, self-murdering *saint*.

I'm now out on the driveway.. very cold.. wet. For all that, being away from the *interior jail-scene*, my spirits are *high*!

I brush the pathways.. collect the debris on the screws' lawns.. note the broken toys, scattered all over the house-porches.. thinking: How *lucky* these screws' kids.. all these toys.. far more than any child needs, thrown about as if *worthless*!

I see Lorraine.. I call: "Hey you.. *blue eyes*.." She looks up.. but I get *no answer*! *Me*.. just a bit sad.. after all.. *she might have waved*! I finish the job *quick*.. it's cold, and I'm sick of all this *screw-opulence*, here in the Quarters! All the screws have cars.. some, *show-off* cars! All the kids have toys.. some, *far too many*! All the wives.. except for a very few.. *indoctrinated* by screws: "Don't have anything to do with those bastard *prisoners*.. they are a *dirty* lot!" Here, in Blundeston, I'm told: "Relate to people, out there in the Quarters.. Carasov.. that's *why we are putting you out there*!" How do you 'relate' with people.. *screws*, their wives, yes, some children, too.. *who don't want to relate with you*?

In going back to the jail I see a dog.. a poor, neglected fellow.. needs a *good scrub*! Also.. he needs love.. affection! He's always dragging himself around.. tired, bored, lonely! I note.. in passing the lamp-posts.. the discarded toys.. yes, some nearby *cycles* and *cars*.. this dog.. much to my amusement, *pissed on every one*!

Around me.. the grounds, walks, gardens, all kept in perfect order. Over there, a rock garden.. the man who made that, working all day long, digging, carrying heavy pieces of rock, lovingly placing those rock-plants! This man . . professes not to *want parole*! He appears to *love this jail-life*! And yet . . 'out there' in the free world . . the same man *could* do wonderfully well as a *dedicated gardener*! No . . no . . this man will go out . . return to villainy . . and . . inevitably, as he is not very clever at beating that rap . . get back to jail! where . . no doubt . . he will resume his *garden work*! It's men like this . . reasonably intelligent, a good worker, a talent for gardening, quite good-looking, fit, the very *stuff of home-life* . . rotting in jail . . that makes me . . feel so useless, so *futile. If* only I could keep such a man from rotting in *jail.*

I get my lunch . . don't feel hungry . . hope for a letter . . return to my peter . . listen to the radio . . *back to work* . . Finally . . finished for the day . . I write to my Empress Dorothy . . She is in New Zealand, visiting her son . . will she *answer*?

End of another day . . bed. . a bloody *bachelor bed*. . of which . . I am heartily sick!

*

A curious day! Weather . . very *odd* . . not *May* at all, or so it seemed till I heard that *blackbird*! Lord! oh, for the *voice* of a *blackbird* . . . The trees, too, all very merry and *green*! Swishing . . swashing . . swooshing in the breeze . . no wonder the poets rave about that *tree*.

I call on Miss Lorraine . . very small . . very fair . . very young! I knock on the door . . Lorraine's mother answers . . she too, rather small, fair, with brown eyes . . unlike Lorraine who has *blue eyes*. "Flowers for Miss Lorraine," I say . . I had picked a bouquet of spring flowers . . mostly *nicked* from the *Bailiff's* garden! "Oh . . thank you . . they are lovely. Lorraine has a cold . . you won't see much of her today," says her mother. At that moment . . *there* is Lorraine! Tiny, fair, soft, tender, blue eyes . . takes the flowers . . sniffs . . sniffs . . *that cold*! Says: "Thank you . . thank you . ." the door closes, and me, happy to have seen Lorraine again, sorry about that cold.

Go to work, brush up, pick the debris up . . see that Dairyland ice-cream van . . hear that *tune* . . think: Bet . . not *one bloody screw* will buy *me* an ice-cream.

I pass the house of Mrs. Gootch . . screw's wife. She often speaks to me on a conversational footing . . all about *socialism* and *welfare work*. She had done much good work for the deprived prisoner, also for handicapped people . . she and her husband had actually befriended two separate prisoners, had been at the wedding celebrations of *both men* after their discharge. Well . . I look at the window . . *hoping* for a glimpse of this woman . . maybe a word or two . . but, *no* . . *no* . . I don't see her. I wonder: Had she been warned to have *nothing to do with that bastard,* Carasov?

Return to the jail . . remembering: *Lock-up early. Today* screws have their weekly *confab* . . the do's and don'ts of the *permissive system.*

After the midday meal, mostly vegetables for me, peas and cauliflower . . don't always care for a meat-meal. Noting: *No letters* for *me*, I go to my peter . . lie down . . time for 'back to work' . . am getting ready . . the door opens . . two screws walk in!

"It's all right, Nick, don't worry . . just a routine search . . we won't bother you too much! *Me* . . tend to resent this search thing . . after all, I am *not* one of these wise guys, everlastingly indulging in contraband activities so as to *sustain their image of toughness*! However, I accept this situation, tell the screws: Go ahead . . you'll find nothing. A screw picks up a book: *Penguin Modern Poets* . . Jackson . . Nuttall . . Bill Wantling . . "You like poetry, Nick?" So the screws and I *relax*. We all sit down and, for the rest of that afternoon, we talk, talk: books, writers and *me* . . *me* . . *me*.

I read some of my work . . had written a bit about the Fish Market, Lowestoft. One of these screws says: "If you don't mind my criticism, Nick, may I point out . . these porters don't wear *sea-boots,* as you have written . . they wear a kind of heavy boot, steel-tipped and shod!" I accept this pertinent criticism . . *that* is how it *is* . . but I'm thinking: Sometimes . . a writer *should* alter a fact . . if it serves the *story*! Finally, one screw looks at his watch, saying: "Blimey! Look at the time! We must go. Nick, you've *surprised me* . . I've learnt a lot about you . . you are a *complex character* . . and . . *you can write*!" Me . . am pleased some screw can *see further than his prejudices*! Also, it was *good* to know, men . . screws right *there,* in the jail scene . . could say to *me*: "Jesus! *that is true* . . what you say there . ."

The searchers gone, I put my writing away, and I think: This communication thing . . *if* only the warring factions . . *if* only the mutually *hostile factions* could *communicate* . . heart to heart . . what *truths would be revealed* !

*

This day started *bad* ! I go down for my gate-pass, and in *there* . . an Orderly Officer . . just slightly *above his station* ! This man, I'd never met before coming here, never *hurt* him, never so much as *looked* at him with hostility.

"Can I have my pass, please?" The man looked at me as if I was a *bad smell* ! Then he says: "I'll send your pass to the gate." *Me* . . having got the pass for weeks now from other staff . . want to know: "Why can't you give me the pass as other staff have done? *or* . . just refuse, point blank, then I can take action . ." This man again looks at me as if I was *shit*, saying: "I am not arguing with you . ." I leave the office . . angry, frustrated . . saying: "Why do you let *personal feelings* into this? You hate my guts . . O.K. but . . you are not permitted to treat me in this fashion . . I've *taken no liberties* . ."

I go to work, thinking: "How . . how . . do you 'relate', friendly fashion, with *staff* who just *don't want to relat*e? On the way to the Front Gate, I *could* have been stopped, by other staff, for *not having that pass* !

I get out . . on the driveway . . see Mr. Wylie, P.O., and Mr. Hill, P.O., too . . I tell them of this absurdity . . this *permissive thing*. One screw is permitted to obstruct for private reasons . . another screw, for the *same reasons* . . that is, *private* but *favourable reasons* . . can, in fact, *help you to help yourself* ! Both of these officers agree that to obstruct me in doing a *good job* . . in preparing for *that freedom thing* . . is bad, stupid and *unfair* ! Mr. Hill said: "It's a liberty, Carasov . . after all, *you can't hit back . . you can't defend yourself*."

I pick flowers for Lorraine, get some sweets for her, and along I go . . knock at Lorraine's door . . *there she is* ! My Lorraine . . sniffing a wrinkled nose . . she's got a *cold* ! It was good to see Lorraine, though sniffing from that cold. She was my heart's delight. There was something about this child . . wayward, moody, charming, *delightful* ! So small . . so defenceless . .

In going around on my job . . notice that one woman, who had talked to me so eagerly, when I met her for the *first time*, now . . *avoided me*. Clearly, she was under the *indoctrination* . .

so peculiar to screws, who hated my guts, without, funnily enough, having any good *reason*. I felt a bit sad about this . . .

Later I meet Mrs. Guymer, Lorraine's mother. She gives me a cup of tea, which I drink on the *porch*, with Lorraine and a little boy . . all three of us having tea, and *biscuits*, too! I tell Mrs. Guymer about a radio show . . I heard last night . . Me . . laugh . . laugh . . so does Mrs. Guymer.

Return to the jail for the midday meal . . being late, I get no dinner . . this is O.K., I *never starve*, I assure the Staff-Cook, "Don't worry . . I'll get something for tea."

Go to my peter . . look out the window . . note the weather . . better than yesterday . . go back to work . .

*

Today is Sunday . . the weather . . *wonderful*! Normally, I'd rest on Sunday . . in other words, I'd stay in my peter, thinking, reading, *writin'*. For today, I decide to go out on the driveway . . brush around the empty car-park . . breathe that *air*!

I'm out there . . meet the Governor. He says: "On my notice-board in the office . . are the letters, V.C., with the word *June* added. That, Carasov, is to remind me: If there is *no* response from the Cheshire Foundation Hospitals re *your* getting a job with them, or somebody coming to see you, then I am going to write to them." I listen . . *very sceptical.* After all, they have had over three months to consider me, for *employment* . . and so far, *no answer*. I'm getting the idea: *No work for Victor* is the *probability* . . and *that knocks out all chance of parole* . . and that seems to be the aim of my so-called *friends* . . who were delegated by the Parole Unit to *try and find a job* for me . .

"Hullo . . will you pick some flowers for us? I look round . . and *there* are two little girls with cycles . . staff-children. One I know is Christine . . a very sweet little one, affectionate and trusting. The other one I don't know . . except . . she is more boy than *girl*! This one . . has cropped fair hair, dark mischievous eyes . . and lots of *cheek*!

"Sure," I say. "When I'm finished the work, I'll get you some flowers."

"No . . no . . I want them *now*," says the cheeky one.

Because I can't say *no* to a *child*, I go and get flowers, as *ordered* by this cheeky one . . gorgeous *rhododendrons* from the

Governor's preserves! The children take the flowers . . say "thank you" . . and . . cycle off . . me . . going back to work.

"Can I come with you . . help you?" I look down, and there is the *cheeky one*!

"Yes," I say. "Come along . . I've got a lot to do."

"Let's see if that bird's nest is still there." This . . from Cheeks. We go and look in the nearby woods. *Yes* . . there it is! Bright eyes, bright yellow beak, and agitated feathers. A *blackbird* . . with nestlings . . we both look . . the child saying: "Let me touch it . . let me touch it!"

"Let's look for *more birds' nests*," says Cheeks. So we look for more . . work neglected . . I'm delighted with this cheeky one . . a bit sorry she is boy-like . . after all, she *is* a girl, and I tell her so, saying, "Little girls shouldn't *act* and *talk* like little boys!" This one . . just *laughs*. So do I. We sit down in the sun, on the grass-edge, *she* . . rambling on. "What's your name? Do you *live in the prison*? Can you have *dinner with me* out here? Hey . . look . . a pond! Worms! Let's stand on our hands!" *Me* . . look at her . . direct . . *no* subterfuge! Speakin' from the heart, that's what I like about these children . . they have got somethin' *we adults have thrown away*.

I ask this little cheeky one, "What's *your* name?" and I'm told, "Karen . . my mother's name is Madeleine . . my Daddy's name is Tony." Me . . think: Christ! Not Tony *Punchard*? *He* . . *he* won't like *his* daughter associating with *me* . . the bastard called Carasov! I say to Karen, "Tell your father it's me you want to eat with, and he will tell you: Not on your *life*! You see, Karen, I'm supposed to be a *bad man*." She says, "*You are not a bad man*." I'm thinking: I wonder if the Governor *would* let me stay out here for the dinner-break . . I could bring the dinner out, and *share it with Karen*.

I see the Governor out there, in front of the Administration Block . . take Karen by the hand, saying: "Let's go and ask the Governor *if* I can bring my dinner out here, and *share* it with you." Karen takes my hand, saying, "Do you think he will?"

"Miss Karen, here, Governor Winston, wants to know, can I stay out here, sharing *my* dinner with her?" The Governor looks at me . . clearly . . *this* situation has to be handled *carefully*!

"I don't think so, Karen . . you see, it would not be easy for Carasov to bring *all* his dinner out . . there is too much to carry . . but . . *one day* . . perhaps . . we can allow *sandwiches* . .

and then you can share with Carasov." I look at the little one . . *not cheeky*, now, just puzzled . . and I say, "Now, Karen, be a good little girl . . and *go home* for your *own Sunday dinner* . . I'll see you again someday." The child reluctantly goes home . . doubtless wondering: *Funny people . . why couldn't I eat with that man*?

The Governor says to me: "You handled that situation very well, Carasov, I was sorry to say 'no' . . but *you understand* . . ." I finish the morning's work, brush up that car-park, put the gear away, return to the jail, thinking: *This* . . is the *jail scene . . no dinner for Victor* . . with the cheeky one . . Karen!

I decide to seek out Mr. Punchard, just in case he got the thing all wrong! I find Mr. Punchard, the father of the cheeky one . . tell him the story, and he says, "Nick, I knew you were with my daughter. At ten o'clock somebody told me . . and . . Nick . . I told him *not to worry* . . she would be *all right*!" *Me* . . am rather relieved . . I am, so to speak, a sort of *wild one*, but *not a child eater*, though some of the screws *here* credit . . or is it *debit*? . . *all* the seven sins to me!

I get some dinner: chops, potatoes, cabbage, a little rice-pudding . . a good dinner. Maybe Karen would have enjoyed sharing it. Go to that peter . . get the typewriter out . . and . . bash this out.

Later . . after dinner . . again, I see the Governor. He is going off by car . . stops: "Thinking of your little dinner-friend?"

"No . . what I'm thinking right now is: Have you just put me out here on this trusty job . . admittedly, a *good job* . . as an *act of kindness* . . or is it intended to lead *somewhere* out there . . is it an *opener* to the free world? *Me* . . Governor . . want *no kindness* of this sort . . no *sops* for *me* . . I only value this kind of break if it's to be an opener to that world out there." The Governor says: "This, Carasov, is not just a sop, a kindness. It is, and it's intended to be, an opener." With that reassurance, he drove off.

I sit down in the sun, shining bright and warm. A boy comes along . . ten . . eleven . . twelve maybe? Jaunty, fair, grey eyes, rather thin. The boy wears overalls . . or jeans . . *patched*! Also a T-shirt . . not too clean . . straight out of Mark Twain. The boy stops: "Hello . ." Sits down. I say: "Where are you off to?" "Nowhere . . just walkin' . . I would like to go for a swim, but my dad says no as I've a cold." This lad talks quietly, and as if I was his own age and his chum! "Let's climb that tree . . let's look for bird-nests . . let's go and look at those machines, over there" . . pointing to a weird collection of prehistoric monsters parked in a corner of this car-park. These monsters . . trench-diggers, earth-movers, are all ready for a drainage-job in the prison. We go along, the youngster rambling on pointing out to me the mechanical *marvels* of these strange-looking *monsters*! Finally, I say, "I must be going." He says, "I'll be seein' you . ." and walks back home. *Me* . . *me* . . thrilled! Children . . boys . . just wonderful . . what a lot I've *missed* . . in my wild rambles.

* * *

At this moment, over four years since my arrival here at the *new look* prison, Blundeston, I'm sitting at a table in my peter. I can see the garden frozen by snow and ice, enlivened by the appearance of gulls and an occasional robin looking for lunch. I think *back* to the day of my arrival . . the days . . the weeks . . the months . . the *years* . . between. I think of my *amazement* . . my *unbelief* . . my *distrust* . . my *anger* . . my *explosions* into near-violence . . my near-*suicidal despair* . . my *disgust*. I also look back at *kindness* . . *tolerance* . . *patience* . . *friendly people* from 'out there'. . *encouragement* . . to *me* to get on with the writing lark. I look back and see something approaching *magic* . . an *unbelievable miracle* . . a *change* . . a *basic change* in my attitude to life, to people, to events . . . Above all a change in my attitude to this villainy-thing . . to the *law* . . to *society*.

Let me add one more *miracle*: the Parole Unit . . has informed me that my parole will come up *again* for serious consideration(third time lucky?) in August this year! By August I'll be sixty-five years of age. I'm finished with the villainy-thing, have an agent waiting for my saga, and I have *friends galore* ready and willing to help where help may be of use . . .

So, for the present, let me say this: The Blundeston story will be written one day . . the *whole story* . . the *truth* . . and *nothing but the truth*. I think it will be a good and *inspiring story* even though centred on a prison.

Those words with which I title my saga—Two Gentlemen to See You, Sir—I hope and trust and *pray* I *will never hear again*.

8